Environmental Sociology
for the Twenty-First Century

Environmental Sociology
for the Twenty-First Century

Nathan Young

OXFORD
UNIVERSITY PRESS

OXFORD
UNIVERSITY PRESS

Oxford University Press is a department of the University of Oxford.
It furthers the University's objective of excellence in research, scholarship,
and education by publishing worldwide. Oxford is a registered trade mark of
Oxford University Press in the UK and in certain other countries.

Published in Canada by
Oxford University Press
8 Sampson Mews, Suite 204,
Don Mills, Ontario M3C 0H5 Canada

www.oupcanada.com

Library and Archives Canada Cataloguing in Publication

Young, Nathan, 1977–, author
Environmental sociology for the twenty-first century / Nathan Young.

(Themes in Canadian sociology)
Includes bibliographical references and index.
ISBN 978-0-19-900329-7 (pbk.)

1. Environmental sociology--Textbooks. I. Title.
II. Series: Themes in Canadian sociology

GE195.Y69 2014   333.72   C2014-903782-1

Cover image: Russ Heinl/All Canada Photos/Getty Images

Oxford University Press is committed to our environment.
This book is printed on Forest Stewardship Council® certified paper
and contains 100% post-consumer waste.

RECYCLED
Paper made from
recycled material
FSC® C103567

Printed and bound in Canada

1 2 3 4 — 18 17 16 15

To Christy, best friend and fellow-traveller

Contents

Preface

I still remember my first encounter with environmental sociology. As a third-year undergraduate at the University of Waterloo, I enrolled in an environmental sociology course mostly out of curiosity. Like many in my generation, I was concerned about the environment, but only casually engaged and aware of the major issues and problems. I had grown up during two major environmental scares—acid rain, which was killing fish and aquatic plant life in lakes and rivers across much of eastern North America, and the depletion of stratospheric ozone (popularly known as the hole in the ozone layer) that threatened to dramatically increase exposure to ultraviolet radiation. These issues were unsettling, but they seemed also relatively straightforward. We (humanity) had made some mistakes in how we go about doing things—generating electricity in the case of acid rain, and making consumer products in the case of ozone. Going into that first course, I assumed that the solutions to environmental problems were relatively straightforward and involved the application of some pretty self-evident lessons to reform how things were done.

The reality, as I soon came to learn, is much more complex than that. One of the aims of this book is to show that we cannot talk about the natural environment without also talking about *people*. Modern humans are among the youngest species on Earth, but we have radically transformed our world over the short time we have been here. The planet that we know—its cities, farms, parks, forests, industries, oceans, and even its atmosphere—has been shaped by generations of decisions and events across space (geography) and time (history). People, governments, and organizations continue to make monumental decisions—both directly and indirectly—about how to treat and shape the Earth. Arguably, the decisions that we make today in the twenty-first century are the *most* monumental. At the time I write this, there are more than seven billion human beings on Earth, and the United Nations expects that there will be close to 10 billion people alive in 2050. The interconnectivity and rapid development of our economies, communications, and technologies mean that the stakes are getting higher—with each passing year we literally have less room to make mistakes, and less time to deal with their consequences.

The environmental sociologist John Dryzek (2005: 9) has said that this is the most difficult area of sociology because it is "doubly complex." On the one hand, Planet Earth is home to life forms, ecosystems, and geophysical processes of such staggering complexity that we still do not fully understand them. On the other hand, human behaviour is equally complicated, mysterious, and often counter-intuitive. Environmental sociology tries to understand environment and society together, not as opposing poles but as things that are **co-constitutive**—that are continually shaped by one another. For people living in wealthier nations, and particularly in affluent urban environments, it is easier to imagine human impacts on nature than the other way around. It is important to remember, though, that despite all of our achievements and skills people are still flesh-and-blood animals who can bend, but not break, biological and ecological rules. As we will see in the following chapters, one of the greatest points of contention—among scholars, activists, politicians, citizens, and corporations—is the question of just how special—just how *exceptional*—we really are as a species. There's a lot riding on the answer.

This book has several aims. First and foremost, it provides an overview of the major theoretical and empirical currents in environmental sociology today. Environmental sociologists are still learning how to study the relationship between humans and nature, which means that theories and research methods are still under development—being proposed, discussed, refined, and debated (sometimes heatedly). This makes environmental sociology a dynamic and exciting field, with plenty of room for intellectual experimentation and innovation.

Second, in writing this book I hope to contribute to a transformation in how we see and understand the human–nature relationship. Western culture and society tend to draw a firm line between the human world and the natural world—between city and country, technology and nature, civilization and wilderness, people and things, exploitation and conservation. According to this logic, the natural environment is something that is "out there," distinct from what is "in here." This book argues that such an assumption is patently false. We are in *constant* dialogue and exchange with the natural world, even if these interactions are masked by the political and economic institutions of a modern consumer society. Each chapter makes the case, in its own way, that the human–nature relationship underwrites both our individual lives and our societies, and that we need to cultivate and reform this relationship to maintain our quality of life in the future.

Third, this book aims to provide a uniquely Canadian introduction to environmental sociology. Canada is a fascinating country when viewed through the lens of environmental sociology. On the one hand, we have a green self-image as a people who value wilderness, conservation, and environmental stewardship. On the other hand, we owe much of our past and present wealth to the extraction and sale of natural resources, from fur to fish to timber to, most recently, fossil fuels. More than almost any other country, Canada embodies the contradictions at the heart of the contemporary human–nature relationship—between our genuine but rather abstract desire to be "green" and "sustainable," and the hard reality that our current standard of living depends on the consumption of staggering amounts of energy, the production of vast amounts of waste, and the ongoing degradation of terrestrial and aquatic ecosystems at home and abroad. By looking at Canada we learn about the environmental dilemmas facing the whole planet, and vice-versa.

The book is organized as follows. The first three chapters provide basic background on the fundamentals of environmental sociology and its subject matter. Chapter 1 outlines the origins of environmental sociology and the unique contributions it makes to the study of environmental problems. Many experts and policy-makers continue to think about environmental problems as being purely "technical" issues that can be solved by the natural sciences alone. In contrast, environmental sociologists argue that we cannot think about environmental problems without also thinking about their social and institutional origins. This chapter introduces sociological thinking on the environment as a launching pad for the remainder of the book. Chapter 2 provides the back story for current environmental problems and dilemmas, looking at human–nature interactions across societies and through time. This discussion shows that environmental problems are not new, and that humans have always had to carefully negotiate their relationship with the natural world. Environmental failure has been extremely common in human history, and we can draw real and tangible lessons from the environmental past to help us today. Chapter 3 looks at the more recent context by examining the environmentalist movement and its opponents. Environmentalism has brought unprecedented public awareness and political pressure to bear on key environmental problems. Environmentalism is constantly changing, however, as new voices and concerns emerge in lesser-developed countries, and as anti-environmentalist forces mobilize to support the status quo and challenge demands for reform.

Chapters 4–6 do much of the theoretical heavy lifting, outlining some of the major concepts, ideas, and debates that have defined environmental sociology to date. Chapter 4 discusses the long-running debate between social constructionist and environmental realist views of the human–nature relationship. Social constructionists tend to see nature as a cultural phenomenon first, shaped by human perceptions, values, symbols, and interests; environmental realists tend to see nature as a semi-autonomous actor that exists independent of society and puts hard limits on human choices and activities. The ongoing relevance of the constructionist-realist debate is illustrated using the example of global climate change—an issue that constructionists and realists approach quite differently. Chapter 5 addresses problems of environmental scarcity and resource depletion, contrasting the sociological "treadmill theory" with notions of "relative scarcity" and "resource substitution" from economics. Treadmill theory argues that the roots of environmental degradation are found in capitalist competition, which compels producers, consumers, and governments to over-exploit natural resources. This chapter also examines controversial theories of "peak production" that are frequently applied to critical resources such as oil and food. Chapter 6 addresses the "risk society thesis," which is one of the most ambitious attempts to theorize the role of environmental problems and hazards in contemporary social life. The risk society thesis, which is strongly associated with the work of German sociologist Ulrich Beck, argues that environmental politics—both at the official and grass-roots level—are increasingly being driven by responses to the "side effects" of prior environmental mistakes. This chapter looks at the strengths and weaknesses of this influential idea, and examines its capacity to explain real-world environmental conflicts.

Chapters 7–9 examine trends in environmental governance. Chapter 7 looks at the increasingly popular idea that environmental improvements can be achieved by reforming how capitalism works. This chapter examines the strengths and weaknesses of several approaches, namely sustainability (and its sister term, sustainable development); neoliberalism, which tends to focus on commodifying and/or "pricing" environmental goods, services, and wastes; and ecological modernization, which is a sociological theory that attempts to explain why "going green" is an increasingly attractive option for businesses, governments, and consumers. Chapter 8 extends this discussion by looking at the effects of globalization on the environment. Globalization is a complex and contradictory force, encouraging some industries and regions to clean up while concentrating pollution and degradation in others. Chapter 9 looks at the role of science and knowledge in expert and democratic decision-making about sensitive environmental issues. This chapter argues that one of the biggest challenges in environmental governance is to find "the right role" for science within an inclusive approach to environmental decision-making that also makes room for local, traditional, and experiential forms of knowledge.

Finally, Chapters 10–11 deal with environmental futures. Chapter 10 addresses the increasingly urgent topics of disaster management, resilience, and adaptation to environmental changes. As the human impact on the natural world accelerates, our capacity to respond to environmental changes will be tested. This chapter draws on lessons from the entire book about how we can better prepare for changes even as we try to prevent or mitigate them. Chapter 11 closes the book by looking at the future of environmental sociology itself. Recent events like the unprecedented and costly flooding in Calgary and Toronto in the summer of 2013 reaffirm the tight links between the human and natural worlds—how each influences and patterns the other. This chapter reviews some of the new theoretical and empirical work in environmental sociology that tries to address, and hopefully to reform, this relationship.

In a sense, I never left that first undergraduate course in environmental sociology. The challenge of understanding humanity's relationship with nature has occupied my academic life since the day I walked into that classroom. This is a field bursting at the seams, with far more questions than we have answers. This book only scratches the surface of current thought and research in environmental sociology in Canada and around the world, but I hope that it begins to explain how and why the environment and sociology belong together. I firmly believe that the first step toward improving our relationship with the planet is understanding the roots and reasons for our sometimes maddeningly short-sighted collective behaviour. As a late colleague of mine used to say, "Good sociology can change the world." Let's begin!

Acknowledgements

My debts, intellectual and otherwise, are too numerous to list here, but I will try nonetheless. I would like to thank Lorne Tepperman and Patrizia Albanese for encouraging me to write this book, as well as the latitude they gave me as series editors to write the book I wanted to. Mark Thompson's work as developmental editor at OUP was truly outstanding. His sage advice and behind-the-scenes efforts helped the book grow from scattered outline to final text. Many thanks to the three anonymous reviewers whose comments helped greatly improve the manuscript.

I am particularly grateful to my friend and mentor, Ralph Matthews, whose broad vision of environmental sociology inspired me into the field. I have greatly benefited from conversations and exchanges with fellow environmental sociologists (although they wouldn't all identify themselves that way), including Richard Apostle, Dean Curran, Riley Dunlap, Brian Elliott, Louis Guay, Randolph Haluza-Delay, Raymond Murphy, Justin Page, John Parkins, John Phyne, Howard Ramos, Bill Reimer, Terre Satterfield, Deborah Sick, Mark C.J. Stoddart, David Tindall, G. Keith Warriner, Rima Wilkes, David VanderZwaag, and others whom I have surely forgotten.

Over the years, I have learned a great deal from the many excellent undergraduate and graduate students who have taken various environment-themed courses with me. Well-researched student essays have deepened my knowledge of many key environmental issues. In particular, Joanne Gaudet's essay on the Great Pacific Garbage Patch inspired the discussion in Chapter 4, and Stéphanie Vaudry's essay on the polar bear hunt did the same in Chapter 9. Other students from whom I've learned a lot include Elodie Button, Alexis Calvé-Genest, Aline Coutinho, Darryn Anne DiFrancesco, Eric Dugas, Isabelle Gingras, Mary Liston, Erica Nickels, Vivian Nguyen, and Mihai Sarbu.

My family has been a constant source of inspiration in everything that I do. Thanks to my parents, Dennis and Marie Young, and to my sisters, Meredith and Elaine, for helping me refine my arguments over holiday dinners and special occasions. The book is dedicated to my wife, Christy, best friend and ruthless editor. Our children, Sam, Elliot, and Nora, are the bright shining lights in our lives. I can't seem to write a book without a child being born in the middle of it. A hallmark of a blessed life.

Thinking about the Human– Nature Relationship

Key Points

◎ Environmental sociology examines how human and natural forces meet, interact, and shape one another. It is a young field in sociology, however, and many of its core ideas are still being developed and debated.

◎ The natural sciences show us that the natural world is extremely complex, while the social sciences tell us that the human world is equally complicated. The human–nature relationship is therefore "doubly complex," because our dependence on nature is often indirect and masked by social structures, institutions, and cultural blind spots.

◎ The great strengths of sociology, namely its attention to culture, structure, and power, are useful for studying environmental problems and can provide fresh perspectives on difficult issues.

Introduction

Human beings are animals. This is a fundamental fact of life that we all must eventually come to terms with. We are born, we have corporeal needs and drives, we follow a more or less rigid life course from youth to old age, and we die. In this, we are no different from any other living organism on the planet. Everyone knows this. And yet, there is more to human existence—something *special*. Children are invariably jarred when they learn that humans are also animals—in a child's world of hard categories, we don't look like animals, we don't act like animals, and animals can't do what we can. Although we share so much in common with other living things, it often seems as though we belong in different categorical boxes—or what Bruno Latour (2004: 13) calls different "houses"—with the human world being (at best) arm's length from or (at worst) fundamentally different from the natural world.

This contradiction—that we are and are not separate from nature—is one of the biggest challenges involved in thinking about the human–nature relationship. If we think about the problem one way, there is no logical boundary between humans and nature. Our bodies follow the same fundamental rules as other organisms in that we need to acquire energy, dispose of wastes, maintain delicately calibrated internal chemistries, and protect ourselves from disease and violence. These facts are widely accepted and anchor the disciplines of biology, genetics, medicine, and ecology. Moreover, our ongoing embeddedness in nature is frequently exposed when things go wrong—in a famine or an epidemic, for instance. At these times it is all too evident what we are: biological creatures whose fate is tied to other life forms and to the land, air, and water upon which we depend.

But it also makes sense to think about the problem the other way—that there is a division of some kind between the human and natural spheres. We are like no other animal currently in existence. This is due in large part to our unique combination of abilities—our capacities for learning, thinking, and abstraction, our ability to intonate an enormous variety of oral sounds (making speech not only mentally but physically possible), our manual dexterity and opposable thumbs, our relative longevity, and our social drives that compel us to live in groups and thus communicate and coordinate our actions. Over time, these skills have allowed us to make our own worlds. Many animals can alter a landscape—think of a beaver building a dam or the enormous desert mounds built by ant and termite colonies. We are the only ones, though, who can do so intentionally, not by instinct but in anticipation of a desired result. Consider the abstraction that is involved in making a spear for hunting or a piece of clothing for warmth, in treating ochre and other natural substances to make dyes and paints, or in planting and caring for crops that will not yield any returns for months. Today, our daily lives rarely if ever bring us into contact with unvarnished "nature." The systems that matter most to our daily lives—financial systems, transportation systems, the health system, education, technology, and so on—on the surface have little to do with nature (although we will challenge this notion later on). From this perspective our embeddedness in nature fades into the background. We are mortal beings, yes, but our quality of life appears much more rooted in the human world—the quality of our jobs, family life, access to technologies, medicine, housing, social networks, and material wealth.

What we need to do is find some middle ground between these two views—that we are *nothing but* organisms tightly bound to nature, or alternatively that we are *exempt from* the natural forces and ecological rules that govern other species. This chapter will argue that environmental sociology is uniquely positioned to find this middle ground because of its emphasis on how human and natural forces meet and interact. This doesn't mean that environmental sociologists see eye to eye on how to understand and study these interactions—they don't. Nevertheless, environmental sociology can provide important conceptual and methodological tools to think about the mutual embeddedness of nature and society. First, however, we need to take a critical look at the discipline of sociology itself to better understand the promises and pitfalls of using this perspective to examine the complex and ever-changing relationship between the environment and us.

Sociology: A Part of the Problem?

One of the curious things about environmental sociology is its relative youth. Depending on your point of departure, sociology has been around for about a hundred years or more, but environmental sociology really only dates from the late 1970s and did not become a major field until the late 1980s and 1990s. Why did it emerge so late, and what does this tell us about the ability of sociology to address nature and the environment? Canonical sociologists such as Karl Marx, Max Weber, Émile Durkheim, and Georg Simmel paid minimal attention to the environment or the natural world, and to this day most sociological research proceeds, in the words of Murphy (1997) "as though nature didn't matter" (see Box 1.1). This is not to say that this work is faulty or inaccurate, but it does suggest that over the years sociology has developed and maintained a significant blind spot (one big enough to hold the Earth!) that is only now being challenged. This blind spot has led many sociologists to conduct their work—often unwittingly—as though the human world is all there is.

Several prominent environmental sociologists have commented on this tendency, including Riley Dunlap (2002; 2010), Raymond Murphy (1994; 1997), and Frederick Buttel (2002). According to them, to fulfill sociology's promise we need to remove the blindspot and find nature again. First, though, we have to understand how it was lost to begin with. A big contributor appears to be the intellectual conditions under which sociology was established as a field of inquiry. Sociology has many antecedents and many founders, but most agree that the contours of the discipline were laid out in the latter half of the nineteenth century and the first quarter of the twentieth century, predominantly in three European cultures—German, French, and English (Maus 1965). These were times and places deeply touched by two seismic cultural-economic events—the Scientific Revolution and the Industrial Revolution—and both had a formative impact on sociology.

While the Scientific Revolution is usually considered to have taken place in the sixteenth to eighteenth centuries, the argument can be made that it has never really ended (cf. Shapin 1996). In the nineteenth century, a series of scholars and thinkers began to apply some of the lessons of the Scientific Revolution, specifically **experimentation, positivism,** and **empiricism,** to human affairs. Among the most famous of these scholars is Auguste Comte (1798–1857), who argued that sociology could mimic and ultimately perfect the methods of the natural sciences. It was he who suggested that the sciences could be organized hierarchically according to the complexity of their subject matter, with sociology at the pinnacle (above biology which was in turn above physics and chemistry). Importantly, Comte argued that sociology depended on the other sciences because, being the most complex, it had to draw on their conclusions in order to understand society. Comte's

Box 1.1   Were Marx, Weber, and Durkheim Theorists of Nature?

While the major founders of sociology did not directly address the natural environment, some scholars argue that they did so implicitly and therefore that sociology is not as ignorant of ecology as it first appears. Buttel (2002: 39), for instance, argues that "not only did Marx, Durkheim, and Weber incorporate what we might regard as ecological components in their work, they did so from a variety of standpoints" that are still relevant today. For reasons discussed in the main text, Durkheim is generally seen as the least ecologically aware of the three. However, Catton (2002) argues that Durkheim's ideas about the increasingly complex division of labour in society were directly inspired by evolutionary theorist Charles Darwin's notion of ecological niches. Animals that occupy niches avoid competition with neighbouring species, which Durkheim interpreted as proof that economic specialization can benefit the common good. Max Weber was more open to considering the environment as a variable, as seen in his work comparing the economies, cultures, and social structures of ancient societies (West 1984). While Weber never did so, Murphy (1994) applied Weber's distinction between *formal* and *substantive* rationality to understand why modern institutions are so good at exploiting the environment and so poor at protecting it. Essentially, exploitation makes sense in the short term and involves solving small, technocratic puzzles (like how to maximize oil production and profits) even though it leads to long-term violations of a more substantive rationality (like the fact we need a clean environment in which to live).

The thinking of Karl Marx was likely the most ecologically informed of the three. It is worth pointing out that Marx was a materialist, which means that he sought explanations for phenomena in the real world rather than in the world of ideas. While materialism for Marx predominantly referred to the workings of the economy, he frequently used agricultural and natural resource examples to illustrate his theories. Foster (1999; 2010) argues that Marx in fact directly addressed environmental degradation as a consequence of capitalism. Specifically, Foster uses the term "metabolic rift" to describe Marx's writing on high-intensity farming, which even in the nineteenth century required the import of fertilizer from as far away as South America and created incentives to overuse soils (Foster 2010: 107). By treating everything as a commodity, capitalism not only alienates people from themselves, their work, and each other, but also from nature. In any case, Marx's thought has had a strong influence on more recent developments in environmental sociology—notably on the concept of the "treadmill of production" addressed in Chapter 5.

thought had a strong influence on Émile Durkheim (1858–1917), who arguably had the most direct role in founding modern sociology. For the most part, Durkheim accepted Comte's positivism but rejected his arguments about the hierarchy of the sciences. Instead, Durkheim was particularly concerned with cementing sociology's independence and uniqueness as a discipline. This gave rise to a specific theoretical and methodological strategy that to this day remains sociology's **epistemological** anchor: the claim that **social facts** can only be explained by other social facts (Catton 2002: 91). This axiom is classically illustrated in Durkheim's book *On Suicide*, which explains variations in suicide rates not by individual factors (psychology) or climate (geography) but by regional variations in social cohesion and social bonds that either discourage or free people to take their own lives. Sociologists continue to work in this tradition when they explain income disparities by factors such as education, social class, ethnicity, and gender (all social constructs and categories) rather than by, for instance, a person's IQ. This has the effect, however, of creating a kind of closed loop, where the human world becomes both the source and the site of explanation to the exclusion of other possible forces and factors (Murphy 1997: 10).

The Industrial Revolution also left a profound imprint on sociology. The transition from a feudal-agricultural society to an industrial one involved profound change in almost every sphere of society. Many early sociologists were critical of these changes, including Ferdinand Tönnies (1855–1936), who wrote about the social consequences of change away from small-scale community (*Gemeinschaft*) and towards a more urbanized, industrialized mass society (*Gesellschaft*). Murphy (1994; 1997), though, argues that sociology has been indelibly stamped with the ideological undertones of the early industrial period (see also Catton and Dunlap 1980). On the one hand, this is evident in sociology's critical stance towards capitalism, social change, and social power—directly inherited from Tönnies, as well as Karl Marx, Max Weber, and Georg Simmel. On the other hand, Murphy (1997: 15–16) argues that "sociology developed in the wealthiest nations during the period when their citizens shared the illusion of being capable of reshaping nature at will." The Industrial Revolution showed that humanity had the means to dominate and change nature. This, combined with the ongoing development of science, medicine, and technology, led to "a socially exuberant sociology" deeply committed to the idea of progress (Murphy 1997: 16). Even today, in a more skeptical era, the core mission of sociology remains in large part to make the (human) world better—more just, equitable, and better functioning. It is not always evident how these "exuberant" goals square with the realities of life on a limited planet.

Finally, Hannigan (2006: 2) argues that sociology has been shaped by its explicit rejection of arguments about biological, geographic, and environmental determinism that were highly influential in the early part of the twentieth century. At that time, it was popular among both sociologists and geographers to speculate about how climate and landscape affected social organization. These arguments, which were tinged with **Social Darwinistic** assumptions about evolution and geographic fitness, suggested among other things that "races" that lived in lush tropical environments had little motive to become industrious, compared to Northern European peoples who had had to cope with harsh climates. Hannigan (2006: 3) argues that sociologists such as Pitrim Sorokin and anthropologists like Franz Boas reacted to these claims "by elevating culture to a primary role in individual and social development, dwarfing both the physical environment and biological inheritance." Rather than looking at how the natural world shaped people, sociology would look exclusively at how people shaped themselves. There is a lesson to be learned here as we go forward. While biology and environment did once play a role in sociology, it was the wrong role. Sociologists were right to reject the use of biology and geography as *the primary* explanation for social phenomena. The claims that determinists made too easily slipped towards justifications of imperialism, colonialism, and racist social policies. If we are to bring questions of environment back into sociology, we have to be careful to do it the right way. The human world has been the near-exclusive focus of sociology for quite some time, and most environmental sociologists would argue that this inability to consider the natural world has hindered our discipline. At the same time, the blind spot needs to be filled carefully. The environment and human society need to be reconceptualized as being mutually embedded or **co-constitutive** (each creating and patterning the other). The lesson from early sociology is that we should avoid oversimplifying the human–nature relationship even as we try to put the two back together.

HEP, NEP, and DWW

Sociology began coming back to nature in the 1970s. It is no accident that this is the time that the modern environmentalist movement, which we will examine in detail in Chapter 3, became a major cultural and political force. Dunlap (2002: 329) suggests, however, that in the early 1970s sociologists approached the environmentalist movement using a traditional disciplinary lens, seeing it as an example of social mobilization and a rising political force. In other words, they approached it as a social fact—as one social movement among many that were challenging the post-war consensus in Europe and North America. More profoundly, Dunlap argues that sociologists at the time did not have the conceptual and theoretical tools to really address the essence of the environmentalist critique—that the human–nature relationship had become so unbalanced as to threaten the future of all societies. By looking at environmentalism only as a social fact, sociologists were missing the point. For example, by examining protests over pollution only through the lens of social movement theory, key questions about the production, proliferation, distribution, and consequences of pollution as a complex social-environmental problem were going unasked. These lacunae are what led Dunlap, along with his colleague William Catton Jr., to propose a now-famous remedy for sociology that would bring it closer to the core concerns of the environmentalist movement: the New Ecological Paradigm or NEP.

To understand the NEP, we first have to consider two other acronyms, the DWW (Dominant Western Worldview), and the HEP (Human Exemptionalist Paradigm). The DWW is a set of cultural assumptions that emerged in Western nations with the advent of modernity and that we continue, more or less, to carry with us to this day. These assumptions could only have emerged in cultures that enjoyed both material affluence and political power. Catton and Dunlap (1980: 16) describe the DWW this way:

> Western culture has a strong **anthropocentric** tradition, seeing humans as separate from and somehow above the rest of nature. Accumulation of scientific knowledge and the growing power of technology converted this ancient anthropocentrism into modern arrogance toward nature, while European expansion into the New World added a strong sense of optimism. . . . It is not surprising that a strong belief in progress developed [based on] the new abundance.

Catton and Dunlap also argue that while many sociologists have been critical of the DWW, they nonetheless have adopted "a more sophisticated version" as the bedrock of their own discipline. This more sophisticated version, adopted for the most part unconsciously, is called the Human Exemptionalism Paradigm (HEP). In a nutshell, the HEP is the implicit assumption that the world as we know it is solely the outcome of human decisions. By this, Catton and Dunlap mean that most sociologists assume that the only limits on human affairs are socially imposed, and therefore highly flexible. Things like social inequality, poverty, and violence exist purely because of human decisions and the (often unintended) consequences of human-generated structures and systems, such as economy, politics, language, symbols, and cultures. This illustrates how sociology is simultaneously a critical and profoundly optimistic discipline. While sociologists are trained to take a hard skeptical look at the world around us, we tend to conceptualize that world as being exclusively human-made and therefore infinitely transformable. The world may be imperfect, but the world is also contingent, and therefore it can become much more fair/equal/prosperous/just through the betterment of human-made systems. Catton and Dunlap did not object to these goals, but rather to the assumption that the human future was open-ended and self-determined, and therefore oblivious to the ongoing depletion and degradation of the biosphere upon which all human societies depend.

To remedy this, Catton and Dunlap suggest that sociology *as a whole* reject the assumptions of the HEP and embrace those of the NEP. The NEP is, at its most basic, a call to acknowledge the reality of ecological limits, and to incorporate these limits into sociological theory and research (Vaillancourt 2010: 49). Against the open-ended optimism of mainstream sociology, Catton and Dunlap argue that political, economic, and social variables are constrained and even shaped by society's orientation towards the environment. For example, consider the core sociological concept of **social class**. Most sociologists see social class as one of the key divisions in society, caused by differential access to resources and power. Sociologists working in the Marxist or **conflict theory** traditions tend to look at class divisions as reflecting different access to the **means of production** or other scarce roles or skills within the production process (Wright 2006). Those with a more Weberian view also look at how **social status** is created, defended, and mobilized by different groups seeking power or advantages over others. Both types would likely agree that the root of these inequalities lies in the ability of certain groups to deny other people access to these means, and that the road to greater equality is therefore to reform the political and economic structures that sustain current class structures so that more (if not all) may share in society's bounties. This is all well and good, but an NEP-informed sociologist would argue that these arguments ignore the role that the environment plays in creating and maintaining social class divisions. If we do indeed live in a finite world with real ecological limits, then the analysis of social class needs to consider **scarcity**. For instance, industrial economies produce wealth, but they also produce spectacular amounts of waste as by-product of both production and consumption (Murphy 1994). This waste, which takes multiple forms, has to be stored somewhere—in the limited land, water, and air that make up the biosphere. Both within nations and globally, we see that waste *intersects* with social class. That is, wastes and waste management facilities (such as incinerators, sewage treatment centres, and dumps) are rarely located in wealthy areas and neighbourhoods, but rather in or near poor areas inhabited by already-marginalized people (Cox 2004: 314). This not only potentially impacts people's health and well-being, but also depreciates what property they may own, thus keeping them locked into a particular class position. Scarcity also works in the other direction—to make the wealthy even wealthier. If we presume that a given resource is scarce and getting scarcer due to degradation and over-use (such as fresh water in much of the world), then that resource rises in value. As value goes up, there is incentive for individuals or companies to "capture" it—to purchase it or secure a licence to access it—in order to sell it to others. Scarcity—be it in water, oil, or food—thus has the effect of transferring capital away from the poor and toward the wealthy. Again, we see how an ecological condition creates and reinforces social class. More profoundly, these examples also show how social equality is not just about sharing benefits, but reorienting our relationship with the natural environment so as to avoid producing these inequalities to begin with.

While it is debatable how much influence the NEP has ultimately had on mainstream sociology, it has certainly had an impact on environmental sociology. This impact, though, has been muted by one major challenge: while the NEP is based on relatively straightforward ideas (see Table 1.1), it is not always clear how these can be operationalized—i.e., turned into researchable questions and variables. If society and nature are indeed co-produced or co-constitutive, what weight ought we give to which variables in order to explain observed phenomena? Should these explanations be symmetrical (giving equal weight to both social and natural variables), asymmetrical, or should we make no distinction at all between the two? Environmental sociologists all agree that natural and social conditions interact. For example, Australia experienced a prolonged and severe drought from 2003–2010 that did not cause a single death by famine. In contrast, the 2011–2012 drought in Somalia—much shorter in duration—resulted in approximately 260,000 deaths by famine. Both droughts are clearly socio-natural events, but these diverging experiences and outcomes are difficult to fit into the four (rather abstract) principles of the NEP. Looking back over 30 years of work in environmental sociology, Manuel-Navarrete and Buzinde (2010: 136) conclude that "regardless of numerous attempts at formulating concepts, formalisms and approaches for addressing the complex interactive character of social and environmental processes, . . . a robust ecological paradigm for sociology is still in the making." We will return to this question in Chapter 11, once we have had a chance to explore the variety of sociological thinking about the environment.

The Promise of Sociology

Although sociology as a whole has been slow to recognize the importance of the natural environment, the discipline brings a lot to the table. Sociology has some real strengths, among them the ability to see the big picture. While some other social sciences focus on specific dimensions of the human experience, such as politics, economics, communication, or geography, sociology is a synthesis discipline that tries to develop comprehensive explanations of observed phenomena. Sociology also pays significant attention to both micro-level interactions—to the (social) spaces between individual people—and the macro-level structures and forces that influence human behaviour. This in turn leads sociologists to examine conflict and

Table 1.1 Major Assumptions of the Dominant Western Worldview (DWW), the Human Exemptionalism Paradigm (HEP), and the New Ecological Paradigm (NEP)

	DWW	HEP	NEP
Assumptions about the nature of human beings	People are fundamentally different from all other creatures on Earth, over which they have dominion.	Humans have a cultural heritage in addition to (and distinct from) their genetic inheritance, and are thus unlike all other animal species.	While humans have exceptional characteristics (such as culture), they remain one among many species that are interdependently involved in the global ecosystem.
Assumptions about social causation	People are masters of their destiny; they can choose their goals and learn to do whatever is necessary to achieve them.	Social and cultural factors (including technology) are the major determinants of human affairs.	Human affairs are influenced not only by social and cultural factors, but also by intricate linkages of cause, effect, and feedback in the web of nature; thus, purposive human actions have many unintended consequences.
Assumptions about the context of human society	The world is vast, and thus provides unlimited opportunities for humans.	Social and cultural environments are the crucial context for human affairs, and the biophysical environment is largely irrelevant.	Humans live in and are dependent on a finite biophysical environment that imposes potent physical and biological restraints on human affairs.
Assumptions about the constraints on human society	The history of humanity is one of progress; for every problem there is a solution, and thus progress need never cease.	Culture is cumulative; thus technological and social progress can continue indefinitely, making all social problems ultimately soluble.	Although the inventiveness of humans and the powers derived therefrom may seem for a while to extend environmental limits, ecological laws cannot be repealed.

Source: Dunlap (2002: 333)

consensus as dynamic forces that shift, change, and co-exist in fascinating ways. For instance, in Canada we have a general *cultural* consensus that a consumer-capitalist economy is desirable, but within that consensus is considerable *economic* conflict among social classes, industrial sectors, regional blocs, and so on. The same can be said about Canadians' views of the natural environment. There is considerable cultural consensus that our environment is worthy of protection and in many ways represents us and our identity (the advertising of governments and beer companies converge on this point). In practice, though, when real interests come into play, the divisions are not hard to find. Sociology is particularly well equipped to explore and understand these dynamics. Environmental sociology brings three strengths in particular to the study of environmental problems: attention to culture, structure, and power.

Culture

Sociology has long had an interest in the systems of symbols and meanings that fall under the umbrella of culture. While Catton and Dunlap have been critical of this tendency (see above), culture is an important lens for understanding human–environment relationships. For instance, the American tradition in sociology has placed substantial emphasis on **symbolic interactionism**, or the study of how people interpret the world through shared understandings (Blumer 1969: 2). This perspective tells us that a great deal of human behaviour can be explained by looking at the "fields of meaning" associated with different contexts and circumstances. For example, individuals are entirely comfortable holding different identities and projecting different presentations of the self in different circumstances (for instance, being the caring parent at home and the ruthless executive at work). This flexibility exists with respect to the non-human world as well. Consider that most North Americans have no difficulty eating beef, while almost none would consider eating dog. While both acts involve the slaughter and consumption of domesticated animals, among North Americans there are symbolic and cultural barriers to eating dog that do not exist for eating cows, and vice versa. It is also noteworthy that this tendency is not universal—dog is consumed in some parts of the world, and beef avoided in still others. Looking at the fields of meaning that surround different actions, species, landscapes, and products can tell us a lot about how people value (and discount) the environment, often in contradictory ways (Macnaghten and Urry 1998).

Sociology also pays significant attention to **discourse**. Discourse is a complicated concept. Sometimes it refers uniquely to language, specifically the implications of using different words to conceptualize things, ideas, and activities. Dryzek (2005) uses the following example to illustrate: What is the difference between a swamp and a wetland? On the one hand, there is no difference whatsoever—both words refer to the same natural phenomenon. On the other hand, the two labels are revealingly different. A swamp is a waste, and "the only sensible thing to do with swamps is to drain them, so the land can be put to useful purpose" (Dryzek 2005: 3). Swamps are also reviled in popular culture, frequently evoked as evil and mysterious settings in both fantasy (*The Princess Bride*, *The Lord of the Rings*) and horror genres (*Creature from the Black Lagoon*, *Swamp Thing*). A wetland, by contrast, has "[inherent] value in providing habitat for wildlife, stabilizing ecosystems, and absorbing pollutants." It is a thing to be protected, nurtured, and defended against urban sprawl and industrial development. This example shows that words matter, not just because of their descriptive power, but the meanings that they envelop and represent. Language is a product of human interactions, but it has real ramifications for how we treat the environment.

Discourse can also refer to how language and practice *combine* to constrain and channel how people and organizations think and act. To illustrate, let us again consider the concept of "waste," which in the common parlance refers to the unwanted by-products of production and consumption. This definition is in fact *the opposite* of what occurs in the natural world. There, wastes of all kinds are incorporated back into the biosphere to nourish other life. Even events that "lay waste" to landscapes, such as forest fires, provide rich soils for the next generation of plant life. If we viewed waste in this more natural way, as an input as well as an output, would we be so eager to discard it? In practical terms, what would our waste management system look like if waste was considered a resource? Such an approach would involve a reorientation of both production and consumption activities, but wouldn't be unprecedented. This is already done on a limited scale with municipally organized recycling and composting programs. Some authors, such as Paul Hawken (1993: 37), have argued that waste is the world's most significant untapped natural resource and the only thing stopping us from using it is the political-economic decision to consider waste as a cost to be borne primarily by taxpayers and by the biosphere (Preston 2012). By freeing manufacturers and consumers from (directly) bearing the full costs of waste disposal, it becomes cheaper to harvest new materials from the Earth than to reuse existing ones. Our concept of waste is thus married to practices of "waste management" that together reinforce the widespread practice of using things for a limited time and then discarding them forever.

Finally, sociology's attention to symbols, meaning, and discourse helps us to understand the often intense competition among groups to define nature (or a part of it) in different ways. A prime example is the Athabasca oil sands in northern Alberta, which have attracted significant domestic and international attention in recent years. The stakes are enormous, as the market value of accessible energy in the oil sands has been evaluated at anything from $342 billion to $1.5 trillion (Sharpe et al. 2008). The oil sands have many powerful backers, including the governments of Alberta and Canada, as well as the Canadian Association of Petroleum Producers (CAPP), a deep-pocketed industry association and lobby group. These organizations have engaged in expensive public relations campaigns to frame the oil sands in a positive way. **Framing** refers to the strategic deployment of symbols, metaphors, and claims to present an "interpretive package" to members of the general public who may be curious but do not yet have strong opinions on a subject (Gamson and Modigliani 1989). These framing activities usually involve images and claims about economic benefits and spinoffs, "regenerated" or restored land (particularly forests), hard-working young people, and continuous scientific innovation (Stokoe 2012). Opponents have engaged in efforts at counter-framing the oil sands. For example, critics frequently refer to the industry as "tar sands" (a term that in fact predates the more neutral-sounding oil sands); compare extraction to "strip mining" or "open-pit mining"; and emphasize carbon intensity, high water use, and tailings waste in labelling this "dirty oil." The point is that many environmental conflicts—even those with deep economic roots—are fought predominantly in the realm of symbols and culture. One of the major strengths of sociology is its attention to how human behaviour is shaped by the shared perspectives (including biases and assumptions) that we pick up through membership in a given culture. These clearly affect how we interact with the environment, and are a major area of study for environmental sociologists.

Structure

Sociologists also have a longstanding preoccupation with structure. **Social structure** refers to the assemblage of formal and informal rules and constraints that produce and enforce patterns in society and its institutions. For example, capitalist societies rely on free labour markets to set wages and meet employer needs. A free labour market, however, is not really free but rather highly *patterned*. Workers who are able to acquire scarce skills and credentials generally fare better than those who cannot, and are thus able to secure better wages, send their children to universities and colleges, and thus reproduce privilege over time. Note that none of these outcomes reflect the worth of the individuals involved—the rules of the game (that is, structure) produce results that channel and constrain people's behaviours. If one wants to better one's labour market chances, the only real way to do so is to engage long-term with the education system to acquire credentials (which are meant to represent skills)—in turn supporting a massive education industry that is largely designed to subsidize the private sector by producing graduates who are ready to work in even the most specialized jobs.

What does this have to do with the environment? Environmental sociology encourages us to look at how our (mis)treatment of the environment is connected to and even compelled by structural conditions. The example above showed how young people are compelled to spend a great deal of time and money on schooling to improve their chances of doing well in the future. The same logic applies to many regions of the world—especially poorer ones—with respect to the environment. For many nations, the easiest path to economic development in an era of global capitalism is through environmental degradation. This can take many forms, including the over-harvesting of natural resources (energy, minerals, fisheries and forestry), the encouragement of cash-cropping and mono-cropping (agriculture), and the privatization and outright sale of environmental assets (water, land, utilities). Economic globalization is worsening this tendency, as resource-hungry industrial economies seek out new sources of commodities and raw materials. Developed countries have of course been doing this for some time, but one example that we will consider at length in Chapter 8 is the case of China. China is presently the world's second-largest economy, having passed Japan in 2010, and may overtake the United States as early as 2016 (Gardner 2011). To sustain this spectacular growth, the Chinese government has worked hard to establish a strong political and economic presence in parts of Africa. Chinese companies are buying up land for agriculture, investing in oil rights and infrastructure, and getting involved in large-scale mining activities (French 2010). While many Africans are grateful for the influx of capital, critics are uncomfortable with the neo-colonial undertones of these activities, and are concerned that Africa's environment will be irreparably degraded to serve the interests of foreign governments, companies, and consumers (Brautigam 2009).

Attention to structure can also tell us a lot about our own environmental challenges in Canada and North America. According to many measures, North Americans are among the worst polluters and heaviest consumers of resources in the world. We generate more waste, use more water, and emit more greenhouse gases (GHG) per capita than nearly all other nations and regions of the world. These embarrassing facts compare very poorly to the countries of Northern and Western Europe, for example, which have had some success curbing fossil fuel use, reducing waste, and increasing energy efficiency (Harris 2007). How can we explain this? Some of it is undoubtedly cultural. Much has been written about how Americans in particular see energy consumption as inextricably linked to individual freedom (Seiler 2008). The ideal of the "open road" is highly salient in the US, building on older ideas about the frontier and early settlers' goals of "opening up the continent" for (white) habitation (Cronon 1995). But culture clearly isn't the whole story. Canadians are right behind Americans in per capita consumption, and we do not make the same associations between energy use and liberty. In fact, Canadians have a relatively green self-image, preferring to see ourselves as responsible stewards of the environment (Young and Dugas 2012). A deeper explanation can be found by looking at structure. According to Paterson (2008), the biggest distinction between North America and Europe is that the former has economies built on "carboniferous capitalism," while the latter is more oriented towards "efficiency capitalism."[1] Carboniferous capitalism is an economy that is based on *an abundance* of fossil fuels (carbon-based energy). For the last 100 years and more, Canada and the United States have enjoyed relatively stable access to low-cost oil, coal, and natural gas. This has led to a particular kind of economic and infrastructural development that has emphasized the consumption of these cheap inputs and de-emphasized efficiency. Consider, for example, the sorry state of North American mass transit systems compared to those that exist in Europe, both within and between cities. The low cost of fuel means that people and goods move within North America primarily by road rather than rail, and much of our electricity is generated by burning coal—an abundant but comparatively inefficient source of energy that is also a major contributor to air pollution and greenhouse gas emissions. Europe, in contrast, is a relatively resource-poor region that imports much of its energy needs (the US imports substantial quantities of oil, but its coal and natural gas supplies are primarily domestic). As such, European governments and companies have had a longstanding interest in energy efficiency. France and Germany, for example, have invested heavily in nuclear energy, which has much higher up-front costs than coal but is substantially more efficient in converting fuel to electricity. Germany, Spain, and Denmark also lead the world in renewable energy development. This is not to say that Europe is an ecological paradise. There are plenty of severe environmental problems currently playing out across that continent, including the depletion of fisheries, problems with nuclear waste disposal, and ongoing disparities between Eastern and Western Europe (Carter and Turnock 2002). York et al. (2010) also note that European nations "export" significant amounts of environmental degradation by drawing resources out of other regions (a theme we will consider in Chapter 8). Overall, though, Europe's economic base—somewhat paradoxically grounded in energy *scarcity*—has allowed European nations to perform substantially better than North American countries in minimizing the environmental consequences of modern living. These different economic realities then have a strong impact on politics. Paterson (2008) notes that it is no accident that the major carboniferous capitalist countries in the world—the United States, Canada, Australia, and Saudi Arabia—have been the most active resisters of coordinated global action to reduce GHGs and combat climate change, while European nations have been the most vocal backers of these efforts, notably the Kyoto Protocol. These are deeply structural questions that sociologists are well equipped to address.

Power

Finally, one of the great strengths of sociology is the attention it pays to the role of power in shaping human affairs. Over the years, sociologists have developed multidimensional perspectives on where power comes from, how it is exercised, and the effects it has on social relations. Power has been shown to reside in access to economic resources, symbols and statuses, and even in everyday language and discourse. It is exercised formally and informally—through rules such as laws and customs, and through softer channels such as expectations, socialization, habits, ideology, and expertise (Savoie 2010). Environmental sociologists pay a lot of attention to how power influences human–nature interactions. First, we need to recognize that powerful people and entities (such as governments and companies) are able to exert substantial control over the natural environment. In our current political-economic system, much of the environment has been **commoditized**—that is, turned into a form of exchangeable property. This is clearest with respect to land, which if not protected or otherwise designated as outside the market, can be bought and sold like any other good. But it is also the case with many natural resources, such as timber. Most forestry in Canada takes place on **Crown land**, or land that is not privately owned but controlled by federal and provincial governments, supposedly in the interests of all citizens. Rights to the resources on or under this land, though, are granted, leased, or sold to private companies, usually in exchange for some kind of royalty. In British Columbia, for example, this has led to a system that favours large, powerful companies that long ago secured rights on a broad scale. This has excluded many smaller, local businesses from access to the forest resources that surround them (Hayter 2000). And it is not just companies that exclude people. In many parts of the world, for instance, women's access to the environment is controlled. In some cases, severe restrictions remain on women's ability to own property. In areas that have suffered widespread environmental degradation, "the impact of scarcity has been particularly hard on women, who are responsible for gathering wood and water [due to] traditional gender roles, making those tasks increasingly arduous and time consuming" (Sontheimer 1991: 2). Additionally, the work of Thomas Homer-Dixon (1999) has highlighted the intersections of ethnicity and the environment, and the particularly troubling conflicts that emerge when groups struggle over **resource capture**, or exclusive control over a source of wealth.

Power imbalances also play a key role in how we protect ourselves from environmental calamities. The 2004 tsunami that left 250,000 people dead along the coastline of the eastern Indian Ocean killed far more women and children than men (Jasanoff 2006). The aftermath of natural disasters in lesser developed countries are invariably most devastating for the poor, many of whom lose what little property they had and are unable to acquire scarce resources such as food, water, and medical attention (Curran 2013). These inequalities extend to the global scale as well. For example, one of the most memorable scenes in Al Gore's celebrated 2007 film, *An Inconvenient Truth*, shows the impact that a dramatic rise in sea levels due to global warming would have on different parts of the globe. In quick succession, viewers are shown the potential devastation of Bangladesh (the world's most densely populated country, much of which is built on river deltas) and the equal impact on the lower Manhattan region of New York City. The truth of the matter is, though, that these places are not equally vulnerable. Let it be said here that the chances of New York City permanently sinking due to global warming are infinitesimally small (temporary storm surges are another matter, as we saw with Hurricane Sandy in 2012). Technologies exist to protect coastlines and (if needed) reclaim land from the sea, and in the United States there is sufficient wealth and political will to protect a place so important to the national economy and sense of identity. Bangladesh, in contrast, is far more vulnerable—in part because a river delta is a more ecologically complex environment, but in greater part because it is *not* an important place in the eyes of those who control much of the world's wealth.

Conclusion

Understanding the human–nature relationship is the great challenge of environmental sociology. A big part of this challenge is that the relationship is highly complex and often contradictory. On the one hand, there is no doubt that we need the natural environment to sustain our bodies and our societies. As animals, we cannot survive for long without the air, food, and water that can only come from the biosphere. This dependency gives us more than enough reason to want to protect the natural environment, minimize degradation, and take a long view of our relationship with the planet. On the other hand, our present behaviours towards the environment appear to be based on the assumption that humans are exempt from ecological limits—that our technology and ingenuity make our relationship with the environment flexible and adaptable. Murphy (1994: 17) describes this as "the plasticity myth"—the assumption that both human beings and nature are malleable and shapeable. With respect to humans, our predominant cultural assumption is that society will continue to be able to solve problems as they arise, including any environmental issues that might threaten quality of life. On the nature side, the plasticity myth assumes that the environment is resilient and has the capacity to absorb a great deal of human excess without fundamentally changing or irreversibly degrading. Environmental sociology looks at all of these issues—how people and their institutions are tied to the biosphere, how and why our actions do and do not reflect that reality, and how our stance(s) towards nature fold back onto society and interact with core sociological concerns about social class, gender, ethnicity, globalization, symbols, and discourse. In particular, I have argued that sociology's core strengths—its attention to culture, structure, and power—allow us to look at the environment as simultaneously a human *and* a natural phenomenon. Next, we will look at how human societies have negotiated their complex relationships with the environment through time.

Questions for Critical Thought

1.   Is sociology capable of analyzing environmental problems? How does it compare to other disciplines?

2.   What can the analysis of culture tell us about environmental problems?

3.   How would you make sociology more "environmentally aware"?

Suggested Readings

Angelo, H., and C. Jerolmack. (2012). "Nature's Looking Glass," *Contexts* 11(1): 24–29. A poignant essay about the intersection of culture and nature, it examines how two red-tailed hawks that built a nest on top of a New York City high-rise spurred city-wide debate about the place of nature in an increasingly human-altered world.

Dunlap, R., F. Buttel, P. Dickens, and A. Gijswijt, eds. (2002). *Sociological Theory and the Environment*. New York: Rowman & Littlefield. This book provides a broad and comprehensive discussion of how different sociological theories view the natural world. It also shows how the work of environmental sociologists draws on different strands of classical and contemporary theory.

Hannigan, J. (2006). *Environmental Sociology*, 2nd edition. London: Routledge. This book contains excellent discussions of the origins of environmental sociology, including its debts to the thinking of Marx, Weber, and Durkheim.

Suggested Websites

American Sociological Association—Environment and Technology Section
www.envirosoc.org/
   This is a comprehensive website for students and researchers working in the field. It includes a regular newsletter updating advancements in the field.

Canadian Sociological Association—Environmental Sociology Research Cluster
www.csa-scs.ca/enviro-home
   This website includes profiles of Canadian environmental sociologists, publication announcements, and a catalogue of resources.

2 Learning from the Past: Taking a Long View of the Human– Nature Relationship

Key Points

◎ Human societies have always faced environmental challenges, most notably resource depletion and land degradation.

◎ Humans are exceptional short-term problem solvers, but we have greater difficulty anticipating the long-term consequences of our decisions and actions.

◎ Today's environmental challenges bear a striking resemblance to those that affected ancient civilizations, suggesting that there are lessons to be learned from the environmental past.

Introduction

In the late 1960s, my grandfather bought some land near the northern tip of the Bruce Peninsula in Southwestern Ontario and built a cottage on it. The Bruce Peninsula juts out into Lake Huron, forming the Western shore of Georgian Bay, and is a geologically and ecologically special place. It is a part of the Niagara Escarpment, an ancient limestone rock formation that arcs from New York State, through Ontario, to Wisconsin and Illinois. "The Bruce" is home to many endangered or threatened plant and animal species, such as Ontario's only surviving rattlesnake, black bears, rare orchids, and a remarkable variety of nesting and migrating birds.

I have known the Bruce my whole life, and I've seen it change. In the mid-1990s, when I was in my late teens, I started to get very alarmed. Our family cottage is on a mid-sized inland body of water unconnected to Lake Huron or Georgian Bay, and over the course of a few years I noticed that the lake was changing. I had canoed over "dead lakes" in Northern Ontario— lakes that were so affected by acid rain that all plant and animal life was destroyed, making them crystal clear. What frightened me was that our lake, which was normally murky, was clearing. I could see rock formations 20 feet farther off the dock than before, and propeller-busting underwater hazards that had been hidden were now obvious even on cloudy days. It seemed that the microbial and plant life so critical to lake ecology was beginning to retreat, and it was painful to imagine what might come next.

It turns out, though, that what I thought was decline was actually *recovery*. The Bruce, I later learned, had been relentlessly logged between the

1880s and the 1940s, to the point that nearly the whole peninsula resembled a clear cut at mid-century. Trees were logged right up to the shores of lakes and streams, leaving no buffer to prevent erosion and run-off into the waterways. Lakes would have been flooded with nitrogen and potassium and seen their average temperatures rise due to increased exposure to sunlight. These changes would have made the lakes more eutrophic than otherwise—encouraging the growth of algae and severely stressing fish and animal populations. These effects were then compounded by early cottagers, many of whom disposed of human wastes in outhouses too close to the shore, and whose "grey water" plumbing (for cleaning and bathing) often emptied directly into the ground and ultimately found its way to the lake. As the forest regenerated and new bylaws required better waste disposal, the lake slowly started to change again. I was wrong—it wasn't dying, it was getting better.

The point of this anecdote is that environmental degradation is *not new*. Human beings have affected the environment for as long as we have existed. Too often, we presume that environmental problems began only recently and therefore that we have little experience dealing with them. In fact, human groups have been altering the environment, and dealing with the consequences of those alterations, for millennia. While it is certainly true that the modern world has spawned serious new environmental issues (think of climate change, nuclear waste, and ozone depletion), there are several reasons why environmental sociologists should pay attention to the past as well as the present. First, there are differing opinions on what exactly are the root causes of current environmental problems. As we will see in later chapters, some environmental sociologists blame the capitalist system, which depends on the continuous increase of production and consumption to sustain itself (Schnaiberg 1980). Others see population growth and affluence as the root cause (York et al. 2003), and still others point to serious but correctable shortcomings in governance and decision-making (Mol and Janicke 2009). By looking at the past, we get a better understanding of what is new, and what is not, about current environmental problems. Second, looking at the past provides us with a window on ourselves as a species. Simply put, humanity's checkered environmental past prompts us to ask: Is there something about us—how we act and think, individually and collectively—that contributes to environmental problems? The answer to this question is unclear, and is clouded in ongoing controversy among sociologists, historians, anthropologists, and archaeologists, but it needs to be posed nonetheless. By looking back in history we can see that human behaviours toward the environment are patterned, and that these patterns give rise to eerily familiar ecological problems. There is much to be learned from these past experiences.

Welcome to the Anthropocene

Geologists, who take an extremely long view of time, classify the Earth's history into **eras**. Eras begin and end with major events—geological or paleontological—that usually result in mass extinctions. Our current era, the Cenozoic, began with the extinction of the dinosaurs 65 million years ago and the rise of mammals as the dominant form of land life (if we ignore insects of course, which are far more abundant even today). The Cenozoic is subdivided into **epochs**, which are usually classified according to glaciation periods (ice ages). Our epoch is the Holocene, literally meaning "the most recent age," which began about 12,000 years before present (BP). In 2008, though, a proposal was submitted to the Geological Society of London to formally reclassify the current period as "the **anthropocene**"—the age of humans (Zalasiewicz et al. 2008). While there is disagreement on when exactly to draw the line—some arguing for 300 years BP, at the dawn of the Industrial Revolution, and others for 8,000–10,000 BP with the emergence of agriculture—the argument is the same: Humans have so profoundly altered the natural environment that our impact will be observable in the future geological record, long after we are gone.

While the finer points may be debated, it is hard to argue with this conclusion. Since modern humans arose as a species roughly 160,000 years BP, we have altered the natural environment in numerous ways. Human beings are tool-makers and tool-users, and in the early years of human existence these tools were used to build camps, erect structures (temporary and permanent), and clear land. There is substantial evidence that early humans used fire as a common hunting and foraging strategy, allowing them to flush out game and expose insects for collection. In the process, humans substantially altered the landscape of southern Africa and possibly Australia by clearing them of trees (Bird 1995). Human impacts dramatically increased with the discovery and widespread use of agriculture, which encouraged populations to settle permanently and develop systematic ways of exploiting key environmental resources, such as water, soil, and timber. The evolutionary trajectory of many plants and animals have been altered (by domestication) or halted (by extinction) as a direct consequence of human activity. Fast forward to today and we see that the landscapes of every continent except Antarctica have been radically modified by the presence of people. Even the places we do not occupy, like the deep oceans and the atmosphere, bear our mark. At this time, there is literally no place on Earth untouched by human activity. We are, in a real way, a force of nature.

The remainder of this chapter will look at some of the profound impacts that humans have had on the biosphere throughout the anthropocene, and will examine some recurring challenges, problems, and tendencies that human groups have exhibited in the face of ecological strain. Recently, there has been much debate regarding the role of ecological problems in the collapse of several pre-historic human societies (Diamond 2005; Tainter 2006; McAnany and Yaffe 2010). First, there is some disagreement as to whether societies collapse at all, or if they simply adapt and change. Second, it will forever be uncertain whether environmental stresses were the *primary cause* for such declines or merely one among several *catalysts* that sent already-fragile societies over the edge. This chapter does not address these debates directly, as for our purposes they are somewhat moot. For environmental sociology, knowing whether or not ecological problems directly caused societies to collapse is less important than knowing (1) how these problems arose, and (2) how people responded to them—sometimes making them better, and sometimes making them worse. In the following, I outline three problems that have recurred through time and profoundly challenged human relationships with the environment: the problem of abundance, the problem of diminishing returns, and the problem of time.

Too Much of a Good Thing? The Problem of Abundance

The historical and pre-historical record shows that one of the biggest challenges facing human groups is dealing with abundance. This is counter-intuitive, because scarcity is clearly the more urgent problem, and more of a direct threat to survival. We will see, though, that the line between abundance and scarcity is thinner than we usually imagine. When European settlers first came to North America, there were an estimated 30 million bison (also known as buffalo) roaming the continent. They had been actively hunted by Aboriginal groups for thousands of years, but were so abundant that their grazing likely had a hand in creating the treeless grasslands of the Canadian Prairies and US Midwest (Knapp et al. 1999). Within approximately 100 years—from 1780 to 1880—the bison were all but extinct, with only a few hundred surviving animals left in the wild. Most disturbingly, the worst years for the bison were the final ones, with "the last 10 to 15 million buffalo on the Great Plains killed in a punctuated slaughter lasting a little more than 10 years" (Taylor 2007: 1). While many bison were killed for sport or for bounty (the burgeoning railroads saw their huge bodies as a threat to trains), the prevailing reason was economic. Buffalo hides made great leather, and there was an insatiable demand in both North America and Europe for this cheap source of raw material. Also, the abundance of the bison blinded settlers and their governments to the fragility of the whole population. When pushed to the edge, the fall came stunningly quickly—tipping abundance into scarcity before any meaningful conservation measures were attempted or enacted.

The story of abundance is a very old one, and begins with the first human migrations. The further back in history we go, the more difficult it is to be certain about how human beings interacted with the natural environment. Archaeology, palaeontology, and palaeobotany, though, provide strong evidence that these encounters were often catastrophic. To begin, it is important to know that anatomically modern human beings first emerged in Africa, and over a period of time migrated across the globe (Flannery 2011). Migrations across the Pacific Ocean were greatly facilitated by the cold climate of the period (45,000 to 10,000 years BP), which locked up much of the world's water in glacial ice, thus lowering sea levels and creating a land bridge between modern-day Siberia and Alaska and shrinking the distance between South East Asia and Australia. Mariners in more recent times then settled the islands of Micronesia, Polynesia, New Zealand, and Hawaii (from 5,000 to 1,500 years BP), completing pre-historic human circumnavigation of the globe.

The world these pre-historic newcomers encountered was radically different than it is today. Each continent was home to a staggering variety of **megafauna**—animals weighing over 220 lbs (100 kgs). Australia, for instance, was home to enormous marsupials many times larger than modern day kangaroos (Burney and Flannery 2005). The *Diprotodon*, a giant creature resembling a wombat, weighed up to 4,500 lbs. The continent was also populated by 10-foot-tall flightless birds, crocodiles up to 20 feet long, and carnivorous tree-dwelling marsupials weighing over 200 lbs. North and South America also had an almost unthinkable richness of animal life compared to today—including vast herds of woolly mammoths and mastodons, the largest cats that have ever lived (with adults reaching up to 1,000 lbs.), and the colossal *Megatherium*, a ground sloth that stood 15 to 20 feet tall (Dilworth 2010).

The story of what happened to these animals is controversial (see Box 2.1), but there is strong evidence that the fate they met was us. The paleontological record shows that much of the world's megafauna disappeared almost in lock-step with the first arrival of migrating human beings. If we set aside humanity's home continent of Africa for a moment (a special case that needs separate consideration), we see a breaking wave of extinctions that mirrors our own spread across the globe—first into Europe and Asia, then to Australia, then through the Americas from north to south. The thesis that human beings caused this great global extinction was first comprehensively proposed by the paleoclimatologist Paul S. Martin. His seminal article on the subject, published in 1972, essentially argued that the disappearance of the world's megafauna could be explained in much the same way as the bison disappeared in the nineteenth century—rapid overkill. At the time, this theory was met with some incredulity—how on Earth could a relatively small number of human beings with limited technologies wreak such ecological havoc, especially on such formidable animals?

Could it Have Been Climate Change?

Not everyone is convinced that the global extinction of megafauna was caused by human overkill. In fact, this is one of the few areas of academic science where open hostility exists between theoretical camps (e.g., Haynes 2007). Some archaeologists and paleontologists argue that the mass extinctions of 45,000 to 8,000 years BP were caused by climate change, and that human activity played little to no role at all (Grayson and Meltzer 2002). The time period in question was one of dramatic changes in global climate, as the world first cooled and then warmed substantially at the end of the last glacial period. This caused parts of the globe to dry, and others to become more humid and moist. It is unclear, though, how these changes would have led to the scale of extinction shown in the fossil record (Dilworth 2010: 86). Many of the animal species in question had survived dramatic climate shifts in the past (the aforementioned *Megatherium*—the giant sloth of South America— had existed for at least five million years before perishing only 10,000 years ago). Most megafauna were also highly mobile animals with access to large continents with varying landscapes and micro-climates. Most importantly, geological data show that this climate shift was not unusual in its speed or severity, which begs the question of how this particular shift could have been so deadly compared to others (Scott 2010: 226).

Recent research has tried to find a middle ground between the two hypotheses. For instance, Haynes (2002) argues that megafauna in the Americas that survived the "human wave" described by Martin would have been further stressed by climate change, particularly in drying regions. Drought would have pushed surviving animals to gather in *refugia*—areas where food and water remained abundant—which in turn would have allowed them to be more easily hunted by humans. Large predators, which would not have been directly hunted by people, would have suffered from the combination of a changing climate and the rapid decline of prey populations. Arguments such as these suggest that the truth is likely somewhere in the middle. Overkill, exacerbated by climate change, has left us, in the words of Bill Bryson, "living on a much diminished planet" compared to the one that existed only a short time ago (2004: 472).

In the years since, archeologists and paleontologists have worked to answer this question (Gillespie 2008). Ultimately, *how* it happened may be easier to understand than *why* it happened. Martin himself proposed the theory of a human wave or "front line" that would have been devastating to large animals. This is best illustrated in the case of the Americas, although it could have also applied in Australia. Remembering that people first entered the Americas from Siberia approximately 13,000 to 16,000 years BP, human beings had spread across both North and South America by 10,000 BP. Archeologist Charles Redman points out that "even at a population growth rate of 1.4 per cent (that is, doubling every 50 years), a band of 100 people entering the New World would saturate the hemisphere with 10 million people in about 800 years" (Redman 1999: 79). Martin calculated that population growth alone would push the human "frontier" progressively south and east from Alaska at a rate of 16 kilometres per year, reaching the southern tip of South America 1,200 years after first arrival. Importantly, Martin also argued that population density on the frontier was likely higher than behind it, as migrants pushed into territories with virgin resources that could (initially) support more people. The frontier, then, was like a wave or a broom that swept over large animal populations, leaving them much reduced and vulnerable to further exploitation (see Figure 2.1).

Another piece of the puzzle has to do with the characteristics of megafauna themselves. First, several scholars have argued that megafauna in Australia, the Americas, and on large islands such as Madagascar and Hawaii, would not have immediately seen people as a threat (e.g., Flannery 2011). Having never seen humans before, our ability to kill at a distance (using spears—a nearly universal technology at the time of global migration) would have caught these animals completely off-guard. This may also explain why Africa retained a larger proportion of its megafauna than any other continent—animals there had a longer history of co-evolution and co-habitation with humans (Dilworth 2010: 87-8). Incidentally, paleontological records also show that extinctions in Eurasia happened over a longer period of time than in the Americas or Australia—perhaps because hominids such as *homo erectus* and *Neanderthal* inhabited these places prior to modern humans (Burney and Flannery 2005). Second, megafauna were vulnerable because of their long reproductive cycles. Modern elephants, for example, have a gestational period (pregnancy) of 22 months; rhinoceros, 16 months; and giraffes, 15 months—and in each case typically only one calf is born per pregnancy. Based on this slow rate of reproduction, "an annual harvest rate of 20% would have been sufficient to push a given species of large mammals to extinction" (Redman 1999: 79).

As mentioned, the question of why this happened is difficult to answer. It is highly unlikely that humans the world over set out to exterminate the large animals upon which they depended. As with the bison of the nineteenth century (which survived the great megafaunal extinction), it appears as though prehistoric humans had difficulty managing abundance. We can draw some evidence about this from what is known about human settlement of the Pacific islands, including Polynesia, New Zealand, and Hawaii, which were populated relatively late (2,000 to 1,000 years BP). Archeological dating shows with a fair degree of certainty that, shortly after arrival, humans

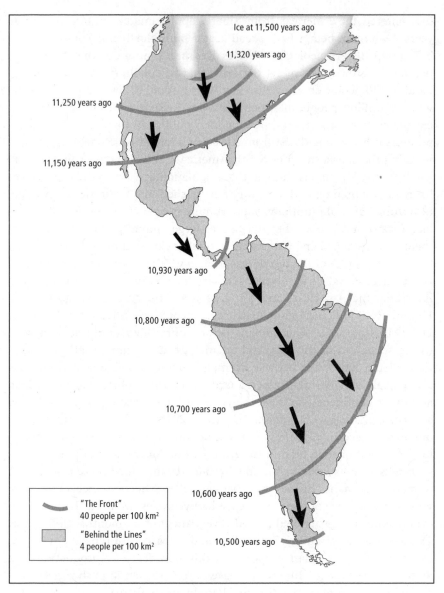

Figure 2.1 The "Human Wave" Across the Americas
Source: Martin (1972)

concentrated their harvesting on species that offered the greatest returns for the effort expended (Dye and Steadman 1990; Simmons 1999). In other words, on entering a new environment people made food choices based on how easy it was capture and kill an animal, and the benefits they acquired (in terms of calories, but also other useful materials such as bones, skins, or feathers). For example, the Pacific islands were populated by a huge variety of sea birds—many of them flightless—that would have yielded a high ratio of calories to effort (Milberg and Tyrberg 1993). In many cases, though not all, these were rapidly driven to extinction. To reiterate, this was likely not people's *intent*. It is most likely that the newcomers harvested what appeared to be an abundant resource and then failed to protect it adequately when it tipped into scarcity. Animals introduced by humans, particularly rats that hitched rides in ocean-going canoes, exacerbated the problem by feeding on eggs and young. In all likelihood, it was over before people could change their behaviours.

This interpretation is backed up by what we know about the major continents. Certain megafauna were likely targeted because they provided plentiful calories to hunters relative to the effort it took to bring one down (Haynes 2002: 397–8). Waguespack and Surovell (2003) analyzed the North American archaeological record and showed that while there is strong evidence that humans ate megafauna, there is little evidence that they ate smaller species that yield fewer returns. This only happens *after* the disappearance of larger options. Globally, the dietary preferences of hunter-gatherer societies vary tremendously (both historically and today), from specialized diets that focus on a few species to generalists who consume a range of plant and animal resources (Kelly 1995). Nonetheless, some archaeologists argue that many pre-historic peoples began as specialists when they entered new areas, and only became generalists after depleting ideal resources. Burney and Flannery (2005: 395), for instance, argue that there is a discernable global pattern in the prehistoric world of people exhausting "ideal" animal populations before turning to less ideal sources (Burney and Flannery 2005: 395). This kind of food ranking would have been an entirely rational response for people entering a new environment that was unknown to them—landscapes that offered both promise and danger. Unfortunately, these rational decisions had staggering long-term consequences that would have been difficult to predict for these first settlers who encountered such tantalizingly abundant natural resources.

The Problem of Diminishing Returns

The problem of diminishing returns is connected to the problem of abundance. Looking back at human history, we see countless examples of human groups developing a good idea, and then pursuing it so thoroughly that it begins to undermine itself. The clearest examples of this come from human experiences with farming. The rise of agriculture is rightly hailed as a watershed moment in human history, allowing people to settle permanently in fewer places, develop more advanced technologies, and sustain more complex divisions of labour and systems of government (Diamond 1997). But agriculture also has a dark side. There is evidence that foraging hunter-gatherer societies enjoyed better overall health than some agricultur-alists who relied too strongly on a few crops—not to mention the hierarchies and larger scale conflicts and wars that agriculture allowed (Barker 2006). Nevertheless, the development of agriculture was a key step towards the complex societies we inhabit today. It is no accident that recorded history begins with the rise of farming, as literacy and numeracy were required to coordinate, plan, and keep records about agricultural practices, land desig-nations, taxes, debts, and so on (Ponting 2007).

Agriculture depends on harnessing energy from the sun (through pho-tosynthesis) and nutrients from the soil. When crops are first planted, they usually enter rich soil. Land that has been recently cleared is typically high in nutrients, especially if it has been cleared using fire (hence the enduring popularity of slash-and-burn agriculture). Over time, though, planting and harvesting—the removal of biomass—takes far more nutrients from the soil than are replenished. Under these conditions, crop yields decline year over year, to the point that soil may be permanently degraded due to erosion or nutrient loss. This illustrates the problem of diminishing returns: when a resource is first used, it frequently provides spectacular returns, but in fol-lowing years it takes greater and greater effort to achieve similar yield.

It is difficult to overstate the challenges that this posed to early societ-ies. One of the earliest farming civilizations—Mesopotamia in modern-day Iraq—suffered tremendously from this ecological dilemma. Mesopotamia is the name for a collection of city-states situated in a region dubbed "The Fertile Crescent" that encompassed the valleys of the Tigris and Euphrates rivers. Evidence suggests that Mesopotamians engaged in agriculture as early as 10,000 years BP (8000 BC). Towns of several thousand people existed in the region by 8,500 BP, undoubtedly supported by livestock and crop agriculture (Montgomery 2007: 28). This early agriculture was aided by a natural advantage that also facilitated the rise of Egyptian civil-ization along the Nile—each year seasonal rains swelled the rivers, which transported nutrients from higher ground onto the cultivated flood plains (Allen 2002). Eventually, population growth—made possible by successful agriculture—pushed farming beyond the river valleys and into marginal lands. There, the Mesopotamians invested in one of the world's first major infrastructure projects, the construction and maintenance of an elaborate irrigation system to draw water out of the rivers year-round. This invest-ment immediately increased crop yields, and was quickly adopted in regions that had been cultivated for some time. There were two problems with this strategy, however. First, even the rich soils of the floodplain could not withstand intensive agriculture of this scale for long, and soon began to lose nutrients. Second, constant irrigation brought groundwater up to the surface through capillary action (essentially, underground water adhering to surface-level water, drawing the former up to mix with the latter). Groundwater in that region (and many others) is more saline than river water—it has a higher salt content. Given that water will evaporate and salt will not, soil became salinated enough to literally poison crops (Montgomery 2007: 39). Crop yields fell by an estimated 66 per cent per hectare between 5,000 and 4,000 years BP (Tainter 2006: 61). There is substantial evidence that Mesopotamian farmers knew about the dangers of erosion and salinization, and worked to mitigate these risks by, for example, improving drainage (Yoffee 2010). A big part of the problem, however, was that large-scale decisions about farming were being driven from above. To compensate for diminishing returns on crops, the rulers of Mesopotamian city-states ordered that agriculture be *intensified* in an attempt to feed their populations and protect themselves militarily from equally desperate neighbours (Chew 2001: 38). The increased use of irrigation also meant that enormous amounts of labour had to be invested in clearing the canals of sediment carried into them from the river (Montgomery 2007: 39). Effort spiralled upwards as returns spiralled downwards. These problems were never resolved, and human-induced soil erosion and salinization played a substantial role in creating the desert landscape we now associate with modern-day Iraq (Pollock 1999: 39).

The problem of diminishing returns is not restricted to agriculture. We are only now, for instance, beginning to understand the extent of global deforestation in early human history (Williams 2003). Forests would have been extremely important for early peoples. They were a source of raw materials for construction, fuel for warmth and cooking, and habitat for food sources such as wild game, plants, and berries. As we saw at the very beginning of this chapter, forests also play a key role in regulating the quality of fresh water, without which people cannot survive. Diamond (2005) argues that forests were *the* most important natural resource of the prehistoric world.

As discussed earlier, fire was an important tool for early hunter-gatherer societies for both hunting and foraging. While it is sometimes difficult to distinguish between natural and human-set fires, there is evidence that much of the landmasses of Africa, Eurasia, Australia, and the Americas were intentionally burned at various times following human arrival (Williams 2000). Where people are mobile, and population densities are low, the forest can easily recover. Things change, though, as people move into the permanent settlements associated with agriculture. Farming requires land, and accessing fertile soil often means clearing trees. According to Williams (2000: 31), "because clearing for agriculture proceeds as the result of one person's effort, or at most that of a family, it is unrecorded, piece-meal, incremental, though in total, massive." Matthews (1983) estimates that the world has lost 10 million square kilometres of forest since the rise of agriculture. The United States alone has lost 94 per cent of its forest cover following the arrival of Europeans, most of it under the plough (Goudie 2006: 33).

Permanent settlements also lock people into place, making them more dependent on local landscapes and resources. This poses a real challenge for their relationship to forests, which provide so much but take a long time to regenerate. Gregg (1988) estimates that a typical prehistoric farming settlement of about six households (or 30 people) would require six square kilometres of forest land to meet long-term needs for construction, maintenance, and fuel. This works out to "a staggering 20 hectares per person," without accounting for poor harvest years, which often forced farmers to turn to the forest for their subsistence needs (Williams 2000: 32). Wood is also a heavy material, which means that people tended to harvest the forest area close to home before going further and further afield. In practice, this frequently meant that "people would completely denude local sources, rather than draw on larger, more distant sources in an effort to conserve forest growth" (Redman 1999: 139). These patterns are still observable in many parts of the world where poverty and lack of infrastructure forces people to scavenge for fuel for heating and cooking (Baland et al. 2010).

Again, deforestation illustrates the problem of diminishing returns. At an early stage of exploitation, forests provide significant benefits that are easily accessible. As the resource is depleted, though, it takes more effort to secure equivalent returns. As local environments are deforested, people have to walk or otherwise travel greater distances to gather fuel. Forests that have been depleted also give fewer returns. A woodland that is recovering has smaller trees that yield less material, meaning that more must be cut in order to satisfy needs. This poses the same dilemma as we saw with soil—when a resource is used on a large enough scale, it becomes *more important* but *less dependable* after a sustained period of exploitation.

The Problem of Time

The final recurring environmental challenge discussed in this chapter is the problem of time. Environmental historians use the term **maladaptation** to describe how groups and societies engage in behaviours that degrade the environment and increase their vulnerability to ecological problems (Redman 1999: 48). We have already considered one example of this— ancient Mesopotamia, where centralized governments responded to the problem of declining soil fertility by extending their control over agriculture and demanding more intensive cropping, rather than allowing farmers to enact conservation techniques such as improving drainage and leaving fields fallow for longer periods (Tainter 2006: 62). In an attempt to solve one problem, a far more serious one was exacerbated.

What does this have to do with time? Humans are exceptionally good problem-solvers. The history of technology—including technologies that have long been abandoned or never caught on—is a fascinating read that shows just how much raw creativity we possess as a species (Diamond 1997). Ancient monuments like the Great Wall of China and the Roman aqueducts demonstrate the lengths to which we go to solve problems. Problem-solving, though, is frequently something that we do ad hoc, even in modern times. It is often difficult to predict where problems will come from, and what shape they will take. Therefore, we frequently approach problems with a short-term bias, addressing them only after they have become apparent and looking to solve them as quickly and expeditiously as possible. The Great Recession of 2008–2010, for instance, was largely the result of monetary and financial deregulation in the United States and Europe to help those economies recover from the dot-com bubble of 2000 and the terrorist attacks of 11 September 2001 (Reinhart and Rogoff 2009). The solution to the two prior problems contributed to a much larger problem down the road—a textbook case of maladaptation. In this case and others, short-term problem-solving which made sense at the time led to longer-term difficulties.

One of the most frequently discussed historical examples of this problem comes from the US southwest, a region of truly impressive social and environmental innovation. As with the other cases discussed in this chapter, this example is controversial, and alternative interpretations exist (e.g., Wilcox 2010). The US southwest is an ecologically varied area that includes the modern-day states of Colorado, Utah, Arizona, and New Mexico. This would have been a difficult place to live, with relatively thin soils, frequent droughts, and extreme temperature variability. Redman (1999) focuses on two major populations in the area—the Anasazi, who lived at the confluence of the four states, and the Hohokam, who lived in what is now southern Arizona. While somewhat distant from one another, the two adopted a similar approach to social and environmental management. In essence, this involved creating regional co-operative and trade networks "that acted to spread agricultural risks over a sufficient number of environmental zones" (Redman 1999: 152). Archaeologist Timothy Kohler (1992) argues that the Anasazi in particular were keenly aware of the fragility of the local environment after long experience with swidden agriculture (which involves the use of temporary slash-and-burn sites, from which the group later moves on). Their eventual response, around 1,200 years ago, was to create a series of permanent settlements. On the surface, this seems counter-intuitive, given how we saw earlier that permanent agricultural settlements are often far harder on local environments. But spreading co-operating settlements out makes sense as a risk management strategy—if the environment degrades somewhere, or is hit by unexpected drought, flooding, conflict, or pests, other areas can pick up the slack.

This strategy allowed the populations to grow and the two societies to become more complex (Anderies 2006). According to Redman (1999: 121),

> This strategy is fraught with risks, but it also is pushed forward by the advantages it bestows upon its participants who organize and cooperate. . . . People would be more willing to share food across groups in a village and to invest in facilities to improve the processing and storage of food. Cooperative labour pools would enable long-distance hunts and participation in trading networks. Overall, village life facilitates the management of cooperative activities and the sharing of production risks over a wider set of individual productive units. These advantages made larger and larger villages possible, but they also made the system vulnerable.

Essentially, the Anasazi and Hohokam built systems to solve "ordinary" problems—or problems that could be expected based on existing knowledge and experience. In both cases, long-term events and ecological fluctuations caught up. The evidence for the Anasazi is hotly contested, but is clearer for the Hohokam. Data from fossilized tree rings shows that the Hohokam system was established during a period of relative stability in the local climate, but that at about 1250 AD climate became more unpredictable, with floods or droughts occurring every 10 years or so. At around 1350 AD, two years of massive flooding were followed by an exceptionally dry one that affected the entire Hohokam region (Redman 1999: 155). After that time, it seems that surviving members of the Hohokam abandoned the village system and a large fraction of the population likely moved elsewhere (Anderies 2006).

These cases show that maladaption is not always about making the wrong decision. In many ways, the indigenous populations of the US southwest made the *right* decisions according to the circumstances in which they found themselves. Their decisions made sense at the time, and resulted in real improvements in quality of life. At the same time, over the long term these decisions were exposed as problematic. While we can't know for sure, it is likely that these people knew something about the long-term risks they were running (Wilcox 2010). They certainly weren't stupid, or naive, given that they survived and prospered for a very long time in a harsh environment. But long-term problems frequently appear abstract compared to the needs of today. We are certainly no strangers to this dilemma in modern times, given our massive consumption of non-renewable resources (a point I return to below). A single human life is short compared to the long ecological processes upon which we depend. One of the biggest challenges facing our species may be to ditch the habit of thinking short term, and start applying our problem-solving genius to the long term.

Drawing Lessons from the Past

The environmental challenges that we face today are both similar to and different from those confronted in the past. They differ primarily in terms of scale. As we will discuss in Chapter 8, environmental problems in the pre-modern era were more localized than today. When the ancient Mesopotamians degraded their soils, they were the ones who suffered the consequences. Nearby civilizations such as Egypt continued to have healthy agriculture well into the last century (see Box 2.2; Montgomery 2007: 43). Today, local problems like erosion or crop failure are also global problems because agriculture has become a complex and delicately balanced international system. A serious drought in Russia in the summer of 2010 destroyed much of the region's wheat crop, which sent global prices up by approximately 50 per cent, which in turn disproportionately hurt poorer wheat-importing nations in the Middle East and North Africa (Trostle 2011).

The similarities are also instructive. Looking back over the examples considered in this chapter, we see that people have always been users of nature, and that this use often (but not always) depletes or degrades the environment. Despite our cultural inclination to think otherwise, the past was not an ecological paradise or Garden of Eden that has only recently been trampled by industrialism and modernity. The most informed environmental historians now suggest that sustainability is the historical exception rather than the norm. In the words of Redman, "the archaeological record encodes *hundreds* of situations in which societies were able to develop long-term sustainable relationships with their environments, and *thousands* of situations in which the relationships were short-lived and mutually destructive" (1999: 4). This is not to say that humans cannot live comfortably within ecological limits, but that it takes a great deal of care in order to do so.

With this in mind, let us return to one of the questions that opened this chapter: Is there something about us as human beings that contributes to environmental problems? According to Dilworth (2010), the answer is yes, and it is that "we are simply too smart for our own good." Dilworth's point is that human beings have one great advantage over others species—our ability to learn. Learning takes multiple forms, including observation, instruction, trial and error (experimentation), and making connections between different things that may at first appear unrelated (abstraction). Humans do all of these things well, which means that we can bend the ecological rules that limit other species. But Dilworth argues that our intelligence also has a down side because it encourages us to experiment with solutions before we really understand the full nature of the problem. Our capacity for learning then means that solutions are shared and replicated by

Box
2.2

What About Historical Successes?

Where are the success stories? Surely there are examples of pre-modern societies that achieved a sustainable relationship with the environment? Yes, there certainly are. But I would caution against applying labels like success and failure to the historical record. The Hohokam, for example, lived comfortably and prosperously for nearly a thousand years in their village system before encountering the ecological calamities that ended their way of life. Is that success or failure? This is why I've talked about recurring challenges and problems rather than classifying people and groups using normative terms.

Generally speaking, environmental historians consider that Ancient Egypt had success in achieving a measure of sustainability. Blessed with the same river ecology as Ancient Mesopotamia, Egypt maintained a more decentralized system of agriculture that allowed farmers more control over land use decisions and practices (Ellickson and Thorland 1996). The Highlands of Peru are also frequently cited as a case of successful long-term agriculture. For thousands of years, farmers there engaged in practices that maintained soil fertility and minimized erosion, principally by terracing (turning hillsides into a series of level steps), building raised fields, and leaving land fallow for long periods of time (Sandor and Eash 1989). These practices were unfortunately abandoned following colonization, leaving the region much diminished today (Erickson and Candler 1989).

Closer to home, the First Nations people of the Pacific Northwest region successfully managed the salmon populations that were (and continue to be) a cornerstone of their culture and economy. Salmon are a particularly vulnerable species, because they migrate from the ocean to freshwater at the end of their lives to spawn. Historically, most salmon were harvested in rivers and streams on their way to reproduce. First Nations people therefore had to temper their catch. A single net strung across a river or stream could destroy an entire salmon population. Salmon numbers are also cyclical—some years are good, and others are bad. In bad years, it would have been extremely tempting to harvest more, leaving less and less for groups further upriver and the overall population in doubt. Anthropologists and others have argued that elaborate rituals such as the potlatch were key to ensuring coordination and sharing across groups—allowing the resource to be maintained over several millennia of intensive human use (Campbell and Butler 2010).

others. Indeed, many of the examples discussed earlier can be interpreted as good ideas that have been pursued too thoroughly. As humans migrated into new areas, and were confronted with abundant resources, it made sense to exploit the ones yielding the greatest returns. When it was discovered that irrigation greatly enhances agricultural productivity, it made sense to irrigate more widely and thoroughly. Once these behaviours have been set, and their benefits demonstrated, it becomes very difficult to alter them.

We need only consider our relationship with fossil fuels to find a corollary in modern times. Fossil fuels such as oil, coal, and natural gas are the good idea that allowed humanity to escape its reliance on agriculture as its primary source of energy. Prior to the Industrial Revolution, all human activities were powered in one way or another by living plant life. Fuel for fires, which was essential not only for cooking but also metallurgy and artisanal manufacturing, came from timber and charcoal. Animal power, critical for transportation, agriculture (ploughing), quarrying, and construction, was fuelled either from grains grown by humans or lands designated as pasture. No matter how advanced pre-historical societies became, their dependence on plant life limited their access to energy. Homer-Dixon (2006: 51) argues that the world's most complex pre-industrial society, the Roman Empire, was ultimately checked by difficulties meeting energy needs. The harnessing of fossil fuels changed this, allowing humans access to *past* energy. Fossil fuels are, at root, the remains of former plant, animal, and microbial life that have been locked up in the Earth by long geological processes. When we burn fossil fuels, we are releasing energy from the sun (via photosynthesis) that has accumulated over a vast period of time. This is how we escape the energy limitations of the present. Many people now argue, though, that this good idea is being pursued too thoroughly. We know that fossil fuels are limited resources (although we don't know how much exists and is accessible to us) and that they cannot be renewed except over enormous periods of time. Fossil fuel use also involves combustion, which releases large amounts of carbon dioxide (a greenhouse gas) as well as particulates that degrade air quality (think of urban smog). Finally, as we will see in Chapter 5, key fossil fuels such as oil may already be showing the same pattern of diminishing returns encountered by Mesopotamian farmers nearly 10,000 years ago.

With all this in mind, why don't we back off on fossil fuels, or use their remarkable gift of energy to power a transition to more renewable sources? While we return to this question later in the book, the short answer is that a good idea is hard to give up. We, like the Hohokam and so many other ancient societies, have urgent problems to solve *now*, and fossil fuels are a tried and tested way of manufacturing more goods, growing more food (through mechanized agriculture), being more mobile, enhancing economic productivity, and improving quality of life. These are the right decisions when looking at the short term; we don't yet know what they will mean over the long term.

Conclusion

The aim of this chapter has been twofold: to establish that environmental problems and challenges are not new, and to see what lessons can be drawn from the past to guide an environmental sociology that is mostly focused on the present day. I have emphasized three main problems that are evident throughout the historical record—the problem of abundance, the problem of diminishing returns, and the problem of time. I have argued that these problems recur because of patterns in human behaviour. The natural environment can be a harsh place, and it is not surprising that human beings, with our penchant for learning and problem-solving, established and maintained practices that made sense in the short term but frequently led to long-term ecological problems. It is not that pre-historic and pre-modern people were stupid, or stubborn, or unable to adapt. I have purposely avoided the ongoing debate about the role of ecological degradation in the collapse or resilience of historic peoples (see Diamond 2005; Ponting 2007; McAnany and Yoffee 2010). In most of the cases discussed in this chapter, problems were frequently caused by good ideas that were pursued too thoroughly. As good ideas are pursued, they become *more central* to the society in question but simultaneously *more precarious*. As was the case with historical extinctions, soil degradation, deforestation, and settlement on marginal lands, the rigorous application of good ideas changes the ecological context in which they originally arose.

The main lesson for the present is that we have already been here, many times. Our tools are different now, and our society far more complex. However, the question *are things different now* is the subject of some controversy. Do the advantages that we have today—science, expertise, democracy, planning, risk management, technology, innovation, communication, global integration—make us better able to exploit and manage the natural environment without encountering these problems? The remainder of the book will show that there is a wide range of perspectives on this question. For a long time, though, the modern world's response to environmental problems was just to ignore them, or to see them as the inevitable consequences of development. In the next chapter, we will look at how environmental issues have recently gotten back on the agenda. Specifically, we will look at the emergence of environmentalism as a social movement that, despite having little access to the traditional levers of power in our society, has had some surprising impacts on mainstream Western and global culture.

Questions for Critical Thought

1. Is our relationship with the natural environment better today than in the past, or worse?

2. How do environmental problems today differ from those encountered in the past? How are they the same?

3. How can we encourage people to think more about the long-term consequences of their actions?

Suggested Readings

Aimers, J.J. 2007. "What Maya collapse? Terminal classic variation in the Maya Lowlands," *Journal of Archaeological Research* 15: 329–377. Numerous scholars are skeptical of the "ecological collapse" narrative that has been popularized by authors such as Jared Diamond in his books *Guns, Germs & Steel* and *Collapse*. Using the Mayan civilization as an example, this article suggests that we are too quick to apply the label "collapse" and should instead focus on how ancient civilizations changed and adapted rather than vanished.

Dilworth, C. (2010). *Too Smart for Our Own Good: The Ecological Predicament of Humankind*. New York: Cambridge University Press. An interesting meta-historical overview of human difficulties in managing the environment, in which Dilworth stresses the limits of human thinking in explaining our poor track record.

Flannery, T. (2011). *Here on Earth: A Natural History of the Planet*. New York: HarperCollins. This is a broad history of ecological triumphs and tragedies from one of the best science writers today.

Suggested Websites

Canadian Archaeological Association
http://canadianarchaeology.com/caa/
 Many of the debates and issues raised in this chapter are hotly debated in archaeological circles. The Canadian Archaeological Association website contains good summaries of current research in the field.

3 Environmentalism and Its Opponents

Key Points

◎ Environmentalism is both a social movement and a broad worldview that has gained a remarkable degree of public acceptance over a short period of time.

◎ Environmentalism has changed and diversified over the years, but has not completely shed its elitist origins.

◎ Anti-environmentalism has evolved as well, directly challenging the influence of environmental activists on key policy issues.

Introduction

As we saw in the last chapter, human groups have always faced difficult environmental choices and circumstances. Modern Western society, however, has had a particularly destructive and exploitative relationship with the natural environment. The so-called developed nations of Europe, North America, Oceania, and Eastern Asia consume far more than their share of the world's resources and export many of their needs and wastes to poorer regions of the globe. And yet Western society has also given rise to the modern environmentalist movement, which has challenged traditional instrumental approaches to the environment, created powerful cultural narratives of conservation and sustainability, and become a force in global affairs. This contradiction is of great interest to environmental sociologists, who see it both as an academic puzzle and an opportunity to push for change in how Western society treats the natural environment.

One of the most fascinating things about environmentalism is just how fast and recent its rise has been. The word "environment" was rarely heard before the 1960s, and it typically referred to human affairs, like the "political environment" in a country or organization (Dryzek 2005: 5). Today, environmentalism is everywhere, from door-to-door fundraising campaigns to slick corporate advertising to children's cartoons. There is now so much environmentalism out there that it is getting harder and harder to precisely define what it means.

Part of the problem is that environmentalism refers to multiple things. In this chapter, I will focus on two distinct meanings. First, environmentalism refers to a **social movement**, or more accurately a broad collection of social movements, driven by people involved in **collective action** to somehow reform or alter human relationships with the natural environment. The target of this action can be open-ended and global, as with the climate change issue, or confined and local, as with land use questions or development projects. Activism in the name of conservation is older than most people realize, extending back into the nineteenth century. Second, environmentalism refers to a shared **worldview** or mindset that emerged relatively recently—in the 1960s and 1970s—and rapidly became part of mainstream culture. This kind of environmentalism is abstract and highly flexible, having more to do with ideas, values, and symbols than organized collective action. It is commonly expressed as a general concern for nature, the sentiment that "we should be doing better" to protect the environment, and support for recognized and uncontroversial eco-friendly activities, like recycling programs, waste reduction, and anti-littering campaigns. Environmentalism as a worldview has become part of the general **cultural consensus** in Western societies, to the point that it is taught in elementary schools as part of the "common sense package" we expect all children to learn.

This chapter outlines the history of environmentalism as both a social movement and a shared worldview. As we will see, environmentalism has changed substantially over the years. From its beginnings as an elite intellectual movement centred in the US, environmentalism has become a truly global phenomenon that resonates with people around the world. In this way, environmentalism can be considered one of the most successful social movements of all time. Internationally, environmentalism has been more widely accepted than the women's movement, the human rights movement, or the labour movement. At the same time, though, its long-term impacts are still unclear. Because environmentalism is about reform, it has always had its share of opponents and adversaries. Social movements frequently attract **counter-movements** that seek to contest or blunt the movement's goals (Meyer and Staggenborg 1996), and environmentalism is no exception. I will end the chapter by arguing that the **anti-environmentalist** counter-movement has evolved and changed as well, and that the most recent shift in strategy—to focus on issues of science and expertise—poses the gravest threat to environmentalism to date.

A Brief History of Environmentalism

In 1995, historian William Cronon published a provocative essay about the history of environmentalism entitled "The Trouble with Wilderness." In it, he argued that Western society has undergone a remarkable about-face in its perceptions of nature over the past 100 years. Cronon suggested that for a very long time European and North American cultures saw nature as an adversary. For people living in pre-modern societies, the natural world would have seemed vast, powerful, and unpredictable. For villagers and settlers, the forests on the outskirts of town were more menacing than bucolic—wild spaces that were mysterious and unknown, full of predators, and home to dangerous and "uncivilized" people such as Aboriginals (in the Americas) and bandits (in Europe). Travel from settlement to settlement was risky, livelihoods and survival depended on weather and climate, and natural disasters such as fire, floods, pests, and storms were devastating and difficult to predict.

Nature, in other words, was where bad things happened. Cronon used Judeo-Christian biblical stories to illustrate how deeply rooted these ideas are in Western culture. Adam and Eve, having sinned, were cast out of the tame Garden of Eden and into the harsh wilderness, where they felt pain, fear, and exhaustion for the first time. Moses and his followers were condemned to wander the barren desert for 40 years following their exodus from Egypt. It was in the wilderness that Jesus, at his most vulnerable, met the Devil and was tempted. We can add secular examples as well—just think of the fairy tales that you likely heard as a child. Little Red Riding Hood, Hansel and Gretel, Snow White—all encounter deep and mysterious evil in the woods and away from settlement and civilization. Nature was a difficult and frightening space, while the good spaces, such as they were, were those that people had carved out of the wilderness.

According to Cronon, this view of nature has changed rather than gone away. While there is great continuity in the narrative, the roles have been reversed. Today, nature is seen as a place of serenity rather than danger, while the crowded (urban) world of people is perceived as more threatening and unpredictable. People now "escape" the city to "get away from it all" and have "authentic" experiences in parks, cottages, hiking trails, and wilderness. It is the urban environment that now corrupts us, exhausts us, and corrodes the soul; and nature is where we relax, recharge, get in touch with ourselves and back to what really matters. More profoundly, whereas the Western project used to be about *protecting ourselves from nature*—by building towns and villages, clearing land, and exterminating predators—we are now much more concerned with *protecting nature from us*. Humans are the menace, and nature the victim that must be preserved, enclosed, and set apart. As mentioned, this has been a remarkably recent change. In the middle of the twentieth century, for instance, provincial and state governments in Canada and the US were still offering bounties for the skins of wolves, cougars, and bears. The Government of Ontario only stopped paying bounties for wolf hides in 1972, three years after the first Moon landing! In a short period of time, environmentalism has become one of our most dominant cultural narratives.

Most histories of environmentalism describe it as emerging in a series of waves. The metaphor is apt, because concern about the environment tends to ebb and flow, with periods of intense interest and activism interspersed with times of relative inattention as other issues come to the fore. The wave metaphor also captures the fact that each "reawakening" of environmental concern tends to build on earlier ones, while also pushing the movement in new directions. In the following, I discuss four distinct waves of environmentalism that have left their imprint on the movement. It is worth mentioning that other scholars have different interpretations of the waves and how they fit together (e.g., Devall 1992; McKenzie 2002).

Preservationism, 1850s–1930s

The first wave of environmentalism is generally thought to have emerged in the nineteenth century. This wave is usually labelled **preservationism,** because it focused on protecting or preserving places of special natural splendour against development. In the United States, the preservationist movement coincided with the closing of the American frontier, as settlement and railroads pushed into the more difficult corners of the US South- and Northwest. The closing of the frontier motivated some American elites to start thinking about nature differently—as something that was limited now that "civilization" had spread across the country (Edwards 1998: 33). Some prominent intellectuals in the US, such as Ralph Waldo Emerson (1803–1882), Henry David Thoreau (1817–1862), and George Catlin (1796–1872), began writing about their experiences in undisturbed and remote nature (Kline 2011). These writings drew on imagery and arguments from the wider **Romantic movement**, which was popular among both conservative and counter-cultural elites at the time (Pagden 1993). Romanticism describes a collection of philosophical and artistic writings that emerged as a critique of the Industrial Revolution, the Enlightenment, and rational modernism more generally—focusing instead on themes of emotion, aesthetics, and nature (Pepper 1996: 169). The carnage of the US civil war (1861–1865), which introduced the world to mechanized warfare, helped to create an audience for preservationist arguments that nature should be protected as a "place apart" from the modern world. The most celebrated American preservationist was John Muir (1838–1914), who is credited with creating over a dozen National Parks through his tireless lobbying of US politicians, co-founding the Sierra Club (in 1892), and popularizing the movement by recruiting celebrities and public figures. Muir also embodied the spiritual side of preservationism. He was a deeply religious man, and saw God's hand in the spectacular landscapes that he sought to preserve (Cronon 1995).

In England, preservationism was less about protecting spectacular landscapes than redefining the relationship between urban and rural areas (Macnaghten and Urry 1998: 37). The Industrial Revolution and the **enclosure movement** had caused mass migrations from the countryside to industrial cities. As such, rural areas became less a place of work and more a place of leisure, particularly for members of the urban upper classes who sought to escape the soot and noise of the city (Urry 1995). New railroads offered the possibility of day trips, and new tourism companies—most famously Thomas Cook and Son—began offering pre-planned packages and tours to wealthy clients. Tourists wanted to experience an aesthetic countryside rather than one under hoe and axe. As in the US, then, the preservationist movement was driven by elites who focused on key "special" places, such as the Lake District in northwestern England not far from Manchester and Birmingham, and the Dover region closer to London.

Preservationism was slower to emerge in Canada, likely because the country was still sparsely settled in the latter part of the nineteenth century, particularly in the West and North. Canada's first National Park, Banff Hot Springs, was founded 13 years after the first US Park, and early Canadian parks were carefully drawn to exclude lucrative timber and mining lands (Dunlap 1999: 119). Canada's small preservationist movement drew intellectually from its counterpart in the US (Muir spent some time in the Georgian Bay area of Ontario), but it also had domestic contributors. Among the more bizarre figures was Grey Owl, a British immigrant who successfully posed as an Aboriginal person, penning books and touring to lecture on living in harmony with nature (McKinnon 2002: 59). Painters such as Tom Thompson (of the Group of Seven) and Emily Carr also played a role, chronicling both spectacular and weather-twisted landscapes far from the cities.

Conservationism, 1900–1950s

In the early twentieth century, preservationism was joined by **conservationism**. In contrast with preservationism, which was a romantic movement driven by elites, conservationism was a **pragmatic** movement driven primarily by governments. Conservationism was motivated by emerging problems in resource management. As we saw in Chapter 2, the abundant resources of the North American continent encouraged a reckless approach to harvesting, epitomized by the decimation of the Plains Buffalo in the 1800s. At the turn of the century some administrators in the US watched in alarm as timber companies started to repeat the pattern, rapidly felling the vast forests west of the Mississippi River. Conservationism was about exerting government control over this recklessness and imposing a more rational, science-based approach to resource management. Specifically, "conservationists believed that through government regulation they would be able to limit excesses and encourage both businesses and individuals to use the nation's vast resources more carefully" (Kline 2011: 61). This approach was championed by US President Theodore Roosevelt (in office from 1901–1909), who pushed legislation to bring water use and forestry under more direct government control. His view of nature, though, was utilitarian—that nature should be conserved for human uses:

> The fundamental idea of forestry is the perpetuation of forests by use. Forest protection is not an end in itself; it is a means to increase and sustain the resources of our country and the industries which depend on them. The preservation of our forests is an imperative business necessity. (Roosevelt, quoted in Kline 2011: 62)

As with preservationism, conservationism was slow to emerge in Canada. According to Dunlap (1999: 235), early twentieth century Canadian governments and policymakers were not convinced that it was necessary to restrict hunting, forestry, mining, and fishing. Macdonald (2007: 69) writes that "prior to World War II, industrial pollution was not subject to any form of regulatory control in Canada," and that the only real environmental legislation in this country was to keep farm animal waste out of public waterways. When conservationism did arrive, it was very business-focused. For example, in the mid-1940s British Columbia became concerned about the long-term fate of its enormous forest cover. In the latter part of that decade, the province overhauled its forestry licensing system in order to preserve timber resources over the long term. Their answer, though, was to take timber rights away from small companies and give them over to large corporations (Hayter 2000: 48). The logic was that large corporations would have more incentive to protect forest resources and invest in regeneration—because they planned to be in business for a long time, they would be good custodians of the resource. Conservationism was less about protecting the natural environment than making sure it could be exploited over the long term.

New Environmentalism, 1960s–1990s

Environmentalism as we know it today began in the 1960s and 1970s. As mentioned earlier, the biggest difference between this "new environmentalism" and previous waves has been its broad acceptance by the general public and integration into mainstream culture. While preservationism was ultimately a limited and elite movement, and conservationism a series of technocratic and utilitarian reforms, the new environmentalism of the 1960s profoundly altered the way many people viewed the world (McCormick 1995: 56).

The new environmentalism was built on three key ideas: (1) that environmental problems were urgent, (2) that they transcended national boundaries, and (3) that they were a direct consequence of scientific, technological, and industrial progress and development. One of the most frequently cited illustrations of these ideas is Rachel Carson's 1962 book,

Silent Spring, which many historians argue played a role in launching the movement (McKenzie 2002; Rome 2003). Carson's book, which sold half a million copies worldwide, outlined the consequences of widespread pesticide use on both wildlife and humans. With respect to wildlife, Carson argued that the careless spraying of pesticides was contaminating food and water sources, and that these chemicals—particularly the compound DDT—were interfering with the reproductive abilities of birds. DDT affects how much calcium is deposited in eggshells, making them brittle and easily broken. Iconic predators such as eagles, ospreys, and falcons were particularly vulnerable because of **biomagnifications**—the tendency of some chemicals to accumulate in animals higher along the food chain (as they consume other animals, they ingest higher and higher levels of toxins already found in their prey). Humans also occupy high places on the food chain, and Carson argued that this made us vulnerable to cancer and other long-term health ailments from a lifetime of accumulating these persistent chemicals. Carson argued that legislators needed to act immediately to ban or otherwise restrict these chemicals or else face rapid population declines in wildlife and escalating human health issues. This was frightening to a lot of people, and enforced the idea that problems were urgent and solving them meant acting decisively. Carson's work also highlighted the transnational character of these types of problems. Birds migrate, and chemicals from crop dusting can travel long distances through the air. Moreover, because the food supply is international, the boundaries of place, region, nation, and continent that had been presumed under preservationist and conservationist conceptions of environment made no sense. Finally, Carson's argument disturbed many people because pesticides were industrial products that were supposed *to solve* problems. DDT in particular had been hailed as a miracle chemical that was helping to increase crop yields and eradicate malaria (more on this in Chapter 6). Instead, Carson argued that this type of interference in the natural world was short-sighted and ultimately catastrophic. According to Macnaghten and Urry (1998: 45),

> Carson painted a picture of a world in mortal danger, a danger systematically and cynically produced by the greed and self-interest of the pesticides industry. Even more significant was the diagnosis that these "elixirs of death" were a direct by-product of the post-war zeal for modernization and technological improvement. While previous [environmental] concerns had centred on the aesthetics of suburbanization, or local pollution incidents, or the loss of particular habitats, Carson's critique centred on a representation of nature as systematically threatened by modern industrial processes.

Rome (2003) argues that the new environmental messages resonated because of two coincidences. The first had to do with youth. The late

1960s and early 1970s saw the baby boom generation entering and moving through post-secondary education. Environmentalism dovetailed nicely with other counter-cultural enthusiasms at the time, including back-to-the-land movements (epitomized in rural communes), drug experimentation, and a general interest in "new age" philosophy and religion. Second, the new environmentalism drew strongly on the more established peace movement. Opposition to the Vietnam War had coalesced by the late 1960s around a more general anti-violence ideology. Perhaps more importantly, the issues of nuclear weapons testing bridged the peace and environmental movements. Throughout the 1950s and 1960s, the United States and Soviet Union engaged in a campaign of mutual intimidation by testing dozens of atomic and hydrogen bombs in the Arctic region (which the two adversaries shared). In the late 1960s, concerned scientists, science fiction writers, and some media outlets began speculating on the effects of wind-borne radioactive fallout from atomic bomb testing (Weart 2008: 40–1). Nuclear fallout and radiation were major themes of the first Earth Day in 1970. The nuclear issue resonated in Canada, which clearly also has a stake in the Arctic region. In 1971, a young group of activists in Vancouver formed the "Don't Make a Wave Committee" to protest an upcoming nuclear test on the Aleutian island of Amchitka off the Alaskan mainland. The group, which would later re-brand itself as Greenpeace, adopted a risky strategy to stop the test—sailing directly into the test area. While unsuccessful in this particular case, the Greenpeace strategy of drawing media attention to issues by performing "action-based activism" (stunts, to their detractors) has been widely adopted by others.

Finally, some historians argue that the new environmentalism resonated broadly because it coincided with the emergence of ecology as a legitimate field of scientific inquiry and investigation. Ecology had been around for some time, but it had been scattered across multiple disciplines (Dunlap 1999: 219). It greatly benefited from the postwar expansion of universities, particularly in the US, and gradually gained in popularity through the 1950s and 1960s. Its real contribution was that it gave a language and formality to environmentalism that simply had not been there during the time of preservationism and conservationism. The basic idea behind ecology—that organisms ought to be studied in their environment and in relation to other living things—is an old notion that can be traced back to Aristotle (McIntosh 1985: 10). But while ecology's subject matter is not revolutionary, its attention to context and interrelationships goes against the **reductionist** approach that has dominated modern scientific inquiry (Forsyth 2003: 5). Reductionism involves the simplification or breaking down of objects and problems to their simplest components in order to better understand "the fundamentals" of what is being observed (Gallagher and Appenzeller 1999). Ecology's emphasis on systems and environments resists reductionism and tends to a more holistic or complex view of the phenomena under examination (Lawton 1992).

The rise of ecology and holism is also notable because it belatedly brought human impacts into environmental science (Forsyth 2003: 5). While most early ecologists focused exclusively on understanding ecosystems in and of themselves, this eventually led to concerns over how they were being disrupted or changed. Beginning in the 1960s, human interference in the biophysical world became an overarching theme in ecological research and education (Worster 1994: 340). According to Forsyth (2003: 4), this combination of resistance to reductionism and de facto critical stance towards human activities meant that ecology had a tense and even "subversive" relationship with other fields in the natural and applied sciences (Shepard and McKinly 1969). This new science posed a strong challenge to traditional narratives of technological and industrial progress, as well as to the role of scientists within these narratives. According to Worster (1994: 340),

> When ecology burst onto the scene during the 1960s, scientists of every sort were accustomed to appearing as society's benefactors. They were expected to show nations how to increase their power and citizens how to increase their wealth. But [ecology] took on a new role in a more nervous, anxiety-ridden time, . . . [based on] a grim hopefulness that ecological science would offer nothing less than a blueprint for planetary survival.

The rise of ecology as a science and as an ideology has been central to the establishment of what Beck (1992: 156) has called "a science-based critique of science" that was not widely present or accepted prior to the 1960s. Simply put, ecology established the *consequences* of science and technology as a legitimate field of scientific study. Ecology became a way for both experts and activists to talk against the excesses of science-guided development—industrialism, technology, and an unwavering faith in progress—using the authoritative language of science itself (Hannigan 2006: 45).

Environmental Justice (1990s–2010s)

The "new environmentalism" that emerged in the 1960s and 1970s is still the one that people are most familiar with. The three core themes discussed above—urgency, globalism, and the unintended consequences of capitalist industrialism—continue to resonate today. Several key issues of the last several decades have reinforced these themes, including acid rain, depletion of the ozone layer, and climate change. Nevertheless, some scholars argue that the environmentalist movement is in the midst of another transformative wave that is accompanying the rise of **environmental justice** concerns. Generally speaking, environmental justice activism combines ecological and socio-economic issues and priorities. It tends to have closer connections to marginalized groups, to be more focused on people's living conditions, and to be more attuned to issues of inequality. Cox (2004) argues that the "new environmentalism" of the 1960s and 1970s was essentially an upper- and middle-class movement that for the most part ignored environmental issues faced by the poor, by ethnic minorities, and by women. It has been known for some time that poor people shoulder a higher environmental burden than most members of the middle-class. For instance, when municipal governments are faced with difficult zoning decisions—like where to put noisy highways, industrial developments, or waste facilities—they are far more likely to place them in poorer neighbourhoods where people have less power and ability to resist them (Maantay 2002). In 1990, the sociologist Robert Bullard published his now-classic book, *Dumping in Dixie*, which showed how toxic waste dumps in the Southern United States were cited in areas predominantly occupied by poor black families—a practice he labelled **environmental racism**. These trends are also observable internationally, as toxic waste from North America and Europe frequently ends up in the developing world, even though this is against international law (Ni and Zeng 2009).

Unfortunately, the mainstream environmentalism of the 1960s–1980s did not see these problems as terribly important. While environmentalism provided an opportunity for marginalized people to articulate their concerns, "these issues were not deemed adequately 'environmental' by environmental groups such as the Sierra Club or the Environmental Defense Fund" (Cox 2004: 293). Part of the problem was that Environmentalist Non-Governmental Organizations (ENGOs) were busy trying to consolidate the gains that they had made. This meant "institutionalizing"—founding big organizational structures with paid staff, media strategies, and donor lists. Again, the archetypal example of this is Greenpeace, which in the space of a few years became a major transnational organization with a corporate governance structure and thousands of employees worldwide (McKenzie 2002: 77). Consolidating their gains also meant investing heavily in scientific research. Many in the environmentalist movement thought that science provided the best arguments for environmental protection (see the discussion of Carson's *Silent Spring* above). Involving poor people, with their "indecorous voices" and "inappropriate concerns," was simply not a priority (Cox 2004: 308).

Since the 1990s, however, environmental justice activism has been widespread and broadly accepted by mainstream ENGOs. For example, significant attention has been paid in recent years to the health issues of Canadian First Nation communities living down river from the Alberta oil sands. The case of Fort Chipewyan in particular has been taken up by several ENGOs, including Greenpeace, the Polaris Institute, and West Coast Environmental Law. In 2006, a local doctor spoke publicly about what he perceived to be elevated rates of rare cancers in the community. This touched off a broad and ongoing series of debates involving

Box 3.1

Speaking for Ourselves

At root, the environmental justice movement is about making environmentalism more inclusive. To do so, one of the main goals of environmental justice activism is to allow marginalized people "to speak for themselves" (Agyeman et al. 2009). One of the great successes of the environmentalist movement has been gaining access to decision-making about the environment. In Canada, for instance, decisions about development traditionally occurred behind closed doors, usually involving negotiation between industry and government (Leiss 2001). Pressure from environmental groups has led to a series of laws and policies to make this more transparent, such as the *Canadian Environmental Assessment Act* of 1992. Today, most major projects undergo reviews at municipal, provincial, and federal levels that involve public hearings and consultations. However, these kinds of forums can be intimidating for ordinary citizens. They are frequently presided by bureaucrats, attended by lawyers representing various interests (including ENGOs), and much of the discussion is about scientific facts and interpretations (Hannigan 2006: 48). When members of the public try to participate, especially people from marginalized groups who have less formal education or are less familiar with the legalistic norms of such settings, they are frequently ignored or dismissed. According to Cox (2004: 309), people who try to describe their experiences or fears in these settings using their own words and observations are often dismissed as irrational, "hysterical," or worse.

Environmental justice activists therefore advocate for more inclusive ways for people to participate in environmental politics. This includes pressing for greater involvement in all steps of the decision-making process, not just the formal hearings that privilege distant experts and entrenched interests. It also means giving greater credibility and weight to the knowledge and experiences of people directly affected by environmental inequalities—to allow marginalized people to speak for themselves, and to have their views reflected in final decisions.

community leaders, Health Canada, the Government of Alberta, and representatives of oil sands companies (Le Billon and Carter 2012). In the meantime, conflicts about air quality, drinking water, and levels of arsenic in local moose and other hunted game have sprung up (Weinhold 2011). If these concerns are founded, then the residents of Fort Chipewyan are clearly suffering from an environmental injustice, as they are bearing the health and environmental consequences of decisions and money made by others.

The Global Face of Environmentalism

The global spread of environmentalist ideas and activism after the 1960s is nothing short of remarkable. As we saw earlier, the new environmentalism of the 1960s was in a way "born global," focusing on major international issues such as nuclear weapons testing, chemical pollution, overpopulation, and resource scarcity. In these early days, though, non-Western voices were almost completely absent. Today, environmentalism of one kind or another can be found in every democratic country in the world. Large international organizations such as Greenpeace and World Wildlife Fund have branches in dozens of countries on every continent. Thousands of grassroots organizations, official and unofficial, have emerged in the developing world to contest domestic and international issues (Longhofer and Schofer 2010). Environmentalism itself has changed due to this global exposure. Dunlap and York (2008) point out that most of the movement's popular heroes now come from non-Western countries, including Chico Mendes and Ken Saro-Wiwa, who were both murdered for their respective opposition to deforestation in Brazil and oil exploitation in Nigeria. Despite these changes, sociologists disagree about whether there really is such a thing as a "global environmentalist movement." More importantly, they disagree about whether or not such a thing is even desirable.

Think for a moment about all of the obstacles that exist to a truly global environmental movement—one that unites people around the world in common cause for environmental protection and reform. Such a movement would have to overcome differences of culture, language, politics, custom, and tradition. Most importantly, it would have to bridge enormous gaps in material wealth. People living in Western societies consume far more resources than do citizens of less developed countries (LDCs). For instance, the average Canadian consumes 1,494 litres of water a day, which is 32 times more than the pan-African average of 47 litres per day (Conference Board of Canada 2011). Environmentally minded citizens in the West often express their concern through purchasing decisions—opting to buy organic produce or a more fuel-efficient car. Needless to say, these behavioural options are not available for most people of the world.

It is this gulf that leads Doyle (2005: 2) to argue that "there is no one [unified] global environmental movement, but many, and the differences between them far outweigh their similarities despite the fact that most share the symbolic nomenclature of 'environmental movements.'" By this, he means that both the motives and the issues are different in developed versus developing regions of the globe. According to some scholars, environmentalism in richer countries is driven primarily by **post-materialist values** (Inglehart 1997). Specifically, the argument is that the high standards of living in Western nations frees their citizens from actively worrying about survival and subsistence. Under these favourable "post-material" conditions, people can then turn their attention to quality-of-life issues, like the desire for a cleaner environment. In contrast, people who live in LDCs are still struggling with material issues such as reliable access to food, clean water, and economic security, and therefore do not have the luxury of prioritizing stringent environmental protections.

The post-materialist thesis has been strongly criticized as simplistic (e.g., Guha 2000; Mostafa 2011). Dunlap and York (2008), for instance, review several international surveys and find that citizens of poorer countries are often *more willing* to pay for environmental protection and clean-up than residents of Western nations, even though they have much lower incomes. This is an important finding that proves that residents of LDCs are just as environmentally conscious, if not more so, than people living in the affluent West (see also Mostafa 2011). However, there is ample evidence that environmentalism *means different things* in developed and less developed nations. For instance, many people in Western nations uncritically accept the notion that environmentalism needs to be global in order to be truly effective. Indeed, it is not at all unusual for Western-based ENGOs to launch campaigns that primarily target other countries. One of the best known examples of this can be seen in the extremely high-profile campaigns during the 1980s and 1990s to protect the rainforests of the Amazon River basin. These campaigns used varying tactics, including appeals to wealthy Europeans and North Americans to help purchase tracts of Amazon land to protect it from settlers (a strategy that continues today). In doing so, Western activists were clearly interfering in the affairs of a less developed nation (Brazil). The Amazon region is socially and ecologically complex, and relations among indigenous people, new settlers, resource companies, and the Brazilian government are delicate (Adams et al. 2009). This complexity was largely papered over by the ENGOs, who justified their involvement by labelling the Amazon as a global rather than a national space—literally as "the lungs of the planet" that provided benefits to all. In contrast, Jasanoff (2004) argues that people living in LDCs who identify themselves as environmentalists are often highly critical of the tendency of Western ENGOs to claim global status. Instead, Jasanoff suggests that environmentalist mobilization in less wealthy places is more closely connected to issues of livelihood. Local activism to reform practices in agriculture, forestry, land use, and sanitation can be far more effective than far-away campaigns to buy up and fence off land. It is also a more legitimate form of intervention in the eyes of people who still have to make a living in the context of any changes.

In sum, the rapid spread of environmentalism should not be misunderstood as a uni-directional transmission of ideas and values from the enlightened West to the rest of the world (Guha 2000). Rather, environmentalism has become a powerful symbol around which highly diverse movements have coalesced (Doyle 2005: 161). Environmentalism means different things to different people in different places. In affluent societies, it tends to be associated with the three ideas discussed previously (urgency, globality, and the unintended consequences of industrial production), and expressed largely through support of organized ENGO campaigns and consumption choices. In less developed societies, environmentalism is more closely connected to material questions such as livelihood. This does not mean, however, that Third World activism is myopically focused on local issues. Some of the most intense environmental conflicts in lesser developed countries involve protests against multinational companies that frequently spill over into the global arena (Rodriguez 2004). It does mean that environmentalism has diversified as it has "gone global," and that the global environmentalist movement encompasses many different viewpoints. This flexibility is a strength and has been an integral part of the movement's success.

Opponents of Environmentalism

As a movement that advocates societal change, environmentalism has always faced a degree of opposition. The early preservationist and conservationist waves in Canada and the United States were strongly opposed by advocates of resource development in the two countries, who saw the designation of protected lands and obligations to slow down exploitation of resources as unreasonable hindrances on private business (Dunlap 1999: 119, 237). Opposition to the "new environmentalism" of the 1960s and 1970s was particularly intense. The chemical industry in the United States, for instance, mounted a vicious campaign to discredit the claims found in *Silent Spring* and to attack Carson herself (Smith 2001). Such attacks, however, which were also directed at "irresponsible youths" and "alarmists," in fact helped to entrench the movement. In the face of a rising tide of public concern, industry attempts to dismiss environmental problems frequently came off as hollow, self-serving, and out of touch (Dunlap 1999: 277). As a consequence, opponents learned that environmentalism was something that was difficult to be *against*, at least in a direct way (Irwin 2001). Many companies and industries got on the green bandwagon and began making pro-environment claims as part of their marketing strategies (see Chapter 7). Opposition did not go away, but tactics would have to change.

The Wise Use Movement

The first evidence of a change in anti-environmentalist strategy was the emergence of the "wise use" movement in the United States in the 1980s. There is controversy about the origins of wise use, with some seeing it as a grassroots movement and others as a sponsored creation of resource compa-nies and anti-environmentalist think tanks (Helvarg 1997: 10). It is a classic counter-movement, in that it emerged in direct response to the perceived successes of the environmentalist movement (Meyer and Staggenborg 1996), arguing that it was better to "use nature wisely" than to set it aside as protected. The first real clashes between environmentalists and the wise use counter-movement occurred in the Pacific region of the US, specifically in logging and milling towns. This region, which includes Washington State, Oregon, and California, is important to US environmentalists, who have long opposed logging in these iconic areas and conducted direct protests by blocking logging roads and camping in trees. In the 1980s and 1990s, con-flict and even violence occasionally erupted between these groups. Helvarg (1997: 11) describes the conflict this way:

> The wise use movement has been primarily about protecting industrial and agricultural access to public lands and waters. . . . [Its] membership consists of workers and middle management in limited-resource industries such as timber and mining whose livelihoods are threatened by industry cutbacks and who are open to the argument that environmental protection means lost jobs. [Unfortunately,] this argument has been reinforced by the disinterest that conservation organizations have historically shown to the social consequences of wilderness protection.

The wise use movement has been less evident in Canada, although traces are definitely observable here. In Western Canada, advocates of resource development frequently draw on the narratives of "responsible development" and environmental stewardship found in US debates. In the late 1980s, a group called "Share the Stein" (referring to the Stein Valley in British Columbia) formed to advocate greater logging in that region. Other "Share" groups were later established in the province, including Share our Resources and Share our Forests (Rowell 1996), although these groups do not appear to be active anymore. Ongoing conflicts over the expansion of the aquaculture industry (fish farming) in British Columbia also exem-plify the wise use movement. Industry advocates, including many workers, frame their activism as being pro-environment and use the slogan "We are Working Environmentalists," while criticizing anti-aquaculture groups for killing jobs in rural communities (Young and Matthews 2010: 2). In other parts of Canada, several new movements have taken up "wise use" rhet-oric around property rights. For example, the Lanark County Landholders Association was founded in 2003 by Randy Hillier (now a Progressive Conservative member of the Ontario Legislature) "to preserve and protect the rights of property owners and to enshrine property rights within the Constitution of Canada" (OLA 2012). The organization re-named itself the

Ontario Landowners Association in 2006, and opposes government interference in a range of issues, including farm practices, zoning, land use, and the establishment of wind turbines in rural areas.

Anti-Environmentalism Gets Technical

Anti-environmentalism has truly matured in the last few decades (1990s–today). While the wise use movement and its subsidiaries have been influential, it has failed to crack the general pro-environmentalist consensus that has held since the 1970s. Recently, however, anti-environmentalist individuals and groups have shifted their focus to issues of science. As mentioned earlier, science has long been a strength of the environmentalist movement, as ENGOs have used scientific findings to argue that their positions are objective and fact-based, and that reforms are necessary and inevitable. Anti-environmentalists now challenge the environmental movement directly on this point, and evidence is showing that this strategy is having an effect.

The best example to illustrate involves the issue of climate change. For some time, members of the environmentalist movement have drawn on the collective expertise of the world's climatologists to make the case that governments worldwide need to start restricting emissions of greenhouses gases (GHGs), notably carbon dioxide that is produced primarily by burning fossil fuels such as oil, coal, and natural gas. This expertise is represented by the Intergovernmental Panel on Climate Change (IPCC) of the United Nations, which periodically reviews and summarizes the state of scientific research on climate issues. With over 1,200 authors and 2,500 expert reviewers, this is the most authoritative scientific body ever assembled on a single topic (we will discuss the IPCC in more detail in Chapter 4). Nevertheless, the conclusions and recommendations of the IPCC have been very successfully countered by a network of think tanks and affiliated experts in a few countries. Many of these groups and individuals are directly funded by energy companies (Hoggan 2008). While key actors in the United States get the lion's share of attention, Canada is home to several organizations—such as the Calgary-based "Friends of Science"—and individuals such as Tim Ball and Steve McIntyre, who participate in the network. This network counters the message of the IPCC by focusing on the uncertainties that are inevitable in any scientific discussion. For example, scientists rarely claim that they are 100 per cent certain about complex natural phenomena. The science of climatology is particularly tricky, as it involves combining knowledge of atmospheric chemistry, geology, ocean circulation, land use, and thermodynamics (just to name a few). As such, there will always be a degree of uncertainty involved in climate science, even if *scientists themselves are highly confident of their findings*. The contrarian network (sometimes called climate skeptics or deniers) focuses almost exclusively on these uncertainties.

Unlike the chemical industry that attacked Rachel Carson directly, contrarians cast themselves as the voice of reason—why act when it is premature, when acting will be expensive, and when there is no proven evidence of harm (Oreskes and Conway 2010)?

This strategy has another important effect. By focusing on uncertainty, the contrarian network implies that anyone arguing for action must have ulterior motives. In short, they suggest that scientists, ENGOs, and politicians who argue for GHG restraint are politicizing science that is not yet complete. Anti-environmentalists argue that climate scientists are just protecting their own research funding, or that they are closet "socialists," supporters of "Big Government," or "liberals" (which in the United States means anyone on the political left). The genius of this strategy is that it pre-empts environmentalist arguments without having to confront them directly (the losing strategy from the 1960s and 1970s). It effectively turns on its head the environmentalist argument that science be used as a rational guide to reform. Acting becomes irrational, while "non decision making" becomes the apparently wiser course (McCright and Dunlap 2010: 100).

As mentioned, there is evidence that this strategy is having a real impact on environmental politics. The great hope for the "new environmentalism" of the 1960s and 1970s was that it would be post-political—that it would be accepted by all political parties and ideologies. For a time it seemed that it might be. Some of the most important environmental legislation in North America has in fact been introduced by right-of-centre governments. Republican President Richard Nixon, for instance, founded the Environmental Protection Agency (EPA) in 1970, which remains the most powerful environmental regulator in the US. Progressive Conservative Prime Minister Brian Mulroney introduced the Canadian Environmental Assessment Act in 1992, and negotiated the Canada–United States Air Quality Agreement with the administrations of Ronald Reagan and George H.W. Bush to combat acid rain. While Reagan was reviled by the environmentalist movement, George H.W. Bush promised to become "the environmental President" in the 1988 election campaign.

Recent evidence, however, shows that anti-environmentalism is having the desired effect of polarizing people on environmental issues. For instance, polling in the Europe, the United States, Canada, and Australia shows that people who self-identify as conservative or who favour right-wing political parties are developing increasingly strong anti-environmentalist views (Dalton 2009; Anderson and Stephenson 2011; McCright and Dunlap 2011; Tranter 2011). Two developments have been particularly important for this polarization. First is the so-called "Climategate scandal" of 2009, which was triggered by the release of hacked personal emails of key climate scientists at the University of East Anglia in the UK. While the emails were embarrassing in some respects (exposing debates about

method alongside more intimate discussions about colleagues and critics), an inquiry later found no evidence of scientific malfeasance (Pearce
2010). Nevertheless, the incident was widely covered in the media, and
provided anti-environmentalists with enough substance to claim that they
were right all along about the politicization of climate science. Second, the
rise of environmental justice activism, while welcome and overdue, has
entrenched the view among many conservatives that environmentalism is
a left-wing project. The attempt to inject environmentalism with a greater
awareness of social inequality has made the movement more inclusive, but
it has also been used as an excuse to tune it out as ideologically motivated.
For example, the Canadian Government under Prime Minister Stephen
Harper has recently moved to scale back public consultations around the
review of major industrial projects, notably oil and gas developments and
pipelines. As we saw in Box 3.1, these are important forums for marginalized people to play a role in decision-making that will affect their lives. The
Government has been clear, though, that it wants to restrict these reviews
to scientific issues and exclude "irrelevant" testimony from people who live
in these areas. Former natural resources Minister Joe Oliver has proposed
that reviews should "group people together who have particular views," so
as not to waste time. Under the proposed rule changes,

> [People] wouldn't all be heard. There would be note of the fact that there's
> a group of them with those views, but those particular views don't have to
> be repeated again and again. . . . You take note of the numbers, but you
> also realize that they are all coming from the same perspective. (Oliver,
> quoted in Canadian Press 2012)

In this case, the response to a more socially aware environmentalism is
to ignore it.

Conclusion

This chapter has argued that there are two faces to environmentalism.
First, environmentalism is a social movement that has evolved over time,
from early waves of preservationism and conservationism, to later waves
such as the "new environmentalism" and environmental justice. Each of
these waves has added new dimensions to the movement, incorporating new
ideas and pushing it into new territory. From its origins in the United States
and other wealthy nations, the environmentalist movement has spread to
all democratic countries of the world. While it is fair to talk about a "global
environmentalist movement," environmentalism varies significantly from
region to region, and issue to issue. Generally speaking, environmentalism in developed countries is built around "post-materialist" values, the

(often implicit) assumption that it is acceptable to interfere in the domestic politics of other nations, and criticism of industrial excesses. By contrast, environmentalism in less developed nations tends to be more "materialist," or linked to issues of livelihood, rights, and work.

The second face of environmentalism is as a shared worldview. While the preservationist movement of the nineteenth century appealed to elites and members of the intelligentsia, environmentalism did not move into the mainstream until the 1960s and 1970s. In a remarkably short period of time, a broad cultural consensus emerged that the natural world is seriously threatened by people, and that steps must be taken to mitigate this harm. As argued by Cronon (1995), this worldview is a notable *reversal* of the dominant narrative in Western society that saw nature as an adversary rather than a victim. The broad acceptance of these ideas was helped along by several coincidences, including the peace movement, youth counter-culture, and the emergence of truly global scale issues such as nuclear weapons testing and pollution.

Environmentalism has always faced opposition, but I have argued that environmentalism is more vulnerable now than it has been in the recent past. Anti-environmentalist strategies have evolved, and current tactics of emphasizing scientific uncertainty and casting environmentalism as a leftist vanity project are having a demonstrable effect on public opinion, at least in the West. It remains to be seen whether this is a minor setback for the environmentalist movement, or whether these new strategies will have a lasting effect by chipping away at the cultural consensus on environmentalism that is crucial to any future reforms.

Questions for Critical Thought

1. Why has environmentalism resonated so strongly with so many people? What is its appeal?

2. While many people are sympathetic to environmentalism, few of us get involved in direct action. Why?

3. Should environmentalists embrace social causes, or is this spreading the movement too thin?

Suggested Readings

Agyeman, J., Cole, P., Haluza-DeLay, R., O'Riley, P., eds. (2009). *Speaking for Ourselves: Environmental Justice in Canada*. Vancouver: UBC Press. This edited volume presents case studies of environmental justice activism from across Canada. Several of the chapters are written by activists, providing direct access to the movement in the words of participants.

Macdonald, D. (2007). *Business and Environmental Politics in Canada.* Peterborough ON: Broadview. This book provides a detailed analysis of the role of business in shaping environmental politics in Canada.

Rome, A. (2003). "Give Earth a chance: the environmental movements of the sixties," *Journal of American History* 90, 525–554. This article provides a good historical overview that analyses why the environmental emerged in the specific political context of 1960s America.

Suggested Websites

Greenpeace Canada
www.greenpeace.org/canada/en/

One of the most sophisticated and best-organized environmentalist groups in Canada, Greenpeace's website contains a wealth of information on current campaigns and events.

Ontario Landowners Association
www.ontariolandowners.ca

The OLA is a grassroots organization that falls into the "wise use" category of anti-environmentalism. It advocates for property rights and against excessive regulation.

The Great Debate: Social Constructionism vs. Environmental Realism

4

Key Points

◎ Environmental sociologists disagree on the best way to conceptualize the relationship between nature and society.

◎ Environmental realists tend to see nature as a semi-autonomous actor that limits and reacts to society's choices.

◎ Social constructionists tend to see nature as a cultural phenomenon first, shaped by human perceptions, values, symbols, and interests.

◎ The case of global climate change illustrates the ongoing importance of the debate.

Introduction

As we saw in the last chapter, the environmentalist movement has had great success drawing public attention to environmental problems and forcing governments and companies to act on certain issues. But this is not quite as straightforward as it sometimes appears. First of all, what exactly is an "environmental problem" worthy of attention and action? In October 2010, a grassroots group called "Citizens for Clean Air" (C4CA) won a major victory when the Ontario government led by Premier Dalton McGuinty cancelled plans for the construction of a natural gas-fired electricity generating station in Oakville, Ontario. As part of their fight, C4CA mounted a slick website, produced brochures and information posters, and lobbied municipal, provincial, and federal politicians to intervene and join them "in opposing the location of Power Plants [*sic*] unreasonably close to homes and schools" (c4ca.org). The group argued that the plant would endanger people's health and create fog and ice that would plague nearby highways, and that if the plant were to go ahead it should in fact be built in the smaller community of Nanticoke which already has a large power-generating station. In this light, the decision to cancel the project was an environmental victory, right?

Perhaps, and perhaps not. The plant was intended as part of the Government of Ontario's Green Energy Plan, which aims to close the province's coal-fired power plants and replace them with less polluting and less carbon-intensive sources of power, which include natural gas (natural gas is also a fossil fuel, but its efficiency rate is much higher, meaning that more electricity is produced per unit of carbon dioxide expelled). It is also worth noting that Oakville is one of Canada's wealthiest cities, and that C4CA was headed by Frank Clegg, local resident and former President of Microsoft Canada. As part of its campaign, C4CA brought in Erin Brockovich, the famous former legal assistant who fought corporate polluters in California, and who is usually paid $25,000 US per appearance (Canadian Press 2010). Brockovich stated that "whether you're rich or poor or black or white, any one of us can be subjected to public health and safety threats. . . . [Citizens of Oakville may] have more flat screens than the average person [but] they shouldn't be told to shut up because they have money" (Daubs 2010).

So, what actually made the proposed power plant "an environmental problem," worthy of public mobilization and extensive media coverage? Was it the *severity of the threat* posed by the plant to nearby residents, schools, and the community at large? Or was it the ability of C4CA to deploy sufficient resources to *publicly define* the plant as an environmental menace rather than a benefit, which was the view of the provincial government?

These questions are emblematic of a long-standing debate in environmental sociology about how best to approach and analyze environmental issues. On one side of the debate are scholars who adopt an **environmental realist** perspective. Realists tend to focus on the characteristics of the threat or the problem itself—arguing that environmental problems often shape or "prompt" social reactions. On the other side are those who adopt a **social constructionist** perspective. Constructionists tend to argue the opposite—that environmental problems are shaped or formed by social and cultural criteria; asserting that problems are "built" or "achieved" through the successful mobilization of claims, symbols, narratives, and other resources.

To be clear, the realist-constructionist debate is not the only disagreement within environmental sociology, as we will see in later chapters. In a way, though, this is the most fundamental and long-standing divide among scholars in the field. I will begin by outlining the two perspectives and why they disagree. I will then discuss the value of each view and its unique contributions to our understanding of how nature and society relate to one another. Finally, I will use the example of climate change to illustrate the differences between constructionist and realist perspectives, and why these differences matter in the broader political arena.

The Debate (A Quick Overview)

The realist-constructionist debate, at root, is about how to best conceptualize the relationship between nature and society. As we saw in Chapter 1, the great challenge of environmental sociology is to try to put the natural world and the human world—long separated in sociology—back together in order to gain a better understanding of both. Generally speaking, realists and constructionists disagree on how to do this.

The Environmental Realist Perspective

Environmental realists tend to focus on environmental conditions first, and then examine how society is constrained by them, and whether society is reacting to these conditions appropriately or not. For example, the problems of ecological limits and **carrying capacity** are common themes in realist scholarship (Harper and Fletcher 2011: 274). We live in a finite world that has only so much land, fresh water, clean air, and fossil fuels. Environmental realists start with these biophysical facts as the basis for their analyses of social phenomena. For instance, Dunlap and Catton (2002) argue that human societies use the Earth in three main ways: as a living space, as a supply depot (a way of getting materials like food, timber, minerals, and energy), and as a waste repository. As human populations and economies grow, however, this puts significant pressure on the planet—to the point that we may now be outstripping the long-term ability of the Earth to absorb, sustain, and recover from these uses (in other words, we are exceeding its carrying capacity). Just as importantly, as our demands on the Earth grow, it is increasingly difficult to avoid "overlaps" in these types of uses (see Figure 4.1). Realists point out that overlap frequently causes conflicts. For example, the conflict in the Alberta oil sands can be interpreted as the outcome of an overlap. Global demand for oil has prompted massive investment in the oil sands to recover what is called "non-standard" or "unconventional" oil, because it is not in liquid form and must be separated from the soil. This creates a fair amount of waste that is deposited into the air (emissions) and water, specifically tailings ponds or vast artificial and converted natural lakes that hold the toxic sludge left over from oil extraction and "cleaning." As we saw in Chapter 3, this is also a space where people live, including several Aboriginal groups who have traditionally depended on the land and water for subsistence activities and who are directly affected by these developments. In other words, the oil sands are a place where the three main uses of the natural environment—living space, supply depot, and waste repository—overlap, thus encouraging (if not guaranteeing) conflict. Other examples of overlap include tropical rainforests (living spaces and supply depots), slums (living spaces and waste repositories), and freshwater lakes and rivers (supply depots and waste depositories). All of these are magnets for conflict as uses, interests, and priorities collide.

Environmental realists also tend to see the natural world as directly shaping human behaviours. Consider this example: Have you ever noticed that the "poor side of town" in major North American and European cities tends to be on the eastern side? This is true for London, England

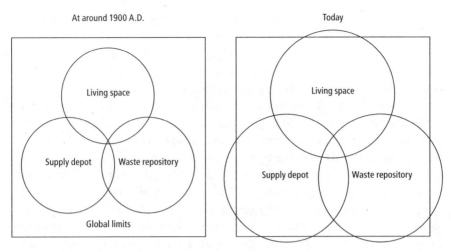

Figure 4.1 Human Uses of the Earth vs. Global Limits
Source: Dunlap and Catton (2002)

(the East End), Los Angeles (Compton), St. Louis (East St. Louis), Vancouver (the Downtown Eastside, East Van), Ottawa (Vanier), Toronto (Scarborough), and Hamilton (East Hamilton). Why? One of the main reasons (although certainly not the only one) is that prevailing winds in the Northern Hemisphere go from west to east. In the world before electricity, smoke from cooking and heating fires would drift eastward, making that part of town far more polluted. As factories sprang up during the Industrial Revolution, air quality got even worse on the eastern side of many cities (unlike today, factories used to be located downtown). Families who could afford to live on the west side enjoyed a real advantage in quality of life, while poorer people settled where prices were lower: the East. In this way, nature can be seen as an actor that affects and shapes human behaviour, even if it acts "without intentionality" or consciousness (Murphy 2004).

According to realists, nature is sometimes a passive and predictable actor (prevailing winds are unlikely to change, for instance), but it can also be active and unpredictable. Nature has only so much tolerance for human activities before it starts to "strike back." For example, reckless industrial development can so pollute local air and water that it begins to affect human life expectancy. This is the current reality in Beijing, China, where rapid growth has created near-constant air pollution and smog that costs the Chinese people billions of dollars in health-care expenses and reduces life expectancy by as much as five years (Mong 2012; Matus et al., 2012). In Murphy's (2006: 193) words, "human practices that amount to ecological recklessness are punished by nature's dynamics." Given our dependency on nature, natural phenomena act as the ultimate check on human activities. This idea is consistent with traditional understandings of ecosystems—that if one species gets out of line, the environmental response will eventually bring it back under control. In the classic example from introductory textbooks, the rapid expansion of a population of deer is brought back down by starvation and predation once local food sources are exhausted. No environmental realist would argue that humans are equivalent to deer, but they do argue that people cannot abuse nature indefinitely and get away with it (more on this in Chapter 5).

Finally, environmental realists tend to argue that improving our relationship to the environment will also help to alleviate social ills. For example, reducing our consumption of resources would minimize the overlaps shown in Figure 4.1, which in turn would reduce the potential for conflict and enhance equity and justice. Realists *do not* argue that all social problems can be addressed this way. They *do* argue that nature constrains our activities, and therefore better harmonization with nature's dynamics leads to better prospects for social reform.

The Social Constructionist Perspective

In a nutshell, realists view nature as being an independent variable (or, more accurately, a set of independent variables) that interact with and affect human decision-making. The arguments about limits, carrying capacity, and constraints that are common in realist scholarship imply that nature sets the ground rules, and people either follow them or they don't. If a society manages to harmonize its activities with nature's rules and realities, it can achieve sustainability; if it does not, the eventual outcome will be far more negative. This can be summarized as an equation: nature's dynamics + society's dynamics = outcome (sustainability or unsustainability).

Social constructionists tend to argue that this equation involves several assumptions that, when looked at critically, are difficult to accept at face value. First, they point out that realists tend to assume that we understand nature well enough to confidently assess how it interacts with human activities, now and in the future (Kroll-Smith et al. 2000: 50). Given the complexity of the natural world, this involves a bit of a leap of faith. Second, constructionists argue that environmental behaviour and politics really have little to do with "realism" in any recognizable form. Consider this example: Quick, name an animal that is currently listed as "threatened or endangered" according to the Canadian Species at Risk Act. Chances are good that you immediately thought of an iconic animal, probably a polar bear, or maybe a bald eagle, a grizzly bear, or a mountain lion. In fact, none of these animals are officially classified as threatened or endangered, but the Pacific water shrew, kangaroo rat, and Townsend's mole are. Would the loss of the Townsend's mole mean more to Canadians than the loss of the polar bear? Why not?

Social constructionists argue that, sociologically speaking, nature is *more of a cultural thing* than a *biophysical thing*. This does not mean that nature is a figment of our imagination, but rather that human relationships to nature are governed more by cultural criteria—specifically symbols, values, narratives, and discourses—than by "objective" physical or ecological criteria. The power of the polar bear as a symbol leads us to care more about its fate than the Townsend's mole, even though objectively speaking the latter may be the more threatened species. In fact, constructionists argue that some of the most objectively serious environmental problems get almost no attention at all. Here is an example of an environmental crisis that you have likely never heard of: the Great Pacific Garbage Patch (Kaiser 2010). The Garbage Patch is a product of the dumping and leaching of waste into rivers, streams, and directly into the ocean. Each of the major oceans of the world have circular currents (called gyres). An unknown percentage of floating surface debris is carried by these currents to the middle of the ocean, where it remains. Prior to the 1950s, the Garbage Patch was likely comprised of wood waste, which would eventually break down, biodegrade, and sink. Unfortunately, the patch is now overwhelmingly made up of plastics, many of which do not biodegrade but instead are worn down through friction and exposure to sunlight into fine particulate that are called "nurdles." Both the raw plastics and nurdles are toxic to marine life. Larger pieces are deadly when swallowed by birds, fish, and sea mammals, while smaller nurdles block sunlight in the water column and can slowly poison animals that ingest them. We are not talking about a small patch of ocean, either. Estimates of the size of the Pacific Garbage Patch vary from being twice the size of Hawaii to almost the full size of the continental United States (Ryan et al., 2009). Nor is the problem restricted to the Pacific Ocean; similar garbage patches exist in the Indian Ocean, the North Atlantic, and likely the South Pacific as well (although one hasn't been found yet!)

This example illustrates a key point made by social constructionists: People don't respond to the environment, or to environmental problems, in a raw and unfiltered way. Our experiences and responses are *mediated* by several things: our senses, our knowledge, our values, and our institutions (Proctor 1998). To most human beings, the Great Pacific Garbage Patch is an invisible problem. A boat can literally sail right through the Garbage Patch because most of the particulate is so small; nor is it visible by air or satellite. More importantly, the Garbage Patch is not something that is frequently discussed in the media or by politicians, likely because it affects people only indirectly. The problem is invisible to humans even as it chokes the life out of huge tracts of the global ecosystem. It is a problem caused by many nations, including Canada, but to us it might as well not exist. The example perfectly illustrates the argument made by Hannigan (2006: 63):

> Central to the social construction [perspective] is the idea that environmental issues and problems do not rise and fall according to some fixed, asocial, self-evident set of criteria. Rather, their progress varies in direct response to successful "claims-making" by a cast of social actors that includes scientists, industrialists, politicians, civil servants, journalists, and environmental activists.

In other words, the natural gas–fired power plant proposed for Oakville, Ontario, was successfully defined as an environmental problem because well-to-do activists were able to grab public attention and convince enough social actors that it was important. The Great Pacific Garbage Patch, lacking such advocacy and attention, fails to register and continues to grow, unnoticed and unable to "fight back."

Strengths and Weaknesses of the Realist and Constructionist Perspectives

Both perspectives have particular strengths and weaknesses in their analysis of human–nature relations. First we will look at these independently, and then examine how they can collide on specific issues, using the timely example of climate change to illustrate.

The Strengths of Environmental Realism

One of the core strengths of the environmental realist perspective is its emphasis on the environmental costs of human activities. Realists are not all on the same theoretical page; some are inspired by Marxist ideas (e.g., York and Clark 2010) and others by Weberian concepts (e.g., Murphy 2009). Nevertheless, all are concerned with studying the intersection of environment, politics, and economy. This has led to some innovative measures and interesting international comparative research. One of the early measures developed by realists is the IPAT model, which conceptualizes environmental degradation as a function of social criteria. Specifically, IPAT is based on the assumptions that I (impact) = P (population) × A (affluence) × T (technology). The model reflects the fact that wealthier societies, like the United States and Canada, produce more ecological damage than poorer ones both through higher levels of consumption (affluence) and more intensive production (technology) (Rudel et al. 2011).

More recently, realists have made use of a concept called "**ecological footprint**," which is "an accounting tool that enables us to estimate the resource consumption and waste assimilation requirements of a defined human population or economy in terms of a corresponding productive land area" (Wackernagel and Rees 1996: 9). In other words, the ecological footprint projects how much of the Earth's finite productive land (a key component of what is called the planet's **"natural capital"**) is required to sustain the consumption and waste of different countries. The different footprints can then be statistically analyzed to see what exactly leads to better or worse environmental performance (York et al. 2003; Dietz et al. 2007). One of the most influential studies was published by Richard York, Eugene Rosa, and Thomas Dietz in 2003. This study used the ecological footprint alongside a more complex version of IPAT, called STIRPAT (Stochastic Impacts by Regression on Population, Affluence and Technology), to analyze what kinds of variables led to smaller or larger environmental impacts across nations. What they found was that "basic material conditions, such as population, economic production, and geographic conditions [i.e., climate] explained the vast majority of cross-national variation in environmental impact," while more cultural-political variables, like political rights, levels of environmental commitment, and civil liberties had little impact (York et al., 2003: 295). This is strong evidence to support realist claims that what really matters is getting production and consumption under control, and that constructionist preoccupations with symbols and meaning are less important—even distracting.

Weaknesses of the Realist Perspective

The main weakness of the realist perspective is that it tends to paint over a certain degree of social complexity. For example, the study by York et al. (2003) mentioned above finds that climate is a significant variable affecting nations' environmental footprint. Specifically, they argue this:

> Nations in temperate regions have 30 percent greater ecological footprints, and nations in arctic regions have 40 percent greater ecological footprints than do nations in the tropics. This finding reinforces the obvious: More resources are required to sustain societies in colder climates. (York et al. 2003: 294)

In a sense, this is indeed self-evident: It takes more energy to heat homes and buildings in non-tropical climates. But the focus on latitude and climate also masks other important socio-political factors, such as the legacy of colonialism. Generally speaking, colonialism has involved the flow of goods, materials, and wealth from tropical nations to temperate and northern ones (particularly in Europe and North America). While colonialism is less evident today, the economic relationships that anchored it continue, particularly in regions of Africa and Asia which provide extensive raw materials to advanced economies and former colonial masters (Yates 1996).

Climate is important, but it is not the whole story as to why "northern" nations consume more than their fair share of world resources. According to Lidskog (2000: 121–2), realists occasionally slip back into a mild form of **environmental determinism**, specifically the assumption that environmental variables are *causing* outcomes that are in fact more attributable to social, political, or economic factors.

The realist perspective is also sometimes accused of pandering to the natural sciences. Over the past several decades, the sociology of science—specifically what is called the **sociology of scientific knowledge**, or SSK—has gone a long way to "demystifying" the natural sciences, showing how even the most complex and sophisticated scientific endeavours are also "social achievements" that involve arguments, disagreements, collaborations, competition, ego, interpretation, and leaps of faith (e.g., Latour 1987; Knorr-Cetina 1999; Hird 2012). This isn't to say that science is made up—it clearly isn't. But it does suggest that science is not a perfect reflection or translator of the natural world. According to Proctor (1998: 353), it is a grave mistake to assume that "nature is simply something out there that scientific knowledge more or less faithfully mirrors." Critics suggest that realists often accept information from the natural sciences uncritically. A famous example of this is the *Limits to Growth* experiment conducted in the 1970s (Meadows et al. 1972). A scholarly group called "the Club of Rome" built a computer simulation of the world's resources and national economies, and concluded that humans would exhaust these by the early twenty-first century. The resulting report was extremely influential, and led to widespread speculation that humanity was headed towards extreme hardship, starvation, and economic collapse in the near future, which in hindsight did not happen. The main problem with *Limits to Growth* was that its model was too limited (including only five variables) and it underestimated the role that economics and technology play in "discovering" new resources (we will discuss this example and these issues again in the next chapter, which deals with environmental scarcity). The deeper issue is that *Limits to Growth* represented cutting edge science at the time. Will the science of today seem just as limited 40 years from now? When social scientists take conclusions such as these as their starting point, they risk building significant error into their own scholarship.

The Strengths of Social Constructionism

The great strength of the social constructionist perspective is that it exposes *how* environmental issues and problems come to be defined that way. The existence of a problem is not enough to make people aware of it. Some of the most iconic problems of the last 30 years—including acid rain, ozone layer depletion, and global warming—were all discovered decades and even centuries before they became public issues taken seriously by citizens and governments (see Weart 2008). The social constructionist perspective encourages us to look at environmental issues like we would any other social problem (Hannigan 2006: 63). Social problems—like crime, poverty, mental illness, and intergenerational conflict—tend to rise and fall in public attention due to *social actions* rather than *real world* ones. For example, crime is currently a hot-button topic in Canada, despite the fact that violent and property crime rates are far lower today than they were in the 1980s and 1990s. The rise of crime in public consciousness and debate has been largely spurred by the actions of the Federal Conservative Party led by Stephen Harper, which has used the agenda setting power of government to focus attention on crime, criminals, and victims to justify new legislation that takes away discretion in sentencing from judges. The logic is the same with environmental issues: For a problem to seize the public imagination and "become" a problem, it needs human actions and voices behind it.

For this reason, constructionists tend to look at the social side of environmental issues, focusing on three things in particular: claims, claims-makers, and claims-making processes (Hannigan 2006: 65). "Successful" environmental problems tend to be ones whose advocates master all three. For example, let's return to the case of the natural gas–fired power plant proposed for Oakville, Ontario. Here, the main opposition group, C4CA, deployed a series of claims against the plant that blended *science-based* claims with claims about *fairness, risk,* and *vulnerability.* This is best exemplified in the group's posters, one of which is reproduced in Figure 4.2. This poster combines images of smokestacks, a nefarious-looking wolf, and a child wearing a respirator with scientific-sounding claims about health effects. Not all the claims are unbiased (see caption), but this bundling of science and moral themes is often highly effective in getting people's emotional and cognitive attention (Young and Matthews 2010: 88).

The C4CA also gained credibility by casting itself, the *claims-maker,* as a grassroots organization made up of ordinary concerned citizens. This is a common tactic that is used by interests on all sides of an environmental issue (large companies, most notoriously oil and energy corporations, do this as well) to present themselves as being motivated by authentic rather than selfish concerns (Dunlap and McCright 2011). Finally, C4CA deftly managed the *claims-making process,* skilfully gaining media attention by recruiting the aforementioned celebrity Erin Brockovich. Her presence not only provided the media with a reason to focus on this story, it also linked the issue with better-known cases of environmental discrimination from the United States.

A second but related strength of the social constructionist perspective is that it examines the role of power in defining environmental issues, rather than just causing them. Not everyone or every issue can get and maintain the public's attention. People have limited disposable time and attention spans,

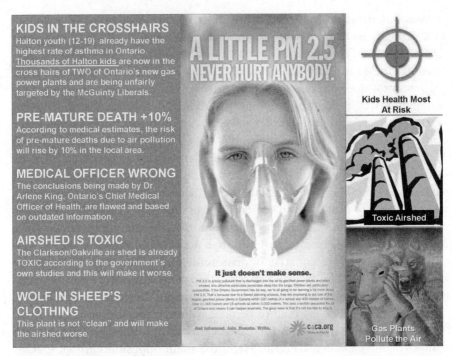

Figure 4.2 C4CA Poster in Opposition to the Proposed Power Generating Station in Oakville, Ontario

Source: www.c4ca.org. Used with permission.

The text under "It just doesn't make sense" reads as follows: "PM 2.5 is a toxic pollutant that is discharged into the air by gas-fired power plants and when inhaled, this ultra-fine particulate penetrates deep into the lungs. Children are particularly susceptible. If the Ontario Government has its way, we're all going to be learning a lot more about PM 2.5. That's because due to a flawed planning process, they are proposing to put one of the largest gas-fired power plants in Canada within 320 metres of a school and 400 metres of homes. Over 11,000 homes and 16 schools sit within 3,000 metres. This is a terrible precedent for all of Ontario and means it can happen anywhere. The good news is that it's not too late to stop it." In reality, PM 2.5 is not a chemical but a technical label for fine particulate matter, which is produced in far higher quantities by *coal-fired* power plants (which the Oakville plant was meant to replace) as well as by cars. It is the main basis for measuring the Air Quality Index and for "smog alerts" during the summer, which have become a regular occurrence in Southern Ontario (Ontario 2010).

and it takes money and resources to seize them. This means that powerful actors have a distinct advantage in the social construction of environmental problems and, equally importantly, the construction of "non-problems" (Liberatore 1995). For example, consider the case of bottled water. The ability of beverage companies—including Coca-Cola and Pepsi—to create a commodity that competes with something that is readily accessible and virtually free (at least in the developed world) is a singularly impressive achievement. Bottled water has an enormous environmental cost, particularly in packaging and transportation (moving it over long distances by truck is far, far worse than by pipes from local sources). The enthusiastic consumer response to bottled water hinged on its successful "construction" as a health issue rather than an environmental one. Manufacturers of bottled water used extensive marketing campaigns to link their product with safety, purity, and desirable lifestyles, while remaining silent on environmental costs (Szasz 2007: 123). Only recently have other organizations, such as Canada's Polaris Institute, gained ground in **framing** bottled water as a cost, to the point that some municipalities and universities (including my own) have banned sales. Constructionists aim to expose the strategies and power relations that go into these struggles over definition.

Weaknesses of the Social Constructionist Perspective

The most salient criticism of the social constructionist perspective is that it focuses on the wrong things. Constructionists' drive to expose how environmental issues are built de-centres questions about the severity of environmental problems themselves (Murphy 2011). Burmingham and Cooper (1999: 310) call this a tendency to "political quietism." In other words, constructionism's attention to claims and claims-making as *social processes* means that they tend to place competing claims on equal ontological footing. For example, Young and Matthews' (2010) analysis of the controversy over aquaculture (fish farming) in Canada examined whose claims were more likely to convince consumers—people who tend to live in big cities rather than the small coastal communities where aquaculture takes place—rather than whose claims were *right*. For some realists, this contradicts environmental sociology's core mission of trying to solve environmental problems rather than just commenting on them (Burmingham and Cooper 1999: 300).

A second and more pointed criticism is that social constructionism may be aiding opponents of environmental reform. As mentioned, constructionists tend to be somewhat skeptical about the ability of the natural sciences to unproblematically represent the true state of the natural environment. They are also interested in **deconstructing** claims to authoritative knowledge to see how they relate to politics, interests, and strategic decisions (see Figure 4.2 above). These ideas have been picked up by corporate lobby groups, among others, to argue against environmental regulations (York and Clark 2010: 489). It is now a common tactic among groups opposed to environmental regulation to "deconstruct" the claims of environmentalists, arguing that they have a political agenda and therefore their claims should not be trusted. Of course, constructionists argue that *all* groups involved in the construction of environmental issues have agendas (Saarikoski 2007: 488), but anti-environmentalists have turned this into a particularly potent line of attack against mainstream environmental science. Mooney (2005) has documented how business associations, think tanks, and allied politicians have drawn on constructionist arguments to label opponents' knowledge as "junk science" and their own as "sound science"—arguing that others have interests while claiming that their own is value-free (see also Demeritt 2006). This is a notable turn of events, given that constructionism is

Box 4.1

Are All Environmental Sociologists Either Social Constructionists or Environmental Realists?

No, definitely not. As mentioned at the outset, there are many active debates in environmental sociology, and this is just one of them. The constructionist-realist exchange, though, is an overarching debate that draws scholars in regardless of their specific theoretical orientation. As Kroll-Smith et al. (2000: 46) argue, this is a "highly visible example of a more generic dispute within sociology between those who believe in the sociological significance of things that exist independent of [our] perception and those who believe that perception [itself] must be the starting point of sociology." In other words, this debate transcends environmental sociology, even if it is particularly intense in this field.

The best way to think about the realist-constructionist debate is as a continuum, with most environmental sociologists somewhere in the middle. Unfortunately, the extremes of the continuum usually get the most attention. For example, social constructionism is sometimes accused of being **relativist** in its approach—of assuming that all types of knowledge and perspectives are equally valid. In practice, though, few constructionists adopt a truly relativist approach to the environment (Proctor 1998: 358), nor do many realists completely ignore the role of culture and symbols in environmental problems. Environmental sociologists usually find a comfort zone between the two poles based on which arguments they find convincing from the two perspectives. This is possible because, as Lidskog (2001: 126) points out, realism and constructionism are not always *directly* contradictory because they ask different types of questions.

about *exposing* the unequal powers behind knowledge production, not aiding them. Nevertheless, constructionist arguments seem to be resonating strongly with conservatively minded groups and politicians, who are generally allied with powerful interests (Gauchat 2012).

A Case Study: Global Climate Change

Climate change is one of the defining issues of our time, and environmental sociologists of all stripes study the issue from a diversity of perspectives. This case also demonstrates the ongoing relevance of the realist/constructionist debate within environmental sociology, and why it matters to the broader shape and politics of this issue.

Global climate change is a monstrously complex phenomenon that has multiple causes and many potential consequences. It is, in the words of

Dessler and Parson (2006: 1), "a new type of environmental problem" the likes of which we have never seen before. It is a problem that is deeply rooted in our economies, politics, and personal habits, which suggests a strong role for sociology (Redclift 2011; Urry 2011). Our collective burning of fossil fuels over hundreds of years, for transportation, electricity generation, heating, and manufacturing, has increased the concentration of greenhouse gases (GHGs) in the atmosphere; meaning that any long-term solution requires collective action on a scale the world has never experienced.

For most environmental realists, the starting point for this issue is the work of the Intergovernmental Panel on Climate Change, or the IPCC. As discussed in Chapter 3, the IPCC is a scientific body that was first assembled by the United Nations in 1988, and produces periodic "assessment reports" that attempt to synthesize all scientific knowledge on global climate change. The latest report, released in 2014, had thousands of authors and reviewers, and "is almost certainly the world's largest-ever scientific endeavour" (Urry 2011: 28). The assessments are based on a consensus model, which means that the IPCC reports contain only those facts that are beyond reasonable dispute. To be clear, the IPCC does no original research; it summarizes and interprets existing research. Realists use the IPCC's conclusions as the basis for research on what needs to be done. For example, Murphy (2011: 168) argues that environmental sociologists should focus on "absolute material indicators that the problem is being solved [or not]." Given that solving the climate change problem means reducing GHG emissions, Murphy focuses on comparing the characteristics of societies that have done so (mostly Northern European) with those that have not (such as Canada and the United States). The aim is to understand the differences "between cases where science wins the struggle, and others where economic and political power drown out scientific assessments" (Murphy 2011: 170). Similarly, Redclift (2011) argues that sociology can help us learn how to "transition from carbon dependency towards more sustainable, lower intensity paths" by proposing innovative economic structures (like encouraging local food production) and policy priorities (such as urban densification). Homer-Dixon (2006) also goes this route, arguing that societies can act constructively or misguidedly to the coming stimuli from changing climates, and that the social sciences can help alleviate the coming ecological and human problems by encouraging more resilient and adaptive institutions.

On the whole, constructionists have approached the issue somewhat differently. A significant literature has developed around issues of claims-making about climate change, particularly in the media and by interest groups (e.g., Boykoff 2009; O'Neill and Nicholson-Cole 2009). Riley Dunlap, usually considered a realist, has also contributed to this research in collaboration with his colleague Aaron McCright (McCright and Dunlap

2003; 2010). More controversially, however, constructionists have taken a critical look at how official climate change knowledge is produced. Urry (2011) argues that, like all environmental issues, climate change was less "discovered" than "achieved":

> [In the beginning,] it was not obvious that climate change would become the environmental issue that would subsequently dominate global agendas. There were many [issues] vying for dominance over the last half-century, including how certain environments and processes are implicated in the production of cancers. . . . Indeed it was not clear that examining long-term climate change was even "do-able" by science. (Urry 2011: 19)

According to this view, many things had to "come together" before climate change could become an important public issue, able to galvanize people and influence politics. First, there needed to be a willingness among governments and other authorities to publicly address it as a global problem. In this light, global climate change owes much to the ozone depletion issue, which arose in the 1980s and, after a period of controversy and negotiation, was addressed by the Montreal Protocol which committed nations to banning the use of CFCs (ozone-destroying chlorofluorocarbons). Fresh off the Montreal Protocol, Canadian Prime Minister Brian Mulroney called a "Toronto Summit" in 1988 to negotiate a "global law of the air" that effectively launched climate change as a global issue (Young and Coutinho 2013). Second, advances in atmospheric, geological, and computer science had to happen to handle the incredibly sophisticated computer models that now anchor future projections of change (Yearley 2009). Third, there had to be means for "creating" climate science. Climate change is such a complex issue that "there is no single science of climate change" (Urry 2011: 23), but rather a collection of specializations that include climatologists, geologists, atmospheric chemists, paleoclimatologists, glaciologists, computer scientists, economists, and so on. Not only did there need to be a mechanism to bring these all together, but also to sort them all out. This brings us back to the IPCC.

Constructionists view the IPCC as a very important institution in the climate change issue, but also as one that reflects the priorities, choices, values, and strategies of its founders and members (Hulme and Mahony 2010). This is where things get extremely controversial. Constructionists argue that if the IPCC is the recognized authority on the global climate change problem, then knowing how it got that status and what it does with it is critical to understanding the role that climate change plays in the world, especially since it has become a touchstone for so many other issues, including ethics, development, justice, and planning (see Hulme 2009). Some realists, though, see critiques of climate science and the IPCC as the ultimate example of misplaced priorities (Lever-Tracy 2008). Given the scale of the climate change problem and its consequences—impacting agriculture, fresh water, biodiversity, oceans, coastlines, and weather—why on Earth would we shoot down the chief messenger and best hope for unbiased information and effective solutions?

Constructionist studies of the IPCC have found substantial evidence of "knowledge hierarchies" in the assessment process, with the social sciences in particular regulated to a "subservient" role (Hulme and Mahony 2010: 708; Yearley 2009). Researchers have also emphasized the fact that the vast majority of IPCC experts are from developed countries, and that their conclusions are slanted towards "northern framings of the problems and therefore biased against interpretations and interests of the South" (Lahsen 2004: 161). Yearley (2009: 391) is also critical of the computer models used by the IPCC, called General Circulation Models, which "depend on assumptions about what people and governments, corporations and households will do. Just as climate models require simplified versions of the atmosphere and the oceans, climate projections demand simplified versions of societal activity" (see also Demeritt 2001). Finally, some constructionists are critical of the relationship between the IPCC's scientific and political mandates (Carolan 2008; Yearley 2009). As mentioned, the IPCC's reports are based on the notion of consensus—the idea being that this is the best way to present unbiased information and conclusions. However, this means that the IPCC sometimes excludes or devalues certain types of information because it is uncertain. Critics point out, though, that the IPCC should be highlighting uncertainties instead of consensus (Petersen 2011). Consensus implies perfect knowledge (which may or may not exist) while uncertainty—outlining what *might* happen or what we *don't know*—is in a way more useful for politicians who have to weigh different options. "The establishment of consensus by the IPCC is no longer as critical to governments as [is] a full exploration of uncertainty" (Oppenheimer et al., 2007: 1506).

Critics of social constructionism argue that these analyses play directly into the hands of the new anti-environmentalism discussed in Chapter 3, which seeks to discredit scientific evidence rather than attacking environmental policies and reforms directly (Lever-Tracy 2008: 457). The notion that the IPCC flawed has become a major part of climate change denialist claims-making, and these activists occasionally draw on constructionist research to make their case. It is perhaps no accident that one of the heroes of Michael Crichton's novel *State of Fear*, which describes climate change as a global conspiracy orchestrated by large environmental groups, is Professor Norman Hoffman, an embattled truth-exposing sociologist! More seriously, Lever-Tracy (2008: 457) argues that constructionist critiques of the IPCC risk angering its members and making it more difficult for environmental sociologists to collaborate with natural scientists in the future. In their defence, constructionists argue that they are only doing honest scholarship, and that their findings will help to improve the IPCC and climate science more generally, ultimately making it more relevant to people and governments that depend on its findings (Grundmann and Stehr 2010: 903–4). The great debate continues. In the case of climate change, though, more people are watching than ever before . . .

Conclusion

The realist-constructionist debate exposes a key division in environmental sociology. This division is not total. Only the most ardent social constructionists would dispute that nature is a "real" thing that responds to societal uses and abuses, and most environmental realists agree that environmental problems have a social and cultural life that deeply influences our responses to them (Young and Dugas 2011). Instead, the disagreement is about which is the *best* way to approach environmental issues—which gives us the most accurate account of what is really going on in the human–nature relationship.

The great strength of the realist perspective is its attention to how natural and social dynamics combine to produce different outcomes. Concepts like the ecological footprint show how dependent our lifestyles are on natural bounty, and how the choices we make today may be setting ourselves up for longer-term difficulties. According to this view, the natural environment should be approached as a powerful entity that follows its own rules. Humans can bend it and shape it, but if we go too far it will strike back and cause great harm to society as it does.

The strength of the constructionist perspective, in contrast, is its claim that people don't react to nature directly, but rather to ideas about nature. These ideas are inconsistent and uneven, and are based more on priorities, values, and interests than any objective reality located beyond society. Constructionists have had great success explaining *how* environmental issues and problems come to be, and *why* some are more successful than others. As we saw with the issue of climate change, their argument that all aspects of an environmental problem reflect uneven power relations—including its discovery, investigation, explanation, and proposed solutions—is deeply controversial within environmental sociology.

In the end, this diversity should be considered a strength. In practice, many environmental sociologists are sometime realists and sometime constructionists, depending on the issue they are looking at and the point they want to make. As we will see in the remainder of the book, realism and constructionism run through many other debates about nature and society, and each make valuable contributions to solving environmental problems.

Questions for Critical Thought

1. Which do you think is the best way to conceptualize the nature–society relationship: realist or constructionist?

2. Do you think the two perspectives can be harmonized? How?

3. Would you say that Chapter 2 and Chapter 3 are predominantly realist or constructionist?

Suggested Readings

Hulme, Mike. (2009). *Why We Disagree about Climate Change: Understanding Controversy, Inaction and Opportunity.* New York: Cambridge University Press. Hulme is an interesting figure whose work has evolved from being predominantly realist to predominantly constructionist. This book is a broad but controversial take on the social and political life of the climate change issue.

Jasanoff, Sheila. (2010). "A new climate for society," *Theory, Culture & Society* 27(2–3): 233–53. Jasanoff reverses the standard constructionist argument by suggesting that climate change is such an overwhelming issue that it challenges our "imaginations of society." It is an interesting piece that challenges core assumptions of both realism and constructionism.

Murphy, Raymond. (2009). *Leadership in Disaster: Learning for a Future with Global Climate Change.* Montreal and Kingston: McGill-Queen's University Press. Murphy's book is a realist take on climate change, focusing specifically on the 1998 ice storm that brought Eastern Ontario, Western Quebec, and Northern New York to its knees. He develops interesting concepts to explain the limitations of societal reactions to unpredictable nature.

Urry, John. (2010). "Consuming the planet to excess," *Theory, Culture & Society* 27(2–3): 191–212. John Urry is usually considered a constructionist, but this stark piece is a fine example of environmental realism, drawing on his new "mobilities paradigm."

Suggested Websites

IPCC
www.ipcc.ch
  Get it straight from the source. The IPCC website contains a wealth of information and data to satisfy realists and constructionists alike.

Social Constructionism in 10 Minutes
www.youtube.com/watch?v=GVVWmZAStn8
  This video from two sociology professors in the United States explains the basics of social constructionism. It does not deal with environmental issues, but provides excellent background information on the topic.

5 Scarcity, Treadmills, and the Age of Peak

Key Points

◎ There is a difference between relative scarcity, which tends to be temporary and remedied by the laws of supply and demand, and absolute scarcity, which refers to fixed limits that cannot be exceeded.

◎ The sociological theory of the "treadmill of production" helps explain why modern capitalist societies consume more and more resources.

◎ Peak theory suggests that we are beginning to encounter the limits of absolute scarcity, but this claim is difficult to verify.

◎ Scholars are both optimistic and pessimistic about potential outcomes of renewed global scarcity.

Introduction

This chapter addresses one of the most urgent questions facing contemporary society: Are we running out of the things we need? Everyone knows that the Earth has limits. There are only so many minerals, fossil fuels, and acres of productive land on the planet. Fortunately, the Earth does receive inputs in the form of energy from the sun, which allows many of our resources to be **renewable**. This energy means, for instance, that plants grow year after year, soil is replenished, and water and nutrients circulate throughout the biosphere. But renewable resources are also vulnerable to disruption—to the point that they can lose productivity and even become non-renewable. As we saw in Chapter 2, fertile topsoil is frequently destroyed and permanently lost from careless use. Fresh water, the ultimate renewable resource, loses nearly all its utility if polluted, and is currently being pumped out of underground aquifers the world over faster than it can be replenished (Wada et al. 2010). Given that we need all of these things to live—especially to *live well* with a high material standard of living—the depletion of the Earth and the resulting consequences are core concerns for environmental sociology.

The spectre that hangs over this chapter is scarcity—that in the near future there may not be enough key resources to go around. It seems strange to think about scarcity at this historical point in time, when we are surrounded by so much wealth and exponential levels of consumption.

Single-family homes built today, for example, have more than twice the square footage as those built in the 1950s. When I was a child, it was almost unheard of for a household to own more than one television, let alone a computer. Today, *each member* of a typical urban household owns several computer-like devices that are jettisoned and replaced every few years. Is all of this sustainable? As we will see, there is profound disagreement about whether scarcity is about to make a big comeback or not. This is a debate that has been going on for some time, and as discussed in the last chapter, many doomsday predictions from yesteryear have gone unrealized. At the same time, we are currently living in a time where talk of "peak oil," "peak food," and "peak water" is commonplace. The idea behind **peak theory** is that demand for these things is beginning to outstrip the Earth's ability to provide them. These claims are not unproblematic (see below) but recent dramatic fluctuations in world energy and food prices mean they cannot be dismissed either.

Sometimes, debates about scarcity get overwhelmed by the logic and concepts of economics. To ensure that things stay sociological, I will locate the scarcity question in what has arguably been the most influential theory to emerge out of environmental sociology—that of the "treadmill of production." **Treadmill theory** seeks to address the structural roots of environmental depletion and degradation. If we are indeed running out of resources—burning too much oil, using too much water, fishing too many fish, paving over too much productive land—how exactly did things get this way? Treadmill theorists argue that the main culprit is the "growth orientation" or "growth ethos" that pervades nearly all of our institutions. Growth—especially economic growth—is the ultimate goal and *sine qua non* of the capitalist system. Growth generates profits, increases government revenues, nourishes innovation, and creates jobs. When growth does not occur, we find ourselves in a crisis (a recession or a depression), and every effort is made to get growth back on track. In other words, growth has long been seen as a way of solving problems and maintaining a stable capitalist system. But the endless pursuit of growth—like a treadmill that burns energy and resources for its own sake—may be leading us to a more difficult future ahead.

What Is Scarcity?

Scarcity is a deceivingly complicated concept that has multiple possible meanings. For our purposes here, we will focus on two types: **relative scarcity**, which tends to be the perspective preferred by economists, and **absolute scarcity**, which tends to be the type adopted by ecologists and environmentalists (Baumgartner et al. 2006). Both types of scarcity are important for understanding our economic relationship with nature.

Relative Scarcity

The idea of relative scarcity is based on a contradiction: that scarcity and abundance are not opposites, but rather go hand-in-hand. How can this be? Looking back through time, one of the things that distinguishes our era from previous ones is the sheer amount of stuff in our lives. The possessions held by a middle-income person in a developed country today would make the most opulent medieval aristocrat blush. Many goods that used to be scarce, such as fresh and preserved foods, books, quality clothing, housing, tools, and medicine, are now abundant—at least in developed countries. Abundance is not just about possession, but access. In the past, services like travel were extremely expensive. People would spend their life savings to cross an ocean or a continent—something many middle-earners now do repeatedly at minimal cost relative to their incomes. The same can be said of other goods and services, like access to medical or legal expertise, specialized equipment or drugs, and esoteric academic textbooks now at your fingertips via Google Books and Amazon.

So where does scarcity come in? An old idea in economics is that people have unlimited desires but limited means to achieve them (Mehta 2010: 13). In other words, any dollar that is spent on one thing is a dollar that cannot be spent on another. If I choose to buy a new laptop rather than put up with my old one, I simultaneously choose to forego something else. Therefore, most economists see scarcity as being *relative* rather than *absolute*. If I don't possess something, it's because I have chosen to spend my money on something else. If people have the desire and ability to pay, they can eat oranges in February, see a Broadway show every night, or drive a gas-guzzling Hummer to their heart's content.

According to this view, scarcity is primarily a function of *demand* rather than supply. Xenos (2010) puts it this way: Plenty of things are rare, but few of these things are scarce. My four-year-old son, for example, enjoys painting. As a solitary painter, his works are quite rare—at best he will produce a few each month. However, his paintings are not scarce because there is simply no demand for them (aside from his immediate family, who receive them as gifts). The point is that scarcity is more about *desire* than rarity or supply (Xenos 2010: 32). Now consider the example of gold. Like my son's paintings, gold is both rare and relatively useless (it is a soft metal that, unlike diamonds, has few industrial applications).[1] What makes gold scarce rather than just rare is that it is desired by many people who compete to acquire it. Scarcity therefore has little to do with limits in the natural world, but the limited means (money and other forms of wealth) that people have to pursue their desires.

So, why does this matter? Capitalism is an economic system that allocates goods primarily through free markets of buyers and sellers. Most economists therefore see modern day scarcity as being self-correcting. If enough people desire something and are willing to pay for it, producers have an incentive to produce more. This is how scarcity leads to abundance in the capitalist system. If, for example, more and more people are willing to pay higher prices for housing, then property developers have an incentive to construct more houses, apartment buildings, townhouse complexes, and so on. Eventually, the increase in supply should bring prices down as competition between people is lessened. This is the apocryphal "invisible hand of the market" that Adam Smith wrote about in his *Wealth of Nations* in 1776. It is the great strength of the capitalist system, and history has shown that this is an unparalleled way to generate the kind of abundance that we take for granted today.

But what about commodities that we cannot just "make more of?" There is only so much clean water available to us, so much oil and minerals in the Earth's crust, and so much clean air for us to breathe. As we will see in a later section, some economists are untroubled by the notion of ultimate limits. For others, though, the link between relative scarcity and abundance works fine until it encounters hard limits of absolute scarcity.

Absolute Scarcity

Absolute scarcity is a problem that is rarely acknowledged in mainstream economics (Baumgartner 2006). The discipline of economics tends to see limits as being temporary things. This view is based on something called the **principle of substitution**. Suppose for a moment that it suddenly became very difficult to grow corn, one of the globe's dietary staples, due to an outbreak of pests or disease. This crisis would make the price of corn increase as people compete for less corn on the world market. According to mainstream economics, eventually more and more people would choose to turn to cheaper substitutes, like wheat, rather than pay higher prices. Tortillas would taste quite a bit different for a while, but eventually the reduction in demand would bring the price of corn down again. The principle of substitution is therefore like a pressure-release valve. When prices exceed willingness or ability to pay, people look for alternatives. This is why economists often say "the cure for high oil prices is high oil prices" (Rubin 2012: 37)—if prices climb too high, people change their behaviours, turning to substitutes (like bicycling and mass transit), that then lead to price decline.

Absolute scarcity occurs when things cannot be substituted for one another; when the pressure cannot be released. Diamond (2005) gives the example of land—specifically the role that land scarcity played in heightening intra-community tensions prior to the Rwandan genocide of 1994. Rwanda is one of the most densely populated countries on the planet. It also is a predominantly agricultural nation, meaning that land is critical for people's economic and subsistence needs. The absolute limits here are the borders of the country. Rwanda is small, and population growth meant that farms became ever smaller as they were handed down from fathers to sons in the years leading up to the conflict. In some regions, "farmers ended up tilling absurdly small parcels of land averaging only 0.09 acre in 1988 and 0.07 acre in 1993," the year before the genocide erupted (Diamond 2005: 321). To be clear, land scarcity did not cause the genocide, but the inability to "substitute" land for something else meant that social and economic tensions continued to build. Most families could not survive on the bounty of these micro-farms, but nor could they easily acquire new land under conditions of absolute scarcity.

Let's also consider the example of water. Water is abundant, but human beings need *clean fresh water* in order to survive, and it is difficult to see how this can be substituted. Other sources of liquids, such as milk, juice, and fruits, are themselves made of water, and would be rapidly depleted under conditions of true shortage. During emergencies, water can be shipped from areas of abundance to areas of scarcity. This is what happened after the 2010 earthquake in Haiti, when countries donated millions of litres of bottled water. The fact remains, however, that humanity has found no viable solution to large-scale water problems such as drought. The only real answers we have to true water shortages are rationing and conservation—actions rooted in the logic of absolute scarcity.

In summary, relative scarcity is understood to be a constructive problem—a perpetual series of challenges that maintain a healthy capitalist economy, balancing desire (demand) and production (supply), encouraging innovation, and substituting one commodity for another when necessary or desirable. Absolute scarcity, on the other hand, is a destructive problem that creates social tensions, restricts growth, and even threatens survival. Whether or not absolute scarcity is becoming more common, and playing a larger role in the global economy, is a subject of intense debate. In the latter half of the chapter, I will discuss how this debate plays out in arguments about "peak oil" and other nature-dependent goods. Next, however, I will introduce the sociological theory of the "treadmill of production," and use it to discuss why our political and economic institutions are so focused on relative scarcity and almost completely ignorant of the problems associated with absolute scarcity.

The Treadmill of Production: On the Road to Disaster?

The treadmill of production is a theory first developed by Allan Schnaiberg (1980) to explain why contemporary society is so reckless in its consumption of resources and treatment of the natural world. In other words, why are we so willing to deplete and degrade the environment regardless of potential consequences? Why are we so eager to gamble that our future will be one of relative scarcity rather than absolute scarcity? Why isn't conservation at the heart of all social, political, and economic policies, actions, and decision-making?

Prior to treadmill theory, most scholars answered these questions in one of two ways. First, much emphasis was placed on the challenges of population growth. This perspective is often called a **neo-Malthusian** view. Thomas Malthus (1766–1834) was an English philosopher who famously argued that population tended to grow exponentially (what he called "geometrically") while food supplies could only grow incrementally (what he called "arithmetically") which meant that human population would ultimately be checked by starvation. In this respect, Malthus was a theorist of absolute scarcity (Baumgartner 2006: 488). Over the years, Malthus's ideas have remained influential, even though the dynamics among population, production, and consumption have proven complex (e.g., Dobkowski et al. 2002). Neo-Malthusians tend to focus on the problems of providing a decent quality of life to ever-growing numbers of people, and the impact that this will necessarily have on the biosphere.

The second way this question has traditionally been answered is to assume deficiencies in human decision-making, such as greed, extreme self-interest, or the inability to consider the long-term consequences of our actions. For example, the famous *Limits to Growth* report discussed in Chapter 4 lamented people's inability to see beyond their immediate lives. The "here and now" bias that most people hold is represented in Figure 5.1.

Treadmill theory accepts that population growth and cognitive deficiencies are challenges, but it argues that environmental degradation is primarily caused by *interests*, specifically the interplay among different powerful economic groups (Buttel 2010: 41). It helps to know that treadmill theory came out of the **neo-Marxist** school of sociological thought. Marx understood modern capitalist society as being shaped by ongoing conflict between the capitalist class (owners of the means of production) and the labouring class (workers who actually produce value). These two groups have competing interests, with capital desiring to suppress wages and thus enhance profits, and labour desiring to maximize wages and gain more control over their work. Neo-Marxists have also paid attention to a third actor, government or the state, as an arbiter and participant in this conflict. Generally speaking, Marx saw the state as an extension of capital (as its "handmaiden") that would need to be reinvented in the transition to socialism. Neo-Marxists such as Antonio Gramsci, Nicos Poulantzas, and Bob Jessop have tried to understand how the state legitimizes capitalism indirectly, by creating shared identities (by promoting nationalism or patriotism), forging alliances between different class groups (by providing tax-funded universal government services), and brokering compromises (such as permitting unionization and peaceful social protest). In other

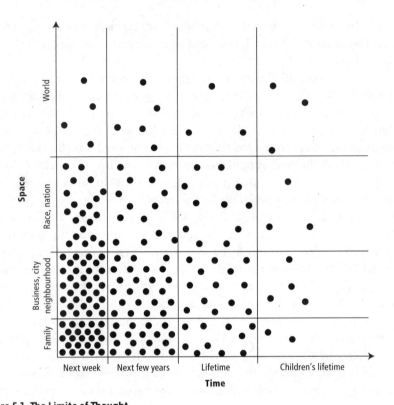

Figure 5.1 The Limits of Thought

Source: Barr (2008); Meadows et al. (1972: 19, figure 1)

Most people spend much of their time thinking about the "here and now"—what is happening to themselves and their loved ones within a short time horizon. Thinking about the long term and the wide scale is rare.

words, neo-Marxists see the relationship among capital, labour, and the state as a triad (see Figure 5.2).

In proposing the theory of the treadmill of production, Schnaiberg (1980) asks how exactly is this triad maintained? While the state has impressive powers to stabilize capitalism, it itself needs resources to function, and these resources predominantly come from taxation. If capital and labour are already struggling over profits, and the state taxes both groups, how does the system stay stable? The question can also be posed a different way: How do you keep the three groups happy? How can we simultaneously increase profits, increase wages, and increase government revenues? Schnaiberg's answer is that it is done through an unwavering commitment to growth. Growth allows the interests of all three groups to be met; it is where their otherwise contradictory interests converge. Growth, of course, involves the ever-increasing generation of wealth. Nearly all forms of generating wealth involve drawing on the natural environment, be it by drilling for fossil fuels, cutting down trees, mining for minerals, or

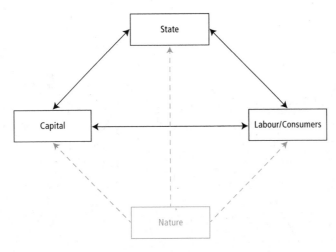

Figure 5.2 The Triad of Modern Capitalism, Supported and Sustained by Nature

The three main actors in the capitalist system—capital, labour, and the state—are each able to represent their own interests. The silent partner that stabilizes the triad is the natural environment. It does not have a voice, and treadmill theory argues that all three groups are complicit in its exploitation.

producing electricity. Therefore, Schnaiberg argues that the triad is in fact sustained by a silent but suffering partner—the natural environment. To keep the triad stable, growth must be continuous, which in turn means that wealth must be drawn from the environment at an ever accelerating pace. Nature has no voice, and therefore cannot represent itself as an interest. The contradictions at the heart of capitalism have not been resolved, but rather downloaded to the point of least resistance—the environment (see Figure 5.2) (O'Connor 1991).

The metaphor of the treadmill is instructive, because it captures the notion that the whole economic system has to consume more and more resources just to maintain itself. In practice, though, the treadmill of production should be understood as a series of interconnected treadmills (Bell 2012: 77) (see Figure 5.3). First, there is a *treadmill of accumulation* occupied by capital. Capitalism is a fiercely competitive system, and private companies have to continually accumulate wealth in order to stave off competitors and potential buyers (Foster et al. 2010: 201). Consider the example of Canada's Research in Motion (RIM), the maker of BlackBerry smartphones. This was a company with deep pockets and no debt but that nonetheless failed because it ultimately misjudged the market and was quickly passed by other players, like Apple and Google. Other fabled companies, like Xerox and Kodak, have also faded as they have failed to keep up with competition.

Second, there is *a treadmill of consumption* occupied by workers and their alter-egos: consumers. At the same time that capitalism tries to keep wages low, it also needs workers to consume its goods and services (Gould et al. 2008: 7). On the supply side, globalization has helped to keep prices

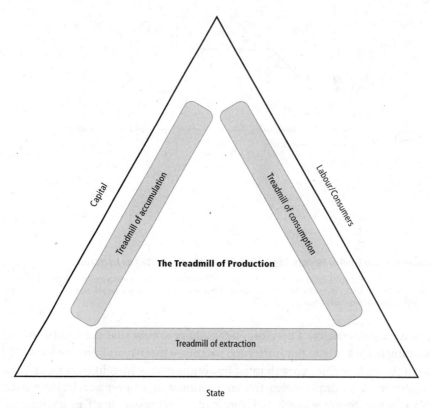

Figure 5.3 The Treadmill of Production as a Series of Interconnected Treadmills

The treadmill of production should be understood as a series of interconnected treadmills—each interest group runs on a different treadmill, but all three are coordinated by the need for perpetual growth (Bell 2012: 77).

for many consumer goods low—the reason that you can buy a plastic lawn chair at Walmart for under $20 is because of low wages in places like China. On the demand side, wages in the developed world have stagnated over the last 20 years, especially for middle- and low-income earners. Harvey (2010: 17) argues that this stagnation has been offset by the dramatic extension of credit and personal lending that began in the 1990s. Credit allows people to keep consuming, while conveniently transferring wealth up the food chain via interest payments, even as wages are depressed. So why do people consume so much even if it puts them at financial disadvantage? The answer is complicated, but sociologists have long argued that consumption has become a major means of personal expression in Western society (Veblen 1899; Lasch 1979; Szasz 2007). Indeed, consumption levels in developed countries have gone far beyond material needs. Most consumption in wealthy societies is discretionary, meaning that it involves the purchase of goods and services we can do without. On the whole, then, consumption is no longer really about improving quality of life, but should instead be understood as an open-ended status-seeking behaviour (Sassatelli 2007). Given that many people consume to "keep up with the Joneses," it has no self-evident limit, making it very much a treadmill.

Third, there is a *treadmill of extraction* occupied by governments. In most parts of the world, governments control access to natural resources. In Canada, for example, nearly all mining, forestry, oil extraction, and fisheries take place on government-controlled territory or waters (often called "Crown lands"). The state controls access, usually by granting or auctioning off licenses in exchange for royalties. To keep the capital-state-labour triad stable, governments open up more and more land to extraction and related activities to assist in accumulation and consumption. Projects such as the proposed Northern Gateway Pipeline to link the Alberta oil sands with the Pacific coast can be understood this way. Ongoing development of the oil sands, critical for accumulation, has filled all existing pipelines to capacity (NEB 2011a). In order to move the glut of Alberta oil to international markets, more pipeline capacity has to be built regardless of its inherent risks. As with the other treadmills, there is no obvious point of "enough" extraction to satisfy a system built to achieve perpetual growth.

In summary, treadmill theory provides us with the tools for understanding the deep dedication to growth that pervades our society. It helps to explain why enough is never enough, and why social stability depends on perpetual movement towards larger and larger economies. It also sheds light on why organized labour, which is usually associated with the political left, sometimes comes into conflict with environmentalists—especially if jobs are at stake (Gould et al. 2008: 12). During recessions, the environment always tumbles down the list of public concerns, and calls for more employment, investment, and growth get louder. Finally, treadmill theory helps us to understand why our political and economic institutions are organized around the idea of relative scarcity and ignore absolute scarcity. The metaphor of the treadmill is apt: There is no logical end to it, no goal to aspire to except more speed (accumulation, consumption, extraction). According to treadmill theory, there is no role for limits in our current economic arrangement. This has led many scholars, including an increasing number of economists, to speculate that we are heading faster and faster towards the wall of absolute scarcity (e.g., Roberts 2005; Homer-Dixon 2006; Rubin 2012). We turn to that debate next.

A New Era of Absolute Scarcity, or Just More of the Same?

In 1956, a geophysicist working for the Shell Oil Company named M. King Hubbert created a stir in the oil business by predicting that oil production in the continental United States would peak and begin to permanently decline in the 1970s. This was a heretical claim at the time, given that oil production in the US had climbed rapidly since the turn of the century and showed no signs of slowing. But Hubbert's argument was based on the geological fact that not all oil is created equal. Some oil is very easily accessible, and by simply putting holes in the ground it will come gushing out (à la *Beverley Hillbillies*). Other oil is more difficult—deeper underground, locked in smaller pockets, and under less natural pressure. Still more oil is stuck in places that are extremely difficult if not impossible to access (more on this below). Hubbert's point was that oil production up until the 1950s had been mostly made up of the easy stuff, and using sophisticated mathematics he estimated that both the discovery of new reserves and actual production would inevitably decline—and rapidly. Building on this, Hubbert (1996: 113) argued that "exponential [economic] growth is a transient phenomenon in human history" that would ultimately be checked by absolute scarcity of natural resources. Hubbert's prediction—which was by and large correct[2]— has achieved mythical status among proponents of "peak theory," which argues that many natural resources go through this cycle governed by absolute scarcity (Bardi 2009). There are, however, strong arguments to be made against peak theory, most of which come from economists and engineers.

The Case for Peak Theory and Absolute Scarcity

Peak theory is ultimately based on the idea of *diminishing returns* that we first encountered in Chapter 2. Hubbert's argument was that, all things being equal, companies will exploit the most easily accessible, and therefore cheapest, resources first. After those stocks are depleted, further extraction gets more difficult, more expensive, and more energy-intensive. Consider an example from Canadian forestry. At the beginning of the twentieth century, new settlers to British Columbia were awed by its vast forest cover. Nearly the entire province was covered by enormous trees that benefited from a long growing season, abundant rain (at least along the coast), and nutrient-rich waterways. As forestry became a major industry in the province, however, it quickly encountered a vexing problem. Given British Columbia's mountainous terrain, it was much easier to harvest trees in valleys and near water (where cut logs could be stored and transported). As these prime areas were depleted, forestry became increasingly difficult and expensive. Cutting on steep slopes must be done without the benefit of large machinery, crews have to be helicoptered to increasingly remote settings, and logs have to be transported further before they get to roads or waterways. Moreover, the new growth in reforested areas is almost always smaller (because it's younger) making a return to easier terrain less profitable than before. In the BC forest industry this dilemma is called "falldown," which refers to what happens to both the quality of wood and industry profits (Marchak et al. 1999). Forestry did not stop, but it became much less profitable over time (Marchak 1983; Hayter 2000).

Coming back to oil, if Hubbert was correct that easily accessible oil was tapped first (just like the valleys and waterfronts in forestry), then the oil industry must be facing diminishing returns as well. In fact, this is precisely what is happening. Conventional oil, which refers to oil extracted using traditional methods, is falling as a share of world production year over year, while unconventional oil, which includes offshore drilling, oil sands, shale oil, and heavy oil production, is increasing (Maggio and Cacciola 2009). Unconventional oil is markedly more expensive to tap, both in cost and energy. In terms of cost, some operations in the Alberta oil sands need oil prices to stay above $80 a barrel to be economically viable (Vanderklippe 2012). If oil prices fall below this threshold, they would lose rather than make money. In terms of energy, the issue is even more problematic. Industry insiders pay a lot of attention to something called "**energy return on investment**" (EROI). Think of EROI this way: The point of harvesting oil is to use it as energy, but it also takes energy to pull it out of the ground. For most conventional drilling, one barrel of oil has to be burned in order to harvest 100 barrels—yielding an EROI ratio of 100 : 1 (Rubin 2009: 46). Unconventional extraction is much more energy intensive. Oil sands production, for instance, currently has a ratio between 6 : 1 and 3 : 1 (Hughes 2009: 68). This means that one barrel of oil has to be invested for every *three* produced. This poor ratio is due to the need to separate the oil from the sands, which is usually done by generating heat. Oil production today is terribly inefficient compared to several decades ago—we burn a lot of energy to get a little bit more.

Diminishing EROI leads peak theorists to argue that there is an absolute threshold to production that has little to do with how much oil is actually in the ground (Hughes 2009). As EROI continues to fall, it gets closer to 1 : 1, and at that point oil production will cease. If it takes a unit of energy to extract an equivalent unit of energy, the exercise is pointless. Some scholars argue that one does not need to get close to 1 : 1 before production falls off, because society couldn't handle investing 50 per cent of its existing energy into generating new (future) energy (Dadeby 2012). This is represented by the idea of a "net energy cliff," whose slope becomes increasingly steep as it approaches the 1 : 1 ratio (see Figure 5.4).

In sum, peak theory *does not* argue that we need to exhaust a resource before we run out of it. What really matters is the point at which we can *no longer meaningfully exploit it*. This threshold is difficult to pinpoint exactly, because it depends on the availability of different technologies and fluctuating prices (Keith 2009). Hubbert, for instance, never predicted the development of the Alberta oil sands because in his day the technology did not exist to exploit it, and oil prices weren't high enough to justify its expensive methods. This is a weakness of peak theory that critics have been quick to seize upon.

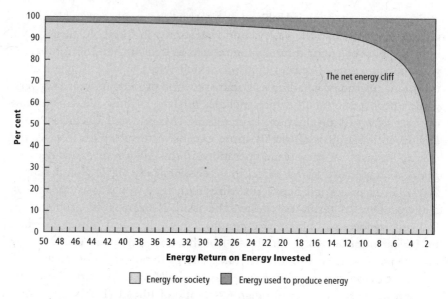

Figure 5.4 The Net Energy Cliff

Source: ASPO-USA: Support for Global Energy Flow modelling and a Net Energy database, Euan Mearns, November 1, 2006. http://europe.theoildrum.com/story/2006/10/31/144929/65

The net energy cliff shows how a declining EROI leaves less and less of society's total energy pool available for other uses.

The Case Against Peak Theory and Absolute Scarcity

There are two main arguments against peak theory and the notion that resource exploitation will soon hit the wall of absolute scarcity. The first is that peak theory fails to account for the impact of the free market. The most famous advocate of this view was the late economist Julian Simon (1932–1998), who wrote several influential books on the subject (Simon 1981; 1996). Simon argued that the world's supply of key natural resources is infinitely flexible. He asserted, for instance, that oil is not found but made. Oil does not fall from the sky, it has to be extracted and then processed into useful things, like gasoline and plastics. Because oil is useful and in demand, the private sector is constantly finding new ways to make more of it. The more something is in demand, the greater the incentive to innovate. For example, natural gas prices in North America increased significantly between 2000 and 2006, reflecting increases in demand and stagnant supplies. In the middle of the last decade, however, a new technique emerged called induced hydraulic fracturing, or **"fracking,"** which dramatically changed the market for natural gas. Fracking uses a high pressure mixture of water and chemicals to break apart rock formations deep underground, allowing the natural gas industry to tap supplies that had been previously inaccessible. In response to this new supply, the price of natural gas fell in North America back to 2003 levels (NEB 2011b).

Coming back to oil, the high prices of recent years have prompted some companies to pursue shale oil development, which also involves fracking. The Bakken region in North Dakota, for instance, has rapidly become one of the US's largest oil fields thanks to fracking, and the technique is also being applied in traditional oil-producing states such as Texas and Louisiana. Experiments are also underway in the Alberta oil sands to use microwave technology to heat the oil sands *in situ* (in place), which may reduce the energy needed to separate oil and sand (Tait 2012a). Copper mining companies, which have long used ugly open-pit mining techniques, are now converting these mines into traditional underground mines to access copper deeper in the Earth's crust (Miller 2012). All of these innovations (theoretically) extend the life of resources and push back absolute scarcity. Ever the economist, Simon argued that future technologies cannot be predicted, but we can be certain that higher prices will provide incentives to develop them. These new technologies will in turn alleviate prices and the cycle can begin anew (Simon 1981: 32). While this argument can be difficult to swallow for non-economists, it should not be dismissed out of hand. The world's estimated oil reserves (the total amount believed to be accessible using current technologies) is currently *increasing* rather than decreasing (by one estimate, it increased from 1.27 trillion barrels in 2001 to 1.65 trillion in 2011) (Tait 2012b). This does not negate peak theory or the EROI problem, but it certainly complicates them.

The second argument against peak theory involves the principle of substitution discussed previously. The suggestion here is that, if high prices and low EROIs become a permanent problem (i.e., we exhaust all technological possibilities around a resource), the market will adopt substitutes. Many potential substitutes for oil exist already. For example, coal can be processed into a synthetic substitute for gasoline. For the moment, coal is abundant (but see Rubin 2012: 109 for a contrarian view) yet also carbon-intensive, meaning that this substitution would be economically viable but ecologically disastrous (Keith 2009: 34). Other substitutions are unexpected. Prior to the 1950s, for instance, uranium was not a "natural resource" like it is today, because nuclear power did not exist. Again, this returns us to the argument that resources are made rather than discovered, and are therefore (theoretically) infinite. In the words of Barnett and Morse (1963: 11), "nature imposes particular scarcities, but not an inescapable general scarcity." As key resources like oil are consumed, new sources of energy will become evident and economical. This involves a leap of faith, however, that what Simon called "the ultimate resource"—human ingenuity—will continue to make new natural resources in response to market demands.

Ultimate Limits? The Problem of Peak Everything

Arguments against absolute scarcity are most convincing when applied to the last 100 years or so. The beginnings of the twentieth century to today have been the glory years of technological development and resource substitution. In this 100-year span, we have greatly increased the amount of energy, food, minerals, and water extracted from the Earth. But can the treadmill really go on forever, brushing up against absolute scarcity but never ultimately running into it? All of our institutions are organized on the assumption that the answer is yes, but here are some things to consider.

First, the arguments made by Simon and other latter day advocates of this view, such as Bjørn Lomborg (2001), rarely address the role of pollution and other undesirable outcomes. For example, the same fracking technologies that are opening up new oil and natural gas reserves may also be threatening groundwater (Manuel 2010). Conflicts over the possible effects of fracking on drinking water are brewing across Europe and North America, and have led to bans in Quebec, Vermont, and all of France. Coal and nuclear power also have serious pollution and waste issues that restrict their long-term potential. In other words, many things that are possible have non-economic costs that may ultimately make them undesirable or even impossible to implement.

Second, the development and implementation of new technologies and substitutions take time. As the treadmill accelerates, the luxury of time is squeezed, if not lost. Homer-Dixon (2006) argues that one of the key characteristics of current problems and crises is that they are coming in bunches. An event like Hurricane Katrina in 2005 knocks out oil production and gasoline refining in the Gulf region for months, starting a run in oil prices that ultimately contributes to the US housing crash of 2007 and the financial crisis of 2008–2009. A fast world is a highly interconnected world, and the lead time to develop solutions in true crises is diminished. It is also critical to realize that there has never been a substitution of a resource as important as oil. Oil is everything today's world: it is used in every sector of the economy, and is critical for transportation, electricity generation, manufacturing, and agriculture. With this in mind, the leap of faith at the heart of this thinking—a position that Murphy (2006) criticizes as "cornucopian"—becomes harder to justify.

Third, and related to this, is the spectre of "peak everything" (Heinberg 2010). The substitution argument makes sense when relatively cheap alternatives are readily available. The example used earlier—of substituting wheat for corn after a hypothetical loss of that crop—works if supplies of wheat and corn are independent of one another. But what if *food* itself is scarce? Substitution, in this dire case, is meaningless. Over the past few years, we've seen troubling convergences of scarcity across several sectors, particularly energy and food. To illustrate how converging scarcities can be problematic, let's again consider the case of water. Fresh water can in fact be created, consistent with Simon's logic, by drawing salt water out of the ocean and desalinating it. This process, however, takes an extraordinary amount of energy that, in arid countries like Saudi Arabia that depend on desalination, comes from oil (Rubin 2012: 98). Scarcity of energy or scarcity of water can be dealt with alone, but not together. The lesson to be drawn is that while single scarcities are almost always temporary, concurrent scarcities pose fundamental problems. Unfortunately, this is exactly where the treadmill threatens to take us.

Scarcity's Children

We have seen thus far that scarcity is a problematic concept. Let us assume for a moment, though, that the logic of the treadmill of production is leading us toward a future of greater scarcity—where resources are less abundant and readily available, and humanity (or at least significant pockets of it) is forced to make due with less. What would that future look like?

As is usually the case, there is disagreement. On the one hand are optimists, who see scarcity as a way of reasserting older values and lifestyles that have been diminished in recent times. On the other hand are pessimists, who see scarcity as a major challenge, especially to the poor and disadvantaged.

An Optimistic Take on Future Scarcity

In a nutshell, the optimistic view of scarcity hinges on the notion of equity. This perspective owes much to the thinking of philosopher Ivan Illich (1974) who argued that "high energy societies" also tend to be highly unequal ones. Illich's model for this is the United States, the archetypal high energy society. Not only is the US a high inequality society, it offers citizens remarkably little choice in terms of lifestyle. Whole cities are built around high energy consumption, beholden to "car culture" and urban sprawl, and ruled by experts and technocrats. Illich argued that high energy societies rob individuals of their autonomy, and the structure of social and economic life means that they have little choice but to "use motors to do most of their work and leisure" (Illich 2012: 48). Low energy societies, by contrast, "allow for a wide choice of lifestyles and cultures" guided by fewer rules, greater autonomy, and more face-to-face interaction (2012: 49).

Sociologically speaking, this view is akin to "easing off the treadmill." In this scenario, scarcity forces us to slow down, and in slowing down become more local, community-oriented, and less obsessed with growth (De Young and Princen 2012). Canadian economist Jeffrey Rubin has written several books on this possibility, including *Why Your World is About to Get a Whole Lot Smaller* (2009) and *The End of Growth* (2012). He argues in these works that energy scarcity will likely lead to a manufacturing renaissance in developed countries as transportation costs put the brakes on globalization. Similarly, he argues that the rampant financial speculation that fuels boom-and-bust economies will diminish, and far-flung suburbs and sprawled cities will likely contract, bringing people closer together and reinvigorating urban life.

A Pessimistic Take on Future Scarcity

Unfortunately, treadmill theory itself suggests that "getting off" may not be as orderly and equitable an experience as suggested by optimists. Treadmill theory focuses on interests, and how the interests of competing groups are reconciled through environmental depletion. If absolute scarcity begins to permanently curtail growth, competing interests and differential power may come rushing back to the fore. In this case, inequalities are likely to be exacerbated. For instance, when food prices spiked in 2008, just prior to the global financial crisis, many Canadians noticed an increase in their grocery and restaurant bills. In poorer countries, however, the price increases brought real hardship (Conceicao and Mendoza 2009). The simple fact of the matter is that poorer people spend a greater proportion of their income on food and energy. Food is especially problematic, because it is difficult to trim back (especially for people getting by on minimal calories to begin with) and prices are set globally now that agriculture has become an internationally integrated activity. Under conditions of absolute scarcity, wealthier people have deeper pockets than poorer people, which means they can almost always outbid them for key goods (Curran 2013). This problem does not have an easy solution, and in the past few years countries as diverse as Russia, Tanzania, Argentina, India, Ukraine, Belarus, Kazakhstan, and Indonesia have imposed export restrictions on agricultural products to try to feed their own people.

Another way that scarcity could exacerbate inequality is through "resource capture" (Homer-Dixon 1999). As a resource becomes more scare, its value increases, which then makes it vulnerable to being "captured" by powerful groups. This is done in various ways. In its most brazen form, the resource is simply seized—often by governments but sometimes by clans, warlords, or criminal organizations (Percival and Homer-Dixon 1998). Other times, pressure increases for the resource to be commodified. This is most evident in the case of water. In much of the world, water has traditionally been seen as a public good that should be available to all at minimal cost. In Canada, for instance, consumers who receive municipal water do not pay for the water directly, but rather for the system that manages it and delivers it to them (people who draw water from their own wells do not pay at all but instead are responsible for the maintenance costs for their own supply). As fresh water has become scarce in many parts of the world, however, it has attracted the attention of large corporations and private investors (Mirosa and Harris 2012). Stock markets such as the S&P 500 now have "Global Water Indexes" that track the value of the for-profit water sector, and brokerage firms now routinely offer pre-packaged water portfolios (as mutual funds or exchange traded funds) for sale to individual and corporate investors. The point is that absolute scarcity can *help* capital (corporations) even as it hurts citizens. Rather than squeezing capital, scarcity can serve as a way to transfer wealth *to* capital. This is consistent with the controversial argument made by Canadian activist Naomi Klein (2007) about "disaster capitalism"—that traumatic experiences like war and scarcity frequently reinforce rather than diminish corporate power. In sum, we don't all suffer equally, and scarcity may make this worse rather than better.

Conclusion

Scarcity is an important concept in environmental sociology, but not a clear-cut one. The question "are we running out of the things we need?" seems simple enough, but it is difficult to answer definitively. According to mainstream economics, scarcity is a flexible and usually temporary thing. If enough demand exists in a market, suppliers have an incentive to make more of a given good, or, failing that, to develop acceptable substitutes. From this perspective, scarcity is *relative*—it exists only within markets and the collective decisions people make about how to spend their money. Other scholars, including ecologists, peak theorists, and some ecologically minded economists, are more concerned with *absolute* scarcity. This perspective sees the Earth as a limited thing that can provide only so many materials and commodities. These scholars point out that our ability to extract things from the planet—notably energy and food—is ultimately limited by the amount of effort required (the EROI). They also argue that while certain substitutions may make economic sense (like making gasoline from coal instead of oil), their environmental consequences would make problems worse, not better. In other words, it is possible that we are at the beginning of a global transition from a system characterized by relative scarcity to one ruled by the hard limits of absolute scarcity.

The sociological theory of the treadmill of production (or "treadmill theory") provides a basis for understanding why we are gambling that this transition *will not* happen. The wager that we are collectively making is that our economies can grow forever without encountering hard limits. Treadmill theory shows how this bet is not wholly voluntary—the logic of the capitalist system compels us to make it. Capitalism is an economic system built on contradictions—among them that competition leads to better outcomes for all. Treadmill theory argues that the only way such contradictions are maintained is through a total dedication to constant growth (Schnaiberg 1980). For the moment at least, growth means drawing ever more resources from the planet, especially materials and energy. In short, treadmill theory shows how the logic of relative scarcity, which builds wealth, leads us into the arms of absolute scarcity.

Assuming that this is our future, what will that future look like? Optimists tend to highlight the creative potential of easing off the tread-mill—allowing us to reclaim locality and community, redesign cities and living spaces, and achieve greater leisure and less inequality. In contrast, pessimists see absolute scarcity as exacerbating existing inequalities. They argue that when competition for critical goods—especially food, water, and energy—gets really heated, the wealthy will always be able to out-bid the poor. Equally troubling is the notion that absolute scarcity may lead to further commodification of the natural environment. As resources get scarcer, their value increases, which make them tempting targets for private companies and investors.

In conclusion, if absolute scarcity is going to be more positive than negative, a lot of effort has to go into making it that way. We need to start planning how we want to manage our resources should supplies ever become truly scarce. Australia, for instance, has been experimenting for decades now with different ways to reduce water demand in both urban and rural areas (McKay 2005). Big investments need to be made now in public trans-portation, and cities need to start adopting "densification" plans, as is being successfully done in places like Vancouver (Berelowitz 2010: 111). Perhaps most difficult in an era of efficiency and austerity, more power needs to be given to municipalities and local organizations to come up with creative and locally tailored solutions. If we are destined to come off the treadmill one way or the other, it is better to slow down and step off intentionally than to hit the wall.

Questions for Critical Thought

1. Do you think global society will encounter absolute scarcity any time soon? Why or why not?

2. Do you have faith in humanity's abilities to "make more resources" should they ever become truly scarce?

3. What do you think a future under scarcity would look like?

4. How could we collectively step off the treadmill? What would that look like?

Suggested Readings

Bardi, Ugo. (2009). "Peak oil: The four stages of a new idea," *Energy* 34(3): 323–326. This article presents a good history of the idea of peak oil, from Hubbert's predic-tion to its resonance with the media and general public.

DeYoung, Raymond and Thomas Princen. (2012). *The Localization Reader: Adapting to the Coming Downshift.* Cambridge MA: MIT Press. This text is an interesting collection of reprinted and original essays that looks at different possible futures under scarcity, with an emphasis on "how a transition that is peaceful, democratic, just, and environmentally resilient" can be achieved.

Dyer, Gwynne. (2008). *Climate Wars*. Toronto: Random House. A hair-raising discussion of how climate change could cause global scarcities in food, water, and security, this volume is a pessimistic vision of absolute scarcity, and not for the faint of heart.

Gould, Kenneth, Pellow, David, and Allan Schnaiberg. (2008). *The Treadmill of Production: Injustice and Unsustainability in the Global Economy*. Boulder CO: Paradigm. This book provides a short and understandable synopsis of treadmill theory, as well as a history of its development.

Suggested Websites

Peak Oil
http://peakoil.com/

This is a discussion forum for people interested in peak oil theory. Many postings also deal with new technologies, and renewable and alternative energy sources.

We Live Simply
http://welivesimply.info/

On this website you will find a discussion forum for people looking to step off the treadmill and live less consumption-driven lives.

6 A Dangerous New World? The Risk Society Thesis

Key Points

◎ The "risk society thesis," which is most closely associated with the thinking of German sociologist Ulrich Beck, is an ambitious attempt to theorize the increasingly central role of danger, fear, and anxiety in modern society.

◎ Beck argues that we have entered a new era in which the "side effects" of industrial production (i.e., risks) are playing an increasingly central role in politics, challenging established authority figures such as scientists, experts, and governments, while creating new opportunities for grassroots mobilization.

◎ Critics of the risk society thesis argue that Beck overstates the role of risk in contemporary politics and assumes (without much evidence) that people will respond collectively to new threats and dangers.

◎ Case studies of "risk in the real world" show that many of the ideas associated with the risk society thesis are valid, but that more attention should be paid to issues of inequality.

Introduction

This chapter presents a markedly different take on the environmental dilemmas facing contemporary society. While treadmill and peak theory assume that environmental problems are primarily economic in origin and consequences, the **risk society thesis** sees environmental problems as key agents in a broad *cultural* and *political* transformation currently underway in many democratic countries. Risk society theorists therefore reach very different conclusions about the character and consequences of environmental problems than those we encountered in the last chapter. To illustrate, consider the following example:

In 1891, a Russian chemist named Aleksandr Dianin created a synthetic chemical that he hoped could serve as a hormone replacement for women suffering from chronically low estrogen. The chemical, now known as bisphenol A (or BPA), turned out to be a disappointment—laboratory tests showed that while it did mimic estrogen, other existing chemicals were more effective—so BPA was duly catalogued and largely forgotten (Szaro et al. 2011). In the 1940s, however, chemists returned to BPA for an entirely different reason: as a key ingredient in the nascent plastics industry. BPA, it turned out, was a "wonder chemical" that worked its way into innumerable consumer products (Erler and Novak 2010). BPA readily binds with other molecules to form polymers, which are the chemical backbone of the hard, clear plastics that have so many consumer uses (such as food storage containers and reusable water bottles). BPA is also used to make the thin plastic lining on the inside of canned foods and beverages, in dental fillings, baby bottles, and "microwave safe" packaging, as well as the coating on paper used for issuing cash register receipts. Approximately 7 billion pounds of BPA are produced by manufacturers every year in a market worth about $370 million US annually (Erler and Novak 2010: 400). BPA, in short, is everywhere, including in our own bodies—ingested through food and drink, and absorbed through the skin.

Given its prevalence, regulators have kept an eye on BPA, and periodic reviews in the United States (in 1976 and 1993) concluded that it was safe. In the late 1990s, however, studies began appearing that suggested otherwise (Erickson 2008). The predominant assumption guiding regulators was that because BPA was a "low dose" chemical that was rapidly processed by the human liver and eliminated in urine, it didn't pose a significant problem. New studies on laboratory animals, though, showed potential links between continuous low-dose exposure and risk of heart disease, mental illness, infertility, and cancer (e.g., Jenkins et al. 2009; Soto Am and Sonnenschein 2010). Human studies quickly followed, suggesting that these links were plausible, and also finding that children were particularly vulnerable because of the chemical's estrogen-mimicking properties and the fact that their livers are not fully developed (Beronius et al. 2010).

After nearly a half-century of use, the wonder chemical with so many applications was exposed as a toxin with potentially serious long-term effects on humans. Environmental activists and consumer protection groups in Europe and North America mobilized to have BPA banned, and anxious parents began throwing out plastic baby bottles and buying old-fashioned glass ones or new "BPA-free" bottles that were rushed to market. The Canadian plastics industry continues to fight these findings tooth and nail, stating that "BPA is one of the most extensively tested materials in use today. Over 40 years of research has demonstrated that consumer products made with BPA are safe for their intended use and there is no basis for human health concerns from exposure to BPA" (CPIA 2012). In 2008, Health Canada responded with a compromise that ultimately satisfied no one: baby bottles containing BPA would be banned from sale in Canada, but all other consumer uses could continue. Environment Canada followed suit by listing BPA as a "toxic substance" in 2010, but has not moved to curb its overall use. Recent estimates suggest that BPA exposure in Canada has declined, but consumers trying to avoid the chemical are frustrated because there is no requirement that it be labelled (Beeby 2012). In the meantime, contradictory studies pile up, exposure continues, and anxious parents and consumers grope in the dark to rid themselves of a chemical they no longer want but can't seem to avoid.

The BPA story resonates not because it is unusual but because it is *so common*. Citizens are bombarded daily with messages about contaminants, toxins, and threats associated with the products, practices, and technologies on which we've come to rely. Claims about hidden dangers and unforeseen side effects are a major trope in both media coverage and environmental activism. Is this just scare-mongering to sell newspapers and promote political agendas, or is there something deeper and more profound going on?

The risk society thesis is a complex, controversial, and theoretically ambitious attempt to address our current obsession with danger and embed it in a broad theory of social organization and change. At root, the risk society thesis argues that messages about danger and harm have a deeper meaning—signalling a profound transition in modern society, where public faith in the achievements of mass industrialism is replaced by anxiety about its (unknown) effects on human health and the environment. This idea is most directly associated with the work of German sociologist Ulrich Beck (1992; 1999; 2009) but many others have made important contributions as well (e.g., Giddens 1990; Luhmann 1993; Strydom 2002; Renn 2008). Briefly put, Beck argues that the pursuit of modern ideals—wealth, technology, progress, and unfettered consumption—have produced a series of "unintended consequences" that are highly dangerous yet extremely difficult to control, and that are now "striking back" at society and challenging some of our most important beliefs and institutions (Beck et al. 2003: 2). All of the major global-scale environmental concerns of today—pollution, toxic waste, contamination, climate change, nuclear accidents, genetic engineering, ozone depletion, extinction—are the direct result of modern society. We didn't set out to produce these problems; they are the unforeseen "side effects" of our efforts to build modern economies, politics, and technologies. For a time, the existence of these side effects was largely ignored by corporate and political leadership, but major incidents like the 1986 Chernobyl nuclear disaster (an example Beck uses throughout his work) made this less tenable. This risk society thesis, then, is that *side effects* of modern living are playing an increasingly *central* role in collective and individual decision-making. Avoiding harm and mitigating risk have become major political, cultural, and personal goals, even if they come at extraordinary cost (Sorenson and Christianson 2013: 10). In the months following the more recent nuclear disaster at Fukushima, Japan, in 2011, for instance, governments around the world abandoned plans to build new nuclear reactors and even began decommissioning existing ones. In Germany alone, the decision to shut down all of its nuclear generators by the year 2022 comes at an estimated cost of anywhere between €55 and €250 billion (Nicola 2011). This logic only makes sense in a society where fear and anxiety have become major motives of public policy and political decision-making.

This chapter addresses the risk society thesis in three parts. The first part outlines the major contours of Beck's ideas and explains why they have been influential in environmental sociology. The second section addresses some of the key criticisms of the risk society thesis that have emerged over the years, while the third section looks at specific cases of the "risk society" in action. Overall, I argue that while Beck's theory has some significant flaws, it is a powerful conceptual tool for investigating some of our most stubborn environmental conflicts and problems.

Beck's Risk Society Thesis

This section breaks the risk society thesis into a series of key ideas. While the risk society concept has been used in a wide variety of fields, including criminology, family studies, economics, and political science, the emphasis here is on its applicability to environmental issues and problems. An excellent and more comprehensive summary of Beck's thinking and writing can be found in Sorenson and Christiansen (2013).

Idea #1: Recent History Can Be Divided into Three Stages: Pre-modern Society, Industrial Society, and Risk Society

The risk society thesis, at root, is a theory of social change, which means that it contains a narrative about why and how contemporary society differs from the past. Beck is in fact interested in two transitions: the one from pre-modern society to what he terms "industrial society"; and from industrial society to "risk society." The three eras can be delineated in different ways, but Beck distinguishes them according to their relationship to dangers. Pre-modern society was a period dominated by traditional institutions and worldviews. This was in fact a dangerous time in which to live, one where people were highly vulnerable to natural disasters such as storms, floods, fires, and plagues. Importantly, however, people typically saw these as "external events" beyond their control (Luhmann 1993: 8). Unpredictable and incomprehensible disasters were collectively explained as "acts of God," Fate, Providence, or chance. This is not to say that people were ignorant of danger. Anthropological studies clearly show that pre-modern people have sophisticated means of identifying and assessing dangers, using their physical senses and collective experience to judge, for instance, which foods are safe to eat and which are not. As we saw in Chapter 2, pre-modern people could and did also prepare for natural disasters like storms and droughts. The difference, however, is that the onset, severity, and duration of such events were attributed to supernatural forces beyond people's immediate control.

The transition from pre-modern society to industrial society occurred gradually in some places and more quickly in others, but was generally associated with the rise of **modernity**. Modernity refers to the package of institutions and values associated with the political, scientific, and industrial revolutions of the eighteenth and nineteenth centuries, and includes a reliance on rationality and reason, a faith in secular science and technology, a commitment to the idea of the nation-state, and a strong notion of progress (Giddens 1990). One of the major achievements of industrial society was to mitigate the dangers that had plagued pre-modern society (Sorenson and Christiansen 2013: 23). Mechanized agriculture removed threats of cyclical famine (at least in more developed parts of the world), while better urban planning mitigated threats from floods and fires, and modern medicine made great strides in combatting infectious disease. At the same time, however, industrial society created new dangers that were "manufactured" rather than natural in origin. New technologies like the automobile turned out to be both convenient and dangerous, while newly built factories spewed industrial wastes into the air and water.

Another distinction is that while pre-modern society "lived with" its dangers, industrial society responded to these new problems by trying to manage them (Sorenson and Christiansen 2013: 16). In other words, industrial society transformed dangers into *risks* (Luhmann 1993: 24). The notion of risk implies that events that may or may not happen can still be predicted and managed. Consider one of the most important tools for "risk management" in the modern world: the notion of insurance. Insurance is a way for individuals and organizations to protect themselves from the unexpected, be it a house fire, an automobile accident, or an unexpected drop in the stock market—anything can be insured so long as there is another party willing to accept the risk in exchange for a premium that the client is willing to pay (Ericson et al. 2003). The insurance industry, however, does not just passively accept premiums and hope for the best. Instead, insurers conduct massive amounts of research on possible future outcomes. How likely is a driver of a certain age, sex, and personal background to get into an accident? How likely is a house in a certain neighbourhood to be burgled? How long is a person likely to live? How likely is it that a given type of individual will break a contract or dishonour a debt? To reach these conclusions, insurers rely on enormous amounts of data about past behaviours and events, combined with models that use key indicators as predictors of future outcomes and means of setting "fair premiums" for customers (Bernstein 1996: 87).

The insurance example tells us several things. First, the notions of risk and risk management involve reaching beyond the physical senses to assess danger in a highly abstract way. Risk involves applying existing knowledge (about the likelihood of a traffic accident occurring to a given "type" of driver, or the link between exposure to a toxin and future development of cancer) to real-world situations that are unknown. Risk is therefore based on *calculations* about *probabilities*—a very different logic than using one's senses to assess immediate dangers. Second, the example illustrates how risk is about *extending human control* over the unpredictable. Threats that used to be considered external (governed by Fate) are increasingly brought into the human realm as "mitigatable" events. Hurricanes, earthquakes, and fires may happen, but rational risk management allows us to mitigate and compensate—mitigate by predicting the effects of a disaster and doing things like strengthening building codes, and compensate by rebuilding using private insurance or, as a last resort, government-backed relief plans.

Beck argues that we are now in the midst of a second transition—from an industrial society to a risk society—that is again based on a transformation in our collective relationship with danger. Essentially, he argues that the *success* of industrial society has created dangers so large and pervasive that they are now *challenging* its key principles. Beck suggests that the fruits of industrial society—increased wealth, scientific and technological breakthroughs, and rampant consumerism—have "unbound" dangers in space and time. Consider the example of pollution. In earlier times, pollution was generally considered a local issue that could be addressed by "cleaning up" a given factory, area, river, or activity. Beck argues that the scale of industrialism, however, along with improved scientific measurements have shattered the illusion that pollution is local (2010: 175). The problems of ozone depletion and global warming have shown us that the impacts of pollution extend far beyond its source, carried by wind, rivers, and ocean currents to the far corners of the world and the upper layers of the stratosphere. The Arctic region is not only being transformed by greenhouse gas emissions from distant places, but its naturally arid climate has made it a major sink for other wandering pollutants that arrive from North America, Europe, and Asia (Fisher et al. 2010). Just as importantly, many pollutants last a long time. Carbon dioxide emitted today will linger in the atmosphere for centuries, long after the factory or consumer who emitted it is dead or decommissioned. Extremely toxic substances such as dioxins and PCBs are highly stable and take dozens and even hundreds of years to biodegrade in the natural environment (Sinkkonen and Paasivirta 2000). Waste from nuclear power generation is expected to remain radioactive for *millions* of years, posing health risks for innumerable generations to come. In short, the risk society thesis assumes that this unboundedness is raising the stakes to unprecedented heights. In Beck's view, the escalation of risk is "turning the world into a laboratory" where our assumptions about the safety of different phenomena are being tested—often against the will of the people who have to live with the results (2009: 36).

One final point: While the risk society is different from the industrial society, it is still a *modern* society. It is important to note that Beck began formulating his ideas at a time when academics were enamoured with the notion of "postmodernism," specifically the idea that society had moved beyond the tenets of modern society and into something new and different from modernity (Sorenson and Christianen 2013: 27). Beck rejects this, arguing that the risk society is pushing us towards "a new modernity" rather than a break with it. This new modernity, though, is a work in progress. The risk society should therefore be thought of as a period of transition to an as-yet unknown future state (Elliot 2002: 297). More accurately, it should be seen as a fork in the road: If we take one path we're in for more of the same—obsessing over our safety while continuing to generate evermore serious problems; if we take the other we have the rare opportunity to reinvent key institutions to make them more environmentally responsible and authentically democratic (through processes Beck calls "reflexive modernization" and "subpolitics"—more on these below).

Idea #2: Risk Is Both Real and Socially Constructed

In the terms outlined in Chapter 4, Beck is both an environmental realist and a social constructionist. Some critics find this frustrating (see below), but it is central to understanding the risk society thesis. On the one hand, Beck posits that risks are objectively more serious today than during industrial society. While the point is debatable, the argument can be made that "unbound" catastrophes such as nuclear fallout, ozone depletion, and global climate change are qualitatively different—and perhaps more serious—than the more "contained" environmental dangers of the industrial period. On the other hand, Beck also argues that what truly demarcates the risk society from the earlier industrial society is people's *recognition* of such risks and willingness to mobilize around them (1999: 138). This brings him closer to the social constructionist camp, implying that the transition between the two eras is predominantly based on a change in public perception. According to Sorenson and Christiansen (2013: 10–11),

> [While] industrial society has always polluted the environment, it is only once the matter of pollution itself obtains the status of a problem in the minds of the population—once pollution becomes a prominent matter of public debate—that the transition from industrial society to risk society occurs. . . . Risk society arises once people start to question whether a particular kind of product or production method can be seen as beneficial and whether the product is worth the pollution it causes, with the knowledge that to put a complete stop to the production of this product or method might entail significant economic drawbacks.

Indeed, Beck suggests that risk is a flashpoint because it is *differently* constructed by different social actors. In the industrial society, issues of risk were dominated by professionals, particularly insurers, accountants, actuaries, doctors, public health officials, and engineers. These professionals typically approached risk as a technical problem that could often be reduced to an equation. Among the most simplistic is this one: risk = probability × harm. In a way, this equation makes sense: A low-probability event can be extremely risky if it generates a great degree of harm (as with a nuclear disaster); and conversely a low-harm event can also generate significant risks if it happens too frequently (as with property crime). One of Beck's key points, though, is that this perspective on risk clashes with the views of people who have to "live" risk. For instance, technical assurances that the probability of a nuclear accident is low are deeply unsatisfactory to many people who live near a nuclear power plant and would have to live with the consequences. Similarly, statements from the Canadian Plastics Industry arguing that "there is no basis for human health concerns from exposure to BPA" are of little comfort to parents concerned about the long-term health of their families. Citizens of the risk society are therefore far more skeptical of experts, decision-makers, and bureaucrats than they were in the industrial society (Beck 2009: 7). The more cultural side of risk (what is sometimes described as "risk perception") causes a dissatisfaction with the technical means established under industrialism to deal with danger.

Idea #3: Risk Issues Are Overwhelming the Institutions of the Industrial Society

Industrial society sought to control risks using several tools, including representative democracy, scientific and technological innovation, insurance, and law. A key pillar of Beck's risk society thesis is that these tools are being overwhelmed by the combined weight of new risks and public skepticism. First, the unbounded nature of new "manufactured" risks means that they are difficult to control using the tools of representative democracy, which are tied to specific jurisdictions. Climate change, for instance, is a truly global danger that cannot be adequately addressed at the national level. With only a few exceptions, however, global climate change negotiations have been derailed by nations intent on defending their own interests, leading to a broad collective failure to meaningfully mitigate risk. Second, science and technology have come under criticism as being *the source* of many risks. In the industrial society, science and technology are generally seen as a force for good, but in the risk society they are perceived more ambivalently. Beck argues that people are now more aware of the tendency of science to solve one problem (or risk) while creating another. For example, the genetic modification of plants and animals is being justified as a way to improve agricultural productivity and thus meet the challenge of feeding an ever growing world population. In doing so, however, critics argue that science is unleashing new risks to human health and to the natural world whose full consequences might not be known for decades (van Assaelt and Vos 2008).

Finally, Beck argues that new risks are so vast that they are essentially beyond the law and increasingly "uninsurable" in any meaningful way. For example, if BPA is shown in the future to have contributed to major health problems, who exactly will be held accountable for these outcomes, and how will victims be compensated for a lifetime of exposure? Will anyone go to jail for having harmed consumers, and will any financial restitution compensate for lost quality of life? Beck (2009: 27) describes this state as one of "organized irresponsibility," whereby the people and institutions that are benefiting from the creation of risks cannot be held fully accountable for their downside.

Idea #4: Risk Is Changing Human Politics

The fourth major idea is that contemporary society is not just obsessed with risk, but actively *reorganized* by it. Beck argues that the industrial society was preoccupied with certain problems, specifically the generation of wealth, the alleviation of poverty, the struggle for fair wages, and the establishment of universal social services (Mythen 2007: 798). These were all struggles for and over *social goods*, as labour, feminist, and minority groups worked to stake a claim to equality, justice, and an enhanced quality of life. In contrast, Beck argues that the risk society is far more concerned about the distribution of *social bads* than goods—specifically the "unintended consequences" of industrial society itself:

> While people were busy making as much money as possible, striving after scientific progress, abolishing poverty [and so on], the risks quietly and swiftly sneaked in, behind the back of a society that had its attention directed elsewhere. . . . These risks are the *unintended side effects* of industrialism: side effects that could not have been planned for, are not wanted or needed and could not have been predicted. They simply appeared wherever industrial society turned out to be prosperous and successful. (Sorenson and Christiansen 2013: 22)

While the industrial society was about achieving a higher quality of life, the risk society is about protecting oneself from harm. This implies a significant shift in politics. Beck argues that the politics of industrial society were predominantly organized around social class—specifically the struggle between workers and capitalists over how best to divide the spoils of industrialism. In the risk society, by contrast, social class loses its hold over politics in the face of what Beck calls "the commonality of anxiety" (1992: 49). His argument is that the "unboundedness" of new dangers such as pollution, toxins, global warming, and nuclear energy means that *everyone* is potentially at risk—even the people and nations that have grown wealthy by creating these risks. Beck calls this the "boomerang effect"

(1992: 37), and it is central to his understanding of the new politics of the risk society. In an oft-quoted phrase, Beck argues that "while hunger is hierarchical, smog is democratic" (1992: 36), implying that the exposure of "ordinary" and otherwise secure people to such dangers creates a new solidarity grounded in fear rather than optimism. Returning to the example of BPA, this is a chemical that affects everyone—its pervasiveness in consumer products makes it nearly impossible to escape. Therefore the push to ban the compound transcends traditional cleavages of social class, gender, race, and age (at least in theory). The struggle to avoid and contain *social bads* promotes an "enforced cosmopolitanism" (Beck 2009: 61) that brings different groups together "that otherwise wouldn't have anything to do with one another."

This leads us to another intriguing argument: As society becomes more pessimistic (more focused on avoiding dangers and "bads"), Beck finds more reason for optimism. Specifically, Beck argues that the risk society is helping to move us from a phase of "simple modernization" to one of **"reflexive modernization."** Simple modernization (which Beck also calls "first modernity") refers to the set of reforms that allowed industrialism to flourish, including the rise of science, capitalism, mass education, and governments dedicated to promoting economic expansion. The emergence of risk issues, however, is now pushing us into a phase of reflexive modernization (or a "second modernity") that is based on "a modernization of modernity itself" (Beck et al. 2003: 1). This is a complicated idea, but essentially Beck is arguing that both the severity of new risks and increased public attention to risk issues are forcing major institutions into a state of "self-confrontation," where they are compelled to address the consequences of past actions and anticipate future problems. For example, Germany's expensive decision to abandon nuclear energy, discussed previously, can be read this way—as an admission that older assumptions about the safety of nuclear power were both technically and socially flawed, even if the chances of an accident remain slim.

Reflexive modernization is not a perfect process, however, and it is rife with contradictions. According to Beck, the "reflexive" in reflexive modernization refers more to "reflex" than to "reflection" (Beck 2009: 109), which implies that society is still stuck in a "reactive" phase to unexpected risks—trying to mitigate harms that arise unexpectedly more often than acting proactively. More importantly, our reactions continue to rely on the tools of first modernity, as we typically try to solve problems by deploying *more* science, *more* technology, and *more* expert calculations (Beck et al 2003: 7). For Beck, deeper solutions to risk issues can be found in the realm of **"subpolitics,"** which refers to political action that takes place outside of traditional institutions (Beck 2009: 95). Risk issues frequently prompt citizens to become "self-taught" experts, learning about dangers themselves (largely via the Internet) and engaging in grassroots organizing for boycotts and pressure campaigns. This type of organization can be local, national, or global, and feeds on the "enforced cosmopolitanism" that Beck argues is promoted by risk issues. This kind of activism can have a profound impact on both private and public organizations. After all, it was public concern and lobbying that forced Health Canada to revisit the status of BPA and prompt private companies to rush "BPA-free" baby bottles to market. In Beck's view, subpolitics are a progressive way of entrenching reflexive modernization from the ground up.

Critiques of Beck and the Risk Society Thesis

Like any ambitious social theory, the risk society thesis has attracted substantial criticism. First, Beck has been criticized for being too abstract in his arguments—relying on vignettes to illustrate his ideas rather than rigorous empirical investigation (Alario 2012: 55). For instance, Beck has largely ignored the voluminous empirical literature on individual risk perception and organizational risk management. For years, psychologists and sociologists have investigated how people and institutions perceive and react to different kinds of risk (e.g., Slovic 2000; 2010). For instance, people take a tremendous risk every time they drive a car. An average of 38 people are killed or seriously injured in automobile accidents every day in Canada (Transport Canada 2011), but no one talks about banning cars the way they do BPA or nuclear power. People react differently to different types of risk, and seem to react particularly strongly to risks imposed on them from the outside (as opposed to risks they voluntarily undertake). This research is critical to understanding the "risk society," but is rarely addressed in Beck's writing.

Second, critics have argued that Beck's distinction between "natural hazards" and "**manufactured risks**" is flawed. Among the most devastating events in pre-modern societies were epidemics and plagues, which are not strictly natural disasters but instead a "side effect" of human decisions about trade, dwelling, and sanitation (Elliot 2002: 300). Alternately, natural disasters are arguably more impactful today than in the pre-modern world. Mythen (2007: 799) points out that the 2004 Indian Ocean tsunami alone killed far more people (approximately 230,000) than all known "manufactured risks" combined, including the use of atomic weapons. Beck's theory about *worsening risk* is similarly questionable. Objective indicators such as life expectancy and infant mortality (particularly in developed countries) suggest that we are living in the safest society that has ever existed, not the most dangerous. In making his arguments, Beck blurs the boundaries between risk and catastrophe, or the worst possible outcome of a given technology or problem (Alario and Freudenberg 2010). This "shrouds the differential impacts of manufactured risks," some of which are more serious than others (Mythen 2007: 800). It also downplays the upside of risk management, which has made the world safer in many ways.

Third, Beck's conceptualization of risks as both real and socially constructed leads to significant theoretical confusion. If risks are socially constructed, then different people should have different perceptions and views on risk (something research confirms—see Slovic 2010), but Beck assumes that all people will react similarly to risks because they have become so large and obvious (i.e., real).

Fourth, critics argue that Beck is projecting European experiences onto the entire world (Mythen 2007: 801). Europe is a prosperous and comfortable part of the world, and freedom from material wants frees people to care more about issues like environmental and consumer protection. (This is consistent with the post-material values thesis discussed in Chapter 3.) Risk issues like the controversy over BPA resonate in the developed world because we have a high level of confidence in other critical systems—like access to food, clean water, and ample consumer comforts.

Fifth, there is profound disagreement over Beck's assertion that class-based struggles over equality are being replaced by risk-based conflicts over safety. This debate has unfolded in two parts. The first disagreement has to do with whether or not the "boomerang effect" is in fact real. Alario and Freudenberg (2010), for instance, reject the claim that risks rebound to affect all social classes equally. While Beck argues that risks "transcend" social divisions, Alario and Freudenberg describe most risks as "Titanic"— referring to the luxury ocean liner that sank off the coast of Newfoundland in 1912. The *Titanic* carried wealthy, middle-class, and poor passengers on its voyage, and when disaster struck clearly everyone was affected. Records, however, show that while only 712 of the 2,200 passengers were saved, 600 of these were "first-class" passengers, while only 70 and 50 came from the second- and third-class compartments. It turns out that the first-class passengers were notified of the accident earlier, evacuated above deck sooner, and had preferential access to the limited lifeboats (Alario and Freudenberg 2010: 501). In other words, their wealth and status provided them with "a private escape route" from an otherwise universal disaster. Similarly, Curran (2013) posits that social class in fact becomes *more important* in the risk society. Curran argues that it is easier for individuals to mitigate their personal risk situation than for society to do so collectively, provided that they have the material means. To illustrate, he points to the devastating cyclone that hit the Indian state of Andhra Pradesh in 1977, killing approximately 14,000 people. The coast of Andhra Pradesh is flat and low-lying, leaving it highly vulnerable to flooding during storms, specifically storm surges that push sea water inland. But "even in the relatively flat delta, where it might be thought there would be an egalitarian distribution of the risks of flooding, there were sites that were slightly higher (3 to 7 metres) than others and thus more secure from storm surges" (Curran 2013: 53). Locals knew this, meaning that homes located on these slightly elevated areas were priced significantly higher than those in lower areas. This in turn meant that wealthy people were far more likely to survive the storm, while poorer people were killed in disproportionately large numbers. This is strong evidence against a uniform boomerang effect, and Beck himself has recently backed off this argument (somewhat), arguing that "risks can be both hierarchical—since the poor cannot protect themselves as efficiently and expansively as the well-to-do—and democratic—since we are all, regardless of status and class, to some extent delivered to them and influenced by them" (Beck, quoted in Sorenson and Christiansen 2013: 76).

The second part of this debate is about whether or not the boomerang effect is creating a new basis for solidarity amongst the general public. As discussed earlier, Beck places a great deal of faith in people's willingness to engage in cosmopolitan subpolitics—to learn about risk issues and organize across social boundaries to put pressure on the institutions of first modernity, specifically governments, corporations, and experts. But there is no guarantee that people will react this way to new threats. Szasz (2007), for instance, argues that in a consumer society people react to new dangers in a highly individualistic rather than collective way. His book *Shopping Our Way to Safety* suggests that people respond to risk by establishing an "inverted quarantine"—isolating themselves from perceived threats rather than mobilizing to defuse it for everyone. Among the many examples he gives is the case of bottled water. Bottled water was a niche market up until the 1980s, when, somewhat ironically, the environmental movement zeroed in on water quality issues (this was when the problem of acid rain first came to light) and people's faith in their municipal tap water systems was shaken (Szasz 2007: 106). The news media began looking into the issue, and the stories they told typically highlighted problems with ageing infrastructure, lax testing and inspection standards, and falsified reporting. People's response, however, has not been to collectively mobilize to demand new water infrastructure that would benefit everyone, but rather to purchase an alternative (and much more expensive) product that will provide immediate individual protection. While Beck argues that risk issues create a new solidarity, Szasz sees the opposite: Risk prompts people to retreat into themselves, focusing on how to protect their own.

Finally, several scholars have taken issue with Beck's conceptualization of reflexive modernization or the "self-confrontation" that society engages in when faced with a major risk issue. As mentioned, Beck argues that this self-confrontation is unavoidable and inevitable—that the dire consequences of manufactured risks force society to respond, which in turn makes us question and often reject older assumptions and actions (Beck et al. 2003). Some critics, though, point out that this argument neglects the formidable forces lined up against such progressive changes. McCright and Dunlap (2010: 104), for instance, argue that agents of "anti-reflexivity" are far more powerful than Beck allows. On the issue of climate change, for instance, coalitions of private companies, business lobby groups, so-called "skeptical" scientists, and sympathetic politicians and governments have played a strong and largely successful role in promoting "non-action" on climate change in key nations such as the United States, Canada, and Australia (McCright and Dunlap 2010; Young and Coutinho 2013). The forces of anti-reflexivity "have mobilized to reassert the dominance of industrial capitalism from the era of simple modernization by directly challenging progressive social movements and the use of [environmental] science in political decision-making" (McCright and Dunlap 2010: 105). This suggests that reflexive modernization is not automatic, but rather a site of significant political struggle (see Chapter 3).

Risk in the Real World

As mentioned earlier, one of the key criticisms of Beck's thinking is that it is highly abstract and not well anchored in real world cases or observations. In this final section we will look at three cases of "risk in the real world" to see how the risk society thesis can help us understand contemporary environmental problems and controversies.

Case #1: Bringing Back the Salmon

In July 2012 the First Nation community of Old Massett on the northern tip of Haida Gwaii (also known as the Queen Charlotte Islands) in British Columbia paid a California entrepreneur $2.5 million to intentionally dump 100 tonnes of iron sulfate shavings into the North Pacific Ocean (Tollefson 2012). The intent was to stimulate the growth of plankton, which provides nourishment to small fish species that are in turn preyed upon by Pacific salmon.

> "We have set off on a path to bring life back to the North Pacific," insists John Disney, economic development officer with the Old Massett Village Council. The community, he says, got involved in the project because a generation ago there was no unemployment in Old Massett, and almost every family had someone working in the commercial salmon fishery. Today the unemployment rate sits at a staggering 70 per cent—and the local rivers that were once full of spawning salmon in the fall are largely empty of fish. (Hume 2012a)

Marine and ocean scientists were stunned by the news. The Old Massett decision was prompted by volcanoes that erupted in 2008 in Asia, spreading ash across the North Pacific and stimulating plankton growth and a temporary spike in salmon populations. Scientists, however, point out that massive plankton blooms often create low oxygen zones that suffocate rather than foster marine life (Joyce 2012). Maite Moldonaldo, an ocean sciences professor at the University of British Columbia, summed it up thusly: "Scientists [everywhere] are really alarmed by this. They are worried, and I personally think it's scary. The consequences of this kind of disturbance to the marine ecosystem can be atrocious . . . and we have to be very careful. I think they should be stopped from doing it again" (Hume 2012b). Mike Brett of the University of Washington agreed: "It's the unintended consequences that [scientists] are really worried about. Fundamentally changing the bio-chemical [basis] of the ocean is a risky thing to do, if you don't know how this experiment is going to turn out—and that's the real concern" (quoted in Joyce 2012). The United Nations has condemned the dumping, and the Canadian government has opened an investigation to see if any national or international laws were broken.

Case #2: DDT and Malaria

Like BPA, DDT was a "wonder chemical" that once occupied a major place in the global economy, in this case as a pesticide liberally used in agriculture. As we saw in Chapter 3, however, DDT gained widespread public attention following the publication of Rachel Carson's *Silent Spring* in 1962, which demonstrated that DDT was a devastating toxin that was poisoning animals and human beings alike. DDT became a powerful symbol for the environmental movement, and was ultimately banned internationally for use in agriculture. One of the unintended consequences of the DDT ban, however, was a resurgence of deadly malaria in many countries. Malaria is one of the world's most devastating preventable diseases, killing approximately 880,000 people a year—with most victims under six years of age (Cone 2009). As a pesticide, DDT offers unparalleled protection from mosquitoes that carry the malaria parasite. For instance, in the 1950s and 1960s Sri Lanka had a policy of spraying DDT *inside* people's private homes, and in the process reduced malaria infections "from 2.8 million cases and 7,300 deaths to 17 cases and no deaths" (Attaran et al. 2000: 729).

In 2006, the World Health Organization (WHO) of the United Nations recommended that countries with a high vulnerability to malaria begin spraying DDT inside residences again. The WHO knew that this decision would be controversial, and Arata Kochi, director of the WHO's malaria control department, implored environmentalist groups to support the spraying program, stating, "I am here today to ask you, please help save African babies as you are helping to save the environment. African babies do not have a powerful movement to champion their well-being" (Sherwell and Chamberlain 2006). The WHO's action deeply divided the environmentalist and development communities, with groups such as Greenpeace resisting any DDT use while others such as Africa Fighting Malaria (AFM) strongly endorsing spraying. Several other environmental groups responded instead by calling for more investment in bed nets and treatment—something that Kochi countered was ineffective given that bed nets only protect people when they are sleeping and that poor farmers often used them to cover livestock rather than themselves (Querengesser 2007). In 2009 the WHO muddied the waters by withdrawing its recommendation and re-endorsing the exclusive use of bed nets and therapeutics. Groups like AFM see this as a betrayal, and continue to press African governments to spray DDT indoors, with AFM board member Roger Bate stating that the "WHO's about-face has nothing to do with science or health and everything to do with bending to the will of well-placed environmentalists. Bed net manufacturers and sellers of less-effective insecticides don't benefit when DDT is employed and therefore oppose it, often behind the scenes" (WSJ 2009).

Case #3: Flood Management in Manitoba

Southern Manitoba is one of the most vulnerable regions in Canada to flooding. Excessive run-off during the spring snow melt routinely swells the Red River, which flows north from the United States through the City of Winnipeg towards the vast basin of Lake Winnipeg. A devastating flood in 1950 prompted the provincial government to build a floodway (completed in 1968) that would carry excessive flood waters around Winnipeg and back to the Red River just south of the community of Selkirk. The floodway helped divert major floods in 1979, 1997, and 2009, and is generally seen as a success in terms of risk management. In 2011, however, both the Red River and the Assiniboine River (a tributary that meets the Red River just south of downtown Winnipeg) flooded simultaneously. The Assiniboine flood took officials completely off-guard, and was described as a "one-in-three hundred year flood" caused by unprecedented rains in Western Manitoba and Eastern Saskatchewan (CBC 2011). Given that the floodway was built on the Red River, it is essentially useless for flooding on the Assiniboine. Faced with the prospect of a massive flood in downtown Winnipeg, provincial officials chose to intentionally breach the river at a community called Hoop and Holler Bend, 90 kilometres west of the city. People living in the area were stunned. Officials were forced to decide quickly, and residents only learned the day before that their homes would be intentionally flooded to save the City of Winnipeg. The CBC interviewed one man who described his shock this way: "This is not an act of God but an act of politics. Officials are making a specific decision to put you and your family in harm's way. That's not something I can accept" (CBC 2011). The intentional breach also sent the floodwaters into Lake Manitoba (not Lake Winnipeg where the Red drains), causing the flooding of several Aboriginal communities.

The community of Lake St. Martin was among the hardest hit, requiring the complete evacuation of its 1,400 residents. Community leadership and the provincial government are still at odds over where to rebuild the community, given that the town site remained underwater for much of 2011 and is now uninhabitable (Galloway 2012).

Lessons from the Cases

On the surface, these are three rather different cases that are only disparately connected. One is about trying to revive a depleted environment, another about combatting a stubborn disease, and the third about responding to a rapidly unfolding disaster. Common threads run through them, however, that provide a glimpse of the "risk society" in action. First, all three are cases of human intervention into the natural world in the name of solving problems. But in each case, solving the main problem—restoring salmon, defeating malaria, protecting a city from flooding—runs into other problems. The attempt to restore salmon may in fact poison the ocean; the attempt to mitigate the spread of malaria may harm the environment and/or the long-term health of people living in DDT-sprayed homes; and the attempt to save Winnipeg depended on intentionally destroying the homes and livelihoods of people who would have otherwise been spared. From this, we can surmise that the risk society is a complicated society that defies easy answers. Problem-solving often creates new problems. While this was undoubtedly the case in the industrial society as well, in the risk society we are painfully aware of the "risk trade-off" involved in almost all of our collective decisions. The widespread deployment of DDT may save lives, but it may also have unintended consequences that we can't predict right now; alternatively, *not using it* will also likely come with a cost of human life. This is not a feel-good problem, no matter what the ultimate decision. Someone, or something, will suffer.

Second, these cases illustrate the limits of the tools that we nonetheless depend on. The best tools that we have for mitigating risk—namely science and technology—have failed us before, contributing to, for instance, the ongoing depletion of the oceans and the climate changes that are altering weather patterns. But these industrial era tools are the best we have. Experts don't definitively know the long-term effects of dumping iron sulfide in the ocean, or whether DDT use will be effective, or how likely it is that another "one-in-three-hundred year flood" will occur in a rapidly warming climate. Our only choice, however, is to keep trying to fill in these knowledge gaps, often using models and projections that are themselves based on assumptions that may or may not reflect reality (see Chapter 4). So while science and technology are our best tools, people are more and more inclined to see them as *problematic* and not always to be trusted (Beck 1992: 156).

Third, the cases illustrate the deep inequalities that characterize risk issues. Risk managers chose to save downtown Winnipeg because it was more important than the farming community of Hoop and Holler Bend and the First Nation communities on Lake Manitoba. This is a coldly rational calculation that will always favour privileged over disadvantaged people and communities. Today, the people of Winnipeg carry on unfazed, while those who were *chosen* to be victims of the flood continue to deal with the aftermath. The case of Old Massett shows the lengths to which a community disproportionately affected by environmental degradation will go to try to revitalize a lost resource, investing a large sum of community money on a collective gamble (both financial and ecological) that might affect the whole region. Finally, in the case of DDT it is notable that the debate over whether or not to spray is taking place predominantly among Western-based environmental and development groups. The back-and-forth shifts in international malaria policy are decided in sheltered offices using the languages of epidemiology, ecology, and pharmacology. "Ordinary" citizens are excluded, even though it is they who have to live with the consequences of these decisions.

Conclusion

Beck's risk society thesis provides a very different interpretation of environmental problems than those advanced by treadmill and peak theory. For Beck, environmental risks and dangers are re-writing the cultural and political foundations of modern society. Scarcity is less important in this transformation than the diffused fear and anxiety that is playing an increasingly central role in individual, institutional, and political decision-making. The risk society thesis has been influential in environmental sociology in large part because it helps us understand why environmental issues and problems that barely registered in the industrial era are so stubbornly intractable today.

The ensemble of Beck's thinking, however, should not be treated as gospel. Beck's critics have raised valid objections to the risk society thesis, but scholars are under no obligation to accept or reject the whole package. For instance, the debate over whether or not today's "manufactured risks" are more severe than the "natural hazards" faced in the past is not terribly relevant. The cases described above show that risk issues are characterized more by their *complexity* than their severity. In the risk society, classic problems of social inequality combine with new questions about environmental inequality. Moreover, in the risk society there are no easy answers. The choice to seed the ocean, to spray DDT, or to divert floodwaters comes with significant social and/or environmental costs. While the industrial society largely ignored the side effects of its collective decisions, the risk society—being one obsessed with safety, science, planning, and unintended consequences—is compelled to address them in one way or another.

Questions for Critical Thought

1. Do you think that environmental risks and dangers are more severe today than in the past?

2. Do you have confidence that traditional authorities such as scientists, experts, doctors, and politicians will be able to predict future dangers and protect us from them?

3. Why do you think people fear some risks like BPA while accepting others such as travelling by car or playing contact sports?

4. In your opinion, is there any upside to risks and risk-taking?

Suggested Readings

Alario, Margarita, and Freudenburg, William R. (2010). "Environmental risks and environmental justice, or how Titanic risks are not so Titanic after all," *Sociological Inquiry* 80(3): 500–12. Alario and Freudenberg take Beck to task for downplaying the role of social inequality in the risk society. Their article uses Hurricane Katrina's disproportionate impact on the poor as a key case study.

Mythen, Gabe. (2007). "Reappraising the risk society thesis: telescopic sight or myopic vision?" *Current Sociology* 55(6): 793–813. Mythen provides a sympathetic critique of Beck's main ideas, including a handy summary of the major complaints against the risk society thesis.

Slovic, Paul. (2010). *The Feeling of Risk.* Washington DC: Earthscan. Paul Slovic's work bridges the gap between sociological and psychological perspectives on risk. His views on risk in some ways complement and in some ways contradict Beck's. His work is strongly empirical, and has been very influential in the policy and business communities.

Sorenson, Mads, and Christiansen, Allen. (2013). *Ulrich Beck: An Introduction to the Theory of Second Modernity and the Risk Society.* New York: Routledge. This book provides an excellent and comprehensive introduction to Beck's thinking about the risk society and other topics. It includes a discussion of his writings in German, which remain under-appreciated among English-speaking academics.

Suggested Websites

Society for Risk Analysis
www.sra.org
The SRA is a multi-disciplinary organization that promotes the study of "risk assessment, risk characterization, risk communication, risk management, and policy relating to risk." The organization runs the influential journal *Risk Analysis*, and its website has information on topics ranging from mathematical risk analysis to social constructionism.

Ulrich Beck's personal website
www.ulrichbeck.net-build.net
Get it straight from the source. Beck's official website contains summaries of his key theories, as well as reprints of newspaper editorials that he regularly publishes in Germany and the UK.

7 Making Capitalism Work? Sustainability, Neoliberalism, and Ecological Modernization Theory

Key Points

◎ Capitalism is firmly entrenched as the dominant global economic system, which has prompted many environmentalists, politicians, and scholars to look for ways to incrementally reform it in order to improve environmental performance.

◎ Much of this conversation has revolved around three concepts or perspectives: sustainability, neoliberalism, and ecological modernization theory. Each one makes different assumptions about what types of reform are needed and how to achieve them, but all are grounded in the notion that economic growth and environmental integrity are not incompatible.

◎ While case studies suggest that each can be effective in particular circumstances, there is little evidence that economy-wide reforms are underway or imminent, suggesting that deeper reforms are needed.

Introduction

This chapter addresses a difficult and politically charged question: Can capitalism and free markets be used to improve environmental performance and help us achieve a more balanced relationship with nature? This is a controversial proposition. As we saw in Chapter 5, critics of capitalism see it as overwhelmingly destructive to the environment, arguing that the competitive pressures inherent in this economic system force both producers and consumers onto a "treadmill of production" based on the ethos that continuous economic growth is both necessary and possible. Those who hold this view often argue that meaningful environmental improvements can only occur if we collectively turn away from capitalism and adopt more egalitarian, modest, and/or localized economies (e.g., Barnes and Gilman 2011; DeYoung and Princen 2012).

Capitalism, however, is more entrenched today than ever before, and has gained a level of global legitimacy that was unthinkable only a few decades ago. In light of this, many environmental groups, politicians, and scholars have adopted a more pragmatic view, asking whether capitalism can be reformed to not only lessen environmental degradation, but actively contribute to solving environmental problems and improving the state of the natural world. This chapter critically examines three inter-related ideas that speak to this issue—the popular but somewhat vague notion of **sustainability**, the political and economic reforms associated with **neoliberalism**, and the sociological perspective called **ecological modernization theory**. While these three ideas differ in many important ways (as we will see), each is grounded in the notion that capitalism can be reformed to generate environmental improvements, and therefore that economic growth and environmental integrity are not incompatible. I will discuss the promise and the problems of each one in turn before coming to an (admittedly incomplete) conclusion on this divisive question.

Sustainability

Sustainability is one of the most commonly heard terms in environmental discourse today. As an idea, sustainability is elegant, easy-to-grasp, and comforting. At root, sustainability is about continuity—ensuring that the progress we have made as a species is maintained despite the large-scale environmental degradation caused by industrialism and capitalism thus far. The notion of sustainability implies that if we can "just get it right"— if we can find the magical point at which the long-term consequences of our actions are minimized to the degree that they become negligible or inconsequential—then we can continue to live in wealth and comfort in perpetuity. This "getting it right" narrative implies that radical changes are unnecessary, and that what is really needed are incremental adjustments—a recalibration of the economy rather than its reinvention (Johnston 2006: 43). The comforting connotations of sustainability have made it a favourite among citizens, environmental groups, politicians, and businesspeople alike who regularly make claims about the sustainability of different activities, products, and practices (Barr 2008: 21). According to Dryzek (2005: 145), sustainability has "arguably [become] *the* dominant global discourse of environmental concern" and a key metaphor for publicly labelling something as being environmentally good ("sustainable") or bad ("unsustainable").

So how did the notion of sustainability gain such prominence in the public sphere? The concept itself is not new. As early as the 1930s, resource managers had identified "maximum sustainable yield"—the maximum degree to which a renewable resource such as fish or forests could be harvested in perpetuity—as a major policy goal (Punt and Smith 2001). The term was also frequently heard in academic circles, particularly following the *Limits to Growth* report from the Club of Rome discussed in Chapter 4 (Meadows et al. 1972). *Limits to Growth* used mathematical models to argue that the world would run soon run out of key resources (in other words, that production and consumption levels were unsustainable) unless significant changes were made. In response, more moderate scholars began looking at how these reforms might occur, specifically how poorer Third World nations might be able to achieve a more environmentally friendly path to development (Dryzek 2005: 148). Up until the 1980s, however, sustainability was a mostly expert term with limited public exposure.

This all changed with the publication of the United Nations' World Commission on Environment and Development (WCED) report entitled *Our Common Future* (often called the Brundtland report) in 1987. Four years previously, the Secretary General of the United Nations had commissioned Gro Harlem Brundtland, the former prime minister of Norway, to conduct an inquiry into the twin problems of economic development and environmental integrity (WCED 1987: ix). Impetus for the inquiry came from two directions. First, senior leadership at the UN was reportedly frustrated with the "apocalyptic" talk associated with the *Limits to Growth* report and wanted to recast the global ecological question in a more positive light (Barr 2008: 25). Second, the UN wanted to counter the perception in many Third World nations that First World environmentalism was little more than "a covert means of holding back developing nations" by insisting that economic development be curbed (Irwin 2001: 36).

Brundtland's report sought to establish an alternative narrative, and in doing so advanced the notion of sustainable development, famously defining it as "development that meets the needs of the present without compromising the ability of future generations to meet their own needs" (WCED 1987: 43). The Brundtland report received a remarkable degree of attention at its release—it was translated into 25 languages and sold over a million copies, making it "the most widely read UN report in history" (MacNeill 2007: 6). Politicians, industry, and the general public now had a recognized means of talking about environmentally responsible economic growth—a discourse that has only intensified over time.

The Promise of Sustainability

Sustainability's rise to prominence has had a substantial impact on how everyone from politicians, to business leaders, to the general public perceives the relationship between environment and economy. In this section, I outline the developments that are generally seen as positive, while in the next I discuss some of the more critical arguments that have been raised by environmentalists and academics alike.

First, the notions of sustainability and sustainable development have provided a way around the economy-versus-environment narrative that characterized much environmental activism prior to the 1980s. As we saw in Chapter 3, much of the early environmentalism of the 1960s and 1970s involved confrontations between activists and authorities—be they government or private industry—who were accustomed to making uncontested decisions about natural resources, pollution thresholds, and technological development. While the economy-versus-environment narrative continues today (as is evident in current conflicts over oil pipelines in Canada and the United States), the notion of sustainability provided a plausible middle ground for both sides. The concept of sustainability contains an implicit endorsement of growth—that economic expansion is acceptable as long as it does not worsen environmental conditions over the long term (Dryzek 2005: 147). By breaking the economy-versus-environment logjam, the notion of sustainability freed politicians and corporations to embrace moderate forms of environmentalism, while also freeing environmental activists to embrace more environmentally responsible policies and companies (Paton 2011: 21). Most importantly, sustainability allowed concerned citizens who might have been uncomfortable with "zero growth" activism to comfortably come on board to a more consensual form of environmentalism that demanded less ideological commitment from its members (Barr 2003).

Second, the twin notions of sustainability and sustainable development have provided a way for other progressive ideas to enter the environmentalist consciousness. As discussed in Chapter 3, early environmentalism was often criticized for being elitist and unconcerned with the human suffering associated with environmental degradation. The concepts of sustainability and sustainable development, by contrast, are unabashedly anthropocentric (oriented towards human interests). Sustainability implies that humans are legitimate exploiters of nature, and that this is acceptable so long as it is done prudently in a manner that respects ecological limits. Sustainable development also contains strong ideas about equity—that it is morally wrong for one country or one generation of human beings to take more than their share of global resources (Langhelle 2009: 396). Moreover, sustainable development implies that local people ought to have the right to refuse projects that they don't feel are in their long-term environmental *or* economic interests. For example, a number of African nations continue to ban the use of genetically modified (GM) seeds in agriculture (or even, in some cases, to allow the import of any foods containing genetically modified ingredients). While the reasons for this are complex, African politicians cite both environmental and economic integrity as key reasons for maintaining the ban—to protect both *farmland* (the environment) and *farmers* (an economic group) from the multinational corporations behind GM technology (Scoones 2008). For many countries, sustainable development means protecting traditional economic practices, and this concept gives them a legitimate avenue to do so.

Third, the notion of sustainability has prompted some interesting innovations in both the public and private sector. Companies large and small have been quick to claim sustainability as a corporate goal, often without justification (see below). At the same time, however, some firms have pursued more concrete reforms, such as adopting a "triple bottom line" approach that attempts to measure a firm's economic, social, and environmental performance using benchmarking and accounting practices (Henriques and Richardson 2004). The idea behind this, as well as the "corporate social responsibility" movement more generally, is that public reporting on social and environmental performance will give companies an incentive to pursue reforms in order to improve their corporate image. A key example of this has been Walmart, the world's largest retailer, which fully endorsed the sustainability narrative in 2005, pledging to become a "zero waste company [using] 100% renewable energy" at some unspecified point in the future (Dauvergne and Lister 2012: 38). While these goals are "aspirational" rather than mandatory, Walmart has used its standing as the world's largest wholesale purchaser to push reforms back through its supply chain, prompting manufacturers to use less packaging and participate in eco-certification programs like the Forest Stewardship Council (Vanderbergh 2007). Gereffi and Christian (2009), however, suggest that Walmart's commitment to sustainability may be motivated more by a desire to rehabilitate the company's reputation than to minimize environmental impact. Specifically, Walmart's sustainability commitment can be seen as an attempt to distract from its poor record on labour rights and willingness to close stores when workers attempt to form or join unions (as happened in Jonquiere, Quebec, in 2004).

Problems with Sustainability

The notions of sustainability and sustainable development have also been subjected to considerable criticism. First, neither term is particularly well-defined or easily operationalized (measurably put into practice). In the sociologist Steven Yearley's words, "simply giving something a name does not indicate that it can actually exist viably" (quoted in Irwin 2001: 31). In other words, when do we know that an action is "sustainable" or more importantly that complex phenomena like regional or national economies have achieved "sustainability?"

One possible measure is given in Figure 7.1, which despite its simplicity illustrates just how difficult it is to achieve true sustainability over the long term. According to this measure, advanced by Canadian economist Peter Victor (2010), sustainability can only be achieved if future economic growth has a diminishing *overall* environmental impact over time. Companies and governments often claim that an activity is sustainable if it becomes more efficient, but Victor's model shows that this is not enough. For example, technological improvements in automobiles mean that cars are on average more fuel efficient than a generation ago (in other words, they are "less intense" in their consumption of resources—which is captured on the x axis of Figure 7.1). However, continuing urban sprawl and under-developed mass transit mean that Canadians are on average spending more time in their cars, commuting longer distances (increasing the scale of the activity, captured on the y axis). For growth to be considered "green," sufficient improvements have to be made in either/both scale and intensity to reduce overall consumption

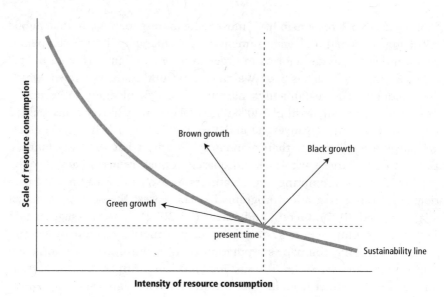

Figure 7.1 A Potential Measure of Sustainability Combining Intensity and Scale of Resource Use
Source: Victor (2010: 241)

of resources (i.e., the growth trajectory must remain below the "sustainability line"). The automotive sector should therefore be considered a case of "brown growth"—as overall emissions continue to rise despite per-unit improvements. This inconvenient truth goes unmentioned in advertising that highlights "better fuel efficiency" and "eco-boost technology."

Second, some scholars argue that the notions of sustainability and sustainable development are *too* compatible with capitalism as it is currently practised (e.g., Johnston, J. 2007; Paton 2011). Sustainability makes a lot of sense in the business world, in which companies are constantly looking to increase efficiencies and eliminate waste as part of surviving in competitive markets (Dauvergne and Lister 2012). While this congruity helped the private sector to embrace the notion of sustainability, Johnston (2007) argues that this embrace has changed what sustainability means. In many cases, when businesses talk about sustainability they are really talking about sustaining *themselves* by "doing more with less [and] identifying new market opportunities for green products" (Johnston 2007: 44). Dryzek (2005: 149) also notes that the "equity dimension" that was central to the Brundtland report has faded with time to be replaced by a more corporate approach that emphasizes accounting over lofty social and environmental goals. In Irwin's words (2001: 43), the early euphoria that surrounded sustainability has given way "to more subtle struggles over how it should be defined in any particular context." According to this view, sustainability has lost whatever transformational potential it had at the beginning and has merged with capitalism to the point that they are indistinguishable in any way that matters—either to the world's poor or to the planet.

Finally, some critics object to the technocratic undertones of sustainability. At its most basic, sustainability means staying below an imaginary line above which consumption begins to diminish the share of resources available to future generations. Identifying this line of "maximum sustainable exploitation" is, however, problematic to say the least. The collapse of the Atlantic cod fishery off Newfoundland is an important cautionary tale (see Box 7.1). In this case, scientists and politicians convinced themselves that they knew how many fish could be sustainably harvested in perpetuity, and failed to appreciate the scope of their errors up until the very end (Bavington 2010a; 2010b). The closure of the fishery in 1992, and the failure of cod stocks to subsequently rebound, shows that science and expertise are not perfect guides to sustainability (more on this in Chapter 9).

Box 7.1

When Sustainability Fails: The Atlantic Cod Fishery as a Cautionary Tale

The collapse of the Atlantic cod fishery (also called the northern cod fishery) off the shores of Newfoundland stands as one of the world's most stunning failures in renewable resource management. Many different explanations for the collapse have been advanced, including overexploitation by foreign fishing fleets, the Canadian government's desire to prop up employment in Newfoundland, new technologies that allowed for bigger catches farther out to sea, and poaching. Environmental historian Dean Bavington (2010a; 2010b), however, argues that the root cause of the collapse was the transition to "scientific management of the fishery" following Newfoundland's entry into Canada in 1949. The federal Department of Fisheries, Bavington argues, was deeply invested in the notion of a scientifically determined "maximum sustainable yield" (a maximum total catch) that could be adjusted each year to ensure "self-regeneration of the population" (2010a: 514). It was thought that sustainability could be achieved by constructing complex models to predict how fish populations would respond to different catch levels and environmental conditions. The overall system was based on the assumption that "managers in Canada's capital city of Ottawa could control fluctuations in harvest to achieve maximum biologically sustainable yields without ever setting foot on a boat in Newfoundland" (Bavington 2010a: 522). Regulators' commitment to this ideal was so strong that when inshore fishermen (those who fish waters close to the coastline) began reporting in the early 1980s that they were having difficulty finding cod, scientists and managers attributed this to changing migration patterns and unusual

continued

environmental conditions rather than questioning their models. The magnitude of their error was not apparent until the fishing season of 1992, when even offshore boats came back to port alarmingly empty, and a total moratorium was announced on 2 July 1992—throwing 30,000 fishermen, dock workers, and processors out of work and ending 500 continuous years of cod fishing in Newfoundland.

Despite the best of intentions and the most advanced science, computer modelling, and mathematics of the time, the Canadian government just got it wrong. In Bavington's words (2010b: 2), "this was an extinction like no other. Unlike the demise of passenger pigeons, the plains buffalo, and innumerable other species, the northern cod was *scientifically managed* out of existence." While the notion of sustainability suggests that we can have both economic growth and long-term environmental integrity, this case shows the inherent risks involved when we try to walk the fine line between sustainable and unsustainable practices. According to Foster (2008), sustainability efforts usually fail because the present always wins out over the future. Authorities are always confident that their knowledge and methods are cutting edge, and today's economic needs always appear more urgent than the abstract needs of the future. Achieving real sustainability would involve abandoning the growth imperative and accepting real reductions in resource use today—something we are stubbornly unwilling or unable to do (Foster 2008: 70). While the Brundtland report argued that "sustainable development requires that those who are more affluent adopt life-styles within the planet's ecological means" (WCED 1987: 9), this has unfortunately been forgotten in today's more technocratic and corporate-dominated sustainability narrative.

Neoliberalism

The label "neoliberalism" refers to the resurrection of ideas associated with classical liberal economists of the eighteenth and nineteenth centuries, such as Adam Smith and David Ricardo. Smith and Ricardo believed that economic liberty, organized through a free market, would benefit all participants by efficiently allocating resources and rewarding specialization and innovation. The most prominent advocates of neoliberalism in the twentieth century were the Austrian economist Friedrich Hayek and the American economist Milton Friedman (Harvey 2005). The best way to describe their views is **"market fundamentalism,"** meaning that they believed that the free market is the ultimate expression of collective will and that government ought to have only a minimal role in public affairs (Castree 2008: 143). While this is an extreme position, many scholars argue that neoliberalism has become *the* dominant political narrative in today's world—replacing the social democratic ideals that anchored the welfare state and saw a strong role for government in economic and environmental regulation (Larner 2003).

Scholars of neoliberalism stress that it is a broad and varied political and economic philosophy that takes different forms in different regions and contexts (Heynen et al. 2007). Neoliberalism's impact on the natural environment exemplifies this. In some contexts, neoliberal policies have clearly had a negative impact on environmental integrity. For example, Prudham (2004) argues that neoliberal policies directly contributed to the tragedy in Walkerton, Ontario, in May 2000, in which seven people died and thousands fell ill from drinking water contaminated with the bacteria *E. coli*. The provincial government at the time had sought to minimize state involvement in environmental regulation by cutting monitoring budgets, shifting responsibility for water quality testing to private laboratories, and replacing mandatory standards with voluntary ones (Prudham 2004: 352). While these changes were made in the name of cost savings and cutting government "red tape," they made the failure of water safety systems more likely.

In other contexts, however, neoliberal policies are not so clearly detrimental. The strategy adopted by Canada and the United States to combat the acid rain problem in the 1980s and 1990s was clearly neoliberal in philosophy and is generally considered to be a success. Acid rain is a major global problem that is most severe in Eastern Canada and the United States, Central and Eastern Europe, and increasingly in rapidly industrializing Eastern Asia. It is predominantly caused by emissions of sulfur dioxide (SO_2) and nitrogen oxide (NO_x) by heavy industry, particularly coal-burning electricity generating stations (Mason 1992). As mentioned in Chapter 2, acid rain has a devastating effect on ecosystems—raising the acidity levels of lakes and soil to the point that indigenous plant and animal life are destroyed. While European nations used traditional regulations to force industry to curb SO_2 and NO_x emissions, Canada and the United States took a different path. As Ellerman et al. (2000) describe in their book, *Markets for Clean Air*, the Reagan administration in the US was concerned that new regulations would increase costs for coal producers and coal-fired power plants and therefore came up with a novel plan: to create economic incentives for companies to reduce emissions "on their own time and in their own way." To do so, they created the first system of "**cap and trade**," where the government distributed emissions credits to companies (essentially "permits to pollute" a certain amount) and allowed these companies to buy and sell these credits amongst themselves. The idea behind this scheme is that companies which reduce emissions by, for example, investing in new technologies can recoup these costs by selling credits they no longer need to other companies who are polluting more (thus also imposing a cost on laggards). Over time, the overall cap on emissions is reduced as credits either expire to be reissued in smaller numbers, or are "retired" by environmental groups that buy them directly from polluters (Israel 2007).[1] In essence, the government created a market for pollution reduction and allowed individual actors to make their own decisions about whether to be buyers or sellers. These changes were implemented in the US in 1990 (as part of amendments to the Clean Air Act), and Canada joined the scheme in 1991 through the Canada–United States Air Quality Agreement. While critics argue that cap and trade is little more than a subsidy to business, because credits are often handed out in large quantities free of charge rather than auctioned off in a truly free market (Gilbertson and Reyes 2009: 10), others are willing to accept this as a necessary cost that is worth the positive outcome. In the case of acid rain, the cap and trade program was more successful in reducing SO_2 and NO_x than the government expected. More companies than predicted moved quickly to reduce emissions, meaning that total pollution has stayed *below* the overall cap since the mid-1990s (EPA 2012).

So how do we understand these two very different examples of neoliberalism—the tragedy of Walkerton and the successful reduction of SO_2 and NO_x emissions in the US and Canada? According to Peck and Tickell (2002), a distinction ought be made between different types of neoliberal programs and agendas, specifically between "roll-back neoliberalism," which is about dismantling existing regulations and freeing companies to pollute, and "roll-out neoliberalism," which involves the creation of new programs based on market principles. While both types are anchored in the market fundamentalist philosophy, roll-back neoliberalism usually takes the form of privatization, deregulation, and cut-backs, and roll-out neoliberalism typically involves *intervention through marketization*, or the pursuit of policy goals by creating market or market-like structures where they did not exist before (Lockie 2010). While most environmental sociologists condemn roll-back neoliberalism as detrimental to the environment, views on roll-out neoliberalism are more varied and ambivalent (e.g. McCarthy 2005). If free market principles can be harnessed to improve environmental performance, should we hesitate to use them?

The Promise of Neoliberalism

Advocates of neoliberalism point out that governments have a less-than-stellar track record when it comes to environmental protection (Schneider 2008). Governments are often slow to act, and when regulations are enacted they are too sweeping—treating all companies in a given sector the same way (Gunningham et al. 1998). Promoters of neoliberalism are particularly critical of what is sometimes called the "**command and control**" approach of traditional government regulation. The command and control approach assumes that it is government's role to set "the rules" or the parameters of acceptable and unacceptable environmental practices, which often includes explicit limits on pollution levels and even what technologies companies are and are not allowed to use (Howlett 2003). Neoliberals argue that this is the wrong role for government. They suggest that individual actors—be they people or companies—have a much deeper knowledge of their own needs and capacities than do governments, and that governments should focus on *outcomes* while leaving *processes* to the individual actors involved. Returning to the acid rain example, the emissions trading program established by the US government set an overall limit (a cap) on pollution for the whole electricity generating industry, while allowing individual companies to decide how they would respond to this new market—either by investing in improvements or buying their way out of them. In other words, market-based programs harness the knowledge and creativity that exists at the individual and company level to reach a collective goal. Instead of one-size-fits-all regulations, actors are free to find their own way to an end point that makes economic sense to them. According to Lockie (2010: 367), this approach is appealing to many people because it blends the notions of liberty and responsibility:

> Through the promotion of market relations, neoliberals have sought to influence the conditions under which people make decisions. . . . Neoliberalism understands the individual as a "manipulable being" who may be counted on to respond rationally and entrepreneurially to changing conditions. Neoliberal rationality thus suggests that to govern better, the state must govern less, optimizing social outcomes through the regulated and accountable choices of autonomous agents.

This is clearly a powerful tool for influencing both individual and corporate behaviour by appealing to—while at the same shaping—actors' own self-interests (Newell and Paterson 2010).

Problems with Neoliberalism

There are several avenues of critique against neoliberal environmental policies. First, as mentioned, environmental sociologists are almost universally skeptical of the kind of "roll back" neoliberalism that removes environmental regulations and privatizes the natural world. The neoliberal logic that sees potential markets everywhere has led to a dramatic leap in **commodification**, or the creation of exclusive property rights where they had not existed before. Consider the example of water. Access to clean and safe drinking water was recognized by the United Nations as a fundamental human right in 2010, and many countries (including Canada) consider fresh water to be a "public good" rather than a tradable commodity (Bakker 2003). Over the past few decades, however, major international institutions such as the World Bank have pushed developing countries to privatize water infrastructure and to allow companies to charge for water—sometimes by means of "pre-paid" water debit cards that have to swiped or scanned at community wells (Goldman 2007). Harvey (2003) calls this type of commodification "accumulation by dispossession," because it involves the confiscation of services or goods that were formerly held in public trust and gives them over to private companies. Harvey thus argues that marketization is about little else than extending corporate power.

Second, critics argue that successful examples of "roll-out" neoliberalism are in fact rare, and that neoliberal programs in the real world rarely live up to their theoretical promise (Gilbertson and Reyes 2009). The cap-and-trade program that worked to curb acid rain in North America, for example, is now a cornerstone of both regional and international efforts to reduce greenhouse gas emissions that contribute to climate change (Newell and Paterson 2010). Unfortunately, however, the complexity of carbon emissions has made these programs extremely difficult to administer (Storm 2009). Whereas the majority of SO_2 and NO_x emissions could be reduced by focusing on a small number of heavy polluters, carbon emissions occur across all facets of the economy. There is also the problem that some polluters are willing to pay extremely high penalties rather than change their behaviours. In the case of acid rain, power plants were able to dramatically reduce pollution by installing relatively inexpensive technologies like smokestack filters and scrubbers, which allowed them to carry on with business as usual. Getting oil companies to get off oil, in contrast, would involve a total reorientation of their business. It is more likely that oil companies would simply pay the penalties, pass on the costs to consumers (as a form of hidden carbon tax), and keep on producing oil so long as there were profits to be made.

Finally, neoliberal theory tends to downplay the existence and consequences of inequality. Consider again the example of water privatization. Advocates of water privatization often argue that because water is a scarce resource, it needs to have a price in order to dissuade waste and encourage conservation (Bakker 2007). The idea is that creating a "water market" will spur investment in better infrastructure (increasing supply) while instilling discipline on consumers (moderating demand). This schema, however, fails to take into account economic inequalities. Overall, poor people spend a higher proportion of their income on necessities such as food and water than do the rich. Basic microeconomics tells us, therefore, that the "market discipline" of paying for water affects the poor far more than the wealthy. In other words, privatization *forces* lower-income households to curb consumption, while merely providing higher-income households with an *incentive* to do so. Critics point out that this is deeply inequitable—shifting the burden of conservation away from the government and directly onto the poor—while allowing the wealthy to escape the same disciplinary forces (Castro 2008).

Ecological Modernization Theory

The third and final perspective examined in this chapter is ecological modernization theory (EMT). Like sustainability and neoliberalism, EMT sees a strong role for capitalism in environmental reforms. EMT, however, has much firmer sociological grounding than the other two perspectives. While both sustainability and neoliberalism have strong (if different) ideological undertones, EMT is more analytical—focused on understanding *how* and *why* environmental reforms occur in capitalist societies and, by extension, how they can be further encouraged (Buttel 2009).

The EMT perspective emerged in the 1980s and 1990s in Northern Europe, specifically Germany and the Netherlands, two of the world's most environmentally progressive nations (Mol and Janicke 2009).[2] These two nations presented a bit of an economic puzzle, in that both had managed to achieve a high level of economic growth while enacting significant environmental improvements in core industries. Early EMT research largely credited technological developments and innovation—arguing that capitalism's relentless drive to reduce costs was beginning to generate measurable environmental progress by encouraging companies to invest in waste- and energy-reducing technologies (Huber 1982). Soon, however, scholars moved past this rather simplistic conclusion to look at the role played by more profound societal changes. Dutch sociologists Arthur Mol and Gert Spaargaren have been central to EMT's later development. Their main argument is that in capitalist society, corporate and individual decisions have been guided by three main "rationalities" or reasonings: economic, political, and cultural (Spaargaren 1993). "Economic rationality" has by far been the most dominant, as individuals are motivated to "find the best deal"; and companies, to maximize profits. The other rationalities, though, also play a role in guiding behaviour. For example, a person might choose to buy an expensive car over a more economical one in order to enhance his or her status (as an act of "conspicuous consumption" that has cultural rather than purely economic roots). Mol and Spaargaren argue, however, that a fourth "rationality" has emerged since the 1980s—an "ecological rationality"—that is powerful enough to challenge the dominant economic rationality. As Mol (2006: 33) puts it,

> European scholars introduced the concept of ecological modernization in the 1980s [because] it was at this point that an ecological perspective started to challenge the monopoly of economic rationality as the all-determining organizing principle in the sphere of economics. . . . [This] means that economic processes of production and consumption are increasingly designed and organized, analyzed and judged, from both an economic *and* an environmental point of view.

For Mol and Spaargaren, this is the only way to explain why individual, corporate, and government behaviours are being "ecologically modernized" (i.e., improved) even when these changes go *against* standard economic logic. For example, consumer commitment to environmentalism often comes at a substantial economic cost, such as choosing to spend more money on organic or "green" products, donating money to environmental groups, purchasing carbon offsets, or buying pollution-reducing technologies like catalytic converters for trucks and automobiles (Spaargaren and Cohen 2009). Even recycling, which most of us now do unthinkingly, involves an uncompensated investment of time (to sort, organize, and "format" waste by crushing and folding all manner of items). We do these things because we are motivated by ecological rather than economic benefits.

Ecological modernization at the corporate and government level are a bit more complex. EMT theorists argue that most ecological modernization takes place at the company level, but not because of altruistic motivations. Instead, ecological improvements occur as a response to companies' institutional environment, which is shaped by both government and the general public (Schofer and Hironaka 2005). According to Buttel (2009: 124), EMT is at root a theory of politics and the state. Governments today take environmental issues more seriously than in the past (even though there are many examples of environmental regress and deregulation). Christoff (2009) argues that this has prompted many companies to reorient their stance on environmental problems. In the past, it was common for companies to ignore problems such as pollution unless it became a major public embarrassment or legal liability. Political attention to environmental issues, however, has made environmental miscreancy more risky for companies. In response, Christoff (2009) suggests that many companies have "shifted away from reactive 'end-of-pipe' approaches towards anticipatory and precautionary actions" that attempt to predict and defuse environmental problems that may harm public perception of a company or industry (see Young and Liston 2010). Much of this is undoubtedly motivated by "brand management," as companies try to protect their image from potential competitors or political opponents (see the Walmart example discussed above). But at the same time, these reforms can be extremely profitable. Toyota, for instance, makes a lot of money from its Prius hybrid car line, as well as benefiting from the reputational windfall of being seen as an eco-leader. EMT scholars argue that this combination of risks and incentives is driving significant change in corporate activities.

The Promise of EMT

EMT offers several conceptual improvements over the concepts of sustainability and neoliberalism discussed previously. First, EMT provides a more complex analytical framework for understanding how and why improvements in environmental performance occur. In other words, EMT fills in some the blanks about how "sustainability" might be achieved. It also allows us to go beyond the narrower neoliberal view of economic incentives to see how changes in other spheres—specifically politics and culture—have helped to "ecologize the economy" (Spaargaren and Mol 2009: 69). With respect to politics, Hajer (1995; 2009) argues that EMT has been widely accepted as a policy goal because it is consistent with many politicians' views on how governments should work. Like "roll out" forms of neoliberalism, EMT sees an active but not heavy-handed role for the state, as a "facilitator" of corporate-driven improvements rather than a source of command-and-control decrees (Buttel 2009: 131). With respect to culture, EMT sees a strong role for progressive social movements in pressing for corporate change (Mol and Janicke 2009: 19)—something that neoliberal theory views as being counter-productive.

Second, EMT's emphasis on politics and culture suggests that there are different possible roads to ecological modernization. Recently, EMT researchers have turned their attention to non-Western developing countries to look for evidence of environmental reforms (e.g., Sonnenfeld and Mol 2006). This has opened an interesting comparative angle to EMT research. For example, studies of China have found that ecological modernization has been discursively embraced by the Chinese government as a way to "catch up" to Western economies, but is being pursued in an exclusively top-down manner with no role for civil society or the general public (Mol 2006; Zhang et al. 2007). Whether this distinction matters is yet to be seen. The Chinese government has invested substantially in green technology development, particularly in the manufacturing of photovoltaic (solar) panels and wind turbines, much to the chagrin of developed economies like the United States and the provinces of Ontario and British Columbia that have tried to do the same (more on this in Chapter 8). At the same time, however, the Chinese government continues to allow rampant pollution in many of its heavy industries without much fear of public protest or embarrassment. Overall, these studies have found that developing countries "do not seamlessly fit the Western version of ecological modernization" (Mol 2006: 51), but that EMT still lends significant insight into environmental progress in non-Western cases.

Problems with EMT

There are two major strains of criticism against EMT—one theoretical and the other methodological. The theoretical critique centres on EMT's understanding of capitalism and corporate decision-making. Foster et al. (2010: 38), for instance, argue that EMT is based on a "Capitalism in Wonderland view" that assumes that small, incremental changes in business-as-usual will somehow lead to a vast ecological restructuring of the global economy. This assumption, they argue, is inconsistent with everything that we know about capitalism's history as a ruthless consumer of all manner of resources in the quest for economic growth. York et al. (2010) also point out that the "grow or die" ethos of capitalism doesn't disappear with the emergence of green product lines. All profits—even green ones—are typically reinvested in expanded production that threatens to wipe out any environmental gains made. Returning to the example of Toyota, profits from the hybrid-powered Prius line rest with a company that also makes gas-guzzling Land Cruisers, Sequoias, and Tundra trucks. In other words, green profits and reputation can easily be used to prop up environmentally destructive products and behaviour.

The second critique is more methodological. EMT research is overwhelmingly based on case studies, which on their own are very convincing. In his classic book, *The Refinement of Production*, Mol (1995) shows how tremendous progress has been made in some of the most traditionally polluting industries in the Netherlands, including pesticides, chemicals, and paint manufacturing. Case studies such as these suggest that a "decoupling" is occurring between economic growth and environmental damage (Connelly and Smith 2003: 68–9), whereby increases in profits are no longer linked to increased pollution or environmental degradation.

Unfortunately, however, when we move beyond case studies it is difficult to find much evidence of economy-wide decoupling. If ecological modernization is occurring across the whole economy, we should see evidence of a phenomenon called an **environmental Kuznets curve** (EKC), which is illustrated in Figure 7.2. Kuznets was an economist who specialized in social inequality. Writing in the 1950s, he argued that the relationship between national wealth and economic inequality in a developing society was not linear but rather a curve—that as national wealth rose, inequality increased at first, but as the nation as a whole became richer inequality fell, largely due to redistributive programs and social services (Kuznets 1955). Ecological economists have adapted this logic to explain why developed nations tend to have cleaner environments than developing ones. Thus the EKC posits that as an economy grows we expect to see increasing environmental damage, but as it matures we should start to see a decoupling of growth and damage as citizens start to demand cleaner environments and societies invest newfound wealth in environmental protection, parks, and conservation. This pattern ought to indicate successful ecological modernization *across* a whole economy (Dietz et al. 2012).

The problem is, however, that EKCs are only observable on specific variables—like SO_2 emissions, deforestation, or the amount of public money spent on parks and conservation (Mills and Waite 2009; Jorgenson and Clark 2009). On larger economy-wide variables, such as amount of waste produced and greenhouse gas emissions, an EKC is simply not observable. For instance, a series of studies by Jorgenson and Clark (2012; Jorgenson et al. 2012) that use CO_2 emissions as a proxy for a country's total pollution output found *no* evidence of decoupling in poorer nations, and only small indications of decoupling in developed nations. In another international study, Dietz and

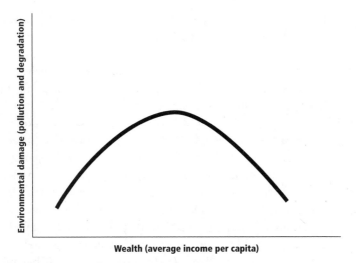

Figure 7.2 The Environmental Kuznets Curve

colleagues (2012) argue that the predominant global trend is in fact the opposite of the Kuznets curve—that high levels of economic development prompt *worse* environmental performance—even if that degradation is hidden because it occurs in another part of the world (a theme we return to in Chapter 8). In other words, critics argue that EMT's methodological focus on small-scale case studies gives false hope about environmental improvements from capitalist reforms that are not evident in large-scale measures.

Conclusion

All three concepts discussed in this chapter—sustainability, neoliberalism, and ecological modernization—are based on the assumption that capitalism can be reformed to achieve environmental progress without breaking radically from current political and economic structures. Each concept, however, is based on an appeal for *more* of something in order to make capitalism work better. Examining these calls for "more" gives us a way of comparing and evaluating the three perspectives.

First, sustainability (and its twin concept of sustainable development) is based on a call for more care and prudence. Rampant, exploitative development should be replaced with more scientifically informed, locally driven, and equitable forms that preserve natural capital for future generations. Unfortunately, sustainability narratives give little guidance about how to achieve these goals. More importantly, the conceptual vagueness around the notion of sustainability means that it is easily co-opted. Governments often view sustainability as a metaphor for "maximum sustainable yield," while corporations frequently twist sustainability into a narrative about their own survival rather than a meaningful environmental strategy. As such, the practical value of sustainability as a template for reform is limited. Sustainability narratives assume that the concept has self-motivating and self-propelling properties—that authorities, be they state or private, will be inspired by the idea of sustainability and find ways to achieve it. This is a naive and occasionally dangerous assumption.

Second, neoliberalism is based on a call for more markets. In the market fundamentalist worldview, markets create incentives that can be harnessed and steered to encourage environmental improvements. The stated logic behind commodification and privatization, for example, is that they encourage investment in and conservation of scarce resources (while also expanding wealth among global elites). More progressive "roll out" forms of neoliberalism try to establish markets for environmental "bads" such as pollution—in the process creating incentives for their eventual elimination. These efforts need to be seriously examined, because they are an attempt to address what economists call the problem of **externalities**, which refers to the fact that many industries have polluted for free for many years (pollution has been "external" or excluded from the costs of doing business). Putting a price on environmental damage is necessary for both rewarding good behaviour and punishing bad behaviour (Newell and Paterson 2010). At the same time, however, neoliberalism's relentless push for "more markets" invariably contributes to the commodification of natural resources and spaces, thus allowing private interests to acquire formerly public or commonly held environmental goods, and shifting the burden of conservation onto the poor. While these policies may lead to short-term environmental gains (by forcing people to pay more for key commodities such as water, for instance), they come at a significant human cost.

Third, EMT is based on a call for more pressure. EMT has the distinction of being both a sociological theory and a programmatic call for action. As a theory, it argues that ecological modernization occurs only when it makes sense for businesses to make environmental performance a priority. This decision is not based on altruism, but as a response to pressures exerted by the market, civil society, and government. The strength of EMT as a sociological theory is that it refuses to credit any single factor for changing corporate behaviour. Instead, it sees companies as reacting to a complex web of forces—including changing consumer tastes, government policies, and the actions of competitors (Mol et al. 2009). This provides a far more nuanced and realistic portrait of what motivates reform than those provided by the sustainability and neoliberal perspectives. Unfortunately, EMT is weaker as a guide for further reform. Critics argue that EMT's prescription for the future is essentially "more of the same," trusting that the processes that have led to improvements in *some* areas of the capitalist economy will spread to the system as a whole—something for which there is little evidence yet (York et al. 2010).

To sum up: Is there evidence that capitalism can contribute to environmental improvements? Certainly, but at a small scale and under certain conditions. Can these improvements be "scaled up" to spur real and lasting global changes? At the moment: unknown, although current evidence suggests this is unlikely on our current track. There are, however, lessons to be drawn from all three of these perspectives. Capitalism is *the* dominant global economic system, and further capitalist development is currently seen among both rich and poor countries as the best way to improve quality of life and standards of living (Bhagwati 2007). Any realistic program for environmental reform has to navigate this reality. Sustainability, neoliberalism, and EMT provide us with an understanding of what tools are currently at our disposal. At the same time, however, all three perspectives can be accused of "tinkering at the edges" of the major problems posed by global capitalism. To effect real change, the conversation must be broadened. For instance, what would a market that had no externalities look like? At the moment, externalities like waste and pollution are borne by taxpayers (in garbage collection, landfill maintenance, health-care costs, etc.) and by the biosphere. A zero-externality economy would, for example, require that companies offset all emissions of carbon dioxide, take back consumer products at the end of their life-cycle, and pay for the restoration of contaminated sites and landscapes. Economists such as Paul Hawken (2000) and Amory Lovins (2011) have conducted thought experiments to predict what such an economy would look like. We would still have capitalism, but it would likely be structured very differently—with companies investing directly in recycling, alternative energy, and waste-reducing technologies (such as biodegradables) rather than relying on a free ride from government and the planet.

Capitalism has proven highly adaptable in the past, adjusting to stronger labour laws, consumer protections, and the rise of the welfare state. This suggests that capitalism can survive more ambitious changes than are proposed by the three perspectives considered in this chapter. The capitalism we have today does not need to be the one we have tomorrow. We need creative thinking on how to more fundamentally reform the practices and institutions at the heart of our current economic system, and we need it now.

Questions for Critical Thought

1. Is sustainability really "too vague" to be meaningfully implemented?

2. The Brundtland report argues that social inequalities worsen environmental problems. What do you think?

3. What would a truly sustainable economy look like? What reforms (big or small) would be needed to get there?

Suggested Readings

Castree, Noel. (2008). "Neoliberalising nature: The logics of deregulation and reregulation," *Environment and Planning A 40*, 131–152. A dense but highly informative piece, this is a good overview article that traces the origins of neoliberal approaches to the environment and analyzes the similarities and differences between types of neoliberal policy.

Mol, Arthur P.J., Sonnenfeld, David A., & Spaargaren, Gert, eds. (2009). *The Ecological Modernisation Reader: Environmental Reform in Theory and Practice*. New York: Routledge. This is the most comprehensive overview of ecological modernization theory in print. It includes selections of key articles and books that have had a particularly strong impact on development of the field.

WCED (World Commission on Environment and Development). (1987). *Our Common Future*. New York: Oxford University Press. The most widely read United Nations report in history, the Brundtland report is still relevant today, as it defined popular understanding of sustainable development. It's worth reading to see how far we have (haven't) come on issues of environment and equity.

Suggested Websites

Canadian Environmental Sustainability Indicators—Environment Canada
www.ec.gc.ca/indicateurs-indicators/default.asp?lang=En&n=47F48106-1
This website provides information on how the Government of Canada measures the sustainability of our economy. A fascinating read, as much for what it includes as what is left out!

Climate Inc.—The Business of Stopping Climate Change
climateinc.org/
This website is run by David Levy, a well-known Professor of Business and environmental specialist at the University of Massachusetts. The site focuses on the intersection of business and climate change, and contains well-informed commentary on how the private sector is (and is not) responding to the issue.

The Fraser Institute—Environment Section
www.fraserinstitute.org/research-news/research/topics-display.aspx?topic=106&name=Environment
The Fraser Institute is a Canadian think-tank that advocates for market solutions to social and environmental problems. It is the leading advocate of neoliberal environmental policies in Canada.

8

Globalization and the Environment

Key Points

◎ Globalization is increasing the speed, scale, and scope of economic activities, thus raising the stakes on key environmental issues and problems.

◎ Scholars are divided on the environmental costs and benefits of globalization. Optimists see globalization as an opportunity to spread green technologies and best practices pioneered in the West to developing countries, while critics see globalization as a deeply unequal process that subjugates the environment to the economy and allows wealthy nations to offload environmental costs to poorer ones.

◎ "Ecologizing" globalization would mean strengthening the enforcement of existing international agreements and creating new agreements that tie opportunities for trade and foreign investment to environmental performance. The "ecological debt" that wealthy nations owe to poorer ones must also be acknowledged and rectified.

Introduction

Let's begin with two stories about **globalization** and the environment:

Story #1: On the morning of 20 August 2006, the three million residents of Abidjan, Côte d'Ivoire, awoke to a bizarre, foul-smelling odour blanketing the city. Coming out of their homes to investigate, people soon discovered the source of the problem—in the wee hours of the night, someone had dumped between 250 and 500 tonnes of toxic waste across 18 different sites throughout the city. The waste included chemicals such as hydrogen sulfide, which is poisonous in high concentrations. In the days and weeks that followed, nearly 100,000 people sought treatment for chemical burns, skin lesions, respiratory tract damage, and vomiting, while authorities estimate that about 15 people died as a direct consequence of exposure to the sludge (Amnesty International 2012). Investigators soon learned that the waste had originated in Europe, and was the property of a Dutch commodities trading and shipping company named Trafigura Beheer BV. In 2005, Trafigura had purchased a large amount of chemical called coker naphtha, which it intended to refine and sell as a gasoline additive. Lacking the facilities to complete the refinement on land, Trafigura contracted a Panamanian-registered vessel, the *Probo Koala*, to conduct the refining at sea and then dispose of the waste. The original plan had been to offload the waste at the port of Amsterdam, the Netherlands. The Dutch waste management company, however, tested the waste at port and determined that it was far more toxic than Trafigura claimed, and subsequently raised the price for its disposal to 40 times the original quote (Plaut 2006). Trafigura refused to pay, and ordered the *Probo Koala* to find an alternate site for offloading the waste. The ship's captain eventually set sail for Africa, and after being turned away from Nigerian ports, the *Probo Koala* arrived in Abidjan, where it contracted a local company called "Compagnie Tommy" to dispose of the waste. The local contractor offloaded the waste from the *Probo Koala* and tried to dispose of it at a local open air landfill. After a few truckloads had been unloaded, workers at the landfill refused to accept any more because of the smell. Unsure what to do next, Compagnie Tommy's drivers dumped the waste wherever they could "at random locations around Abidjan, close to houses, workplaces, schools, fields of crops, and the city prison" (Amnesty International 2012: 47). Trafigura has repeatedly denied responsibility for the incident, but in 2007 agreed to pay the Ivorian government US $195 million in exchange for immunity from prosecution.

Story #2: Electricity generation is one of the most serious environmental challenges facing the world today. Electricity is crucial for social and economic development. Reliable access to electricity is necessary for modern health care, sanitation, and hygiene, not to mention for the development of manufacturing and service industries. It is therefore unsurprising that global electricity consumption has increased dramatically, from an average of 1,300 kilowatt hours per person per year in 1975 to more than 2,800 kw/h in 2009 (World Bank 2012). The problem is not electricity itself, but where it comes from. Approximately two-thirds of the world's electricity comes from burning fossil fuels (coal, oil, diesel, and natural gas), which emits substantial amounts of greenhouse gases linked to climate change. Since the Kyoto Protocol was negotiated in 1997, major efforts have been made in Europe and, to a lesser extent, North America to promote and enhance renewable or "green" energy sources, such as wind turbines, solar panels, tidal power, and geothermal electricity generation. In 2009, for example, 20 per cent of electricity consumed in European Union countries came from these sources, up from 15 per cent in 2005 (EREC 2012).

The story of renewable energy, however, has been turned on its head since 2009 because of the rise of an unlikely green superpower: China. While developed countries have cut back on green energy spending in the aftermath of the Great Recession, China has become the world's leading investor in renewable energy development. In 2012 alone, China invested $68 billion US into the sector—substantially more than any other nation. These investments have reverberated around the world, for example causing the global price of solar panels to drop dramatically. While this price drop is welcome news for environmentalist groups that want to encourage greater household and industrial use of renewables, it is bad news for North American and European manufacturers, several of which have declared bankruptcy even after receiving big government subsidies. The US and the European Union have even gone so far as to slap tariffs on Chinese solar panels, accusing them of "dumping" or flooding their markets with panels sold below cost. The Chinese have responded in part by shifting investment away from copy-cat manufacturing and towards "research and development and advanced education in the hopes that clean technology can help shift China from being merely the low-cost factory of the world to being a global leader in developing innovative [green] technology" (McMahon 2013). The Chinese government has thrown its full weight behind this plan, and despite trade sanctions we can expect the global price of renewable electricity technologies to continue to come down, making them more attractive for both industry and retail consumers alike (Zhang et al. 2012). As Europe and North America falter, it is looking increasingly likely that this green revolution will be led from the developing world.[1]

These two anecdotes illustrate the complexity of globalization and its relationship to the natural environment. As Newell (2012: 10) argues, globalization is too often thought of as a monolithic "thing" or a "fact" rather than a complex collection of (sometimes contradictory) processes that are experienced differently by people in different parts of the world. While globalization is difficult to define (see below), one thing that is clear is that it *makes things possible* that were not possible before. On the one hand, the case of toxic dumping in Abidjan shows how globalization makes it possible for Western countries to export or off-load many of the worst consequences of modern consumer-driven lifestyles to other countries (Dauvergne 2008). By moving hazardous waste to a less developed nation, a European company saves a great deal of money, and Europe itself stays a little bit cleaner. While the movement of toxic waste is regulated by international treaties (the Basel Convention), we will see later on that such quasi-legal international movements of waste occur regularly, and that this particular incident would never have come to light if it had not been for the deplorable behaviour of the local contractor. On the other hand, the case of Chinese investment in renewable energy shows how globalization makes it possible for green technologies to spread—not only from "cleaner" developed countries to "dirtier" developing ones—but as part of a global network of innovation, manufacturing, and trade. In principle, globalization allows good ideas to make it onto store shelves more quickly, more cheaply, and in more markets than ever before (Clapp and Dauvergne 2011: 142).

This chapter examines two interrelated questions: What impact is globalization having on the natural environment? And what impact is globalization having on our prospects for solving environmental problems?

Just as we have seen in other chapters, scholarly opinion is divided on these issues. The more optimistic view sees globalization as a vehicle for greater efficiency and the worldwide spread of environmental best practices as the global economy becomes more integrated. The more critical view, in contrast, sees globalization as a means for wealthy nations to extend their control over poorer ones, exploiting their natural resources to maintain unsustainable levels of consumption while using them to banish dirty industries and unwanted wastes. This chapter sketches out both views, but ultimately returns to a question posed by Newell (2012)—"which kind of globalization" is most helpful for tackling environmental problems? If globalization can be both good and bad for the environment, how do we tip the scales to favour environmental progress over degradation?

What Is Globalization?

The first step in answering these questions is to clarify what we're talking about. Like *sustainability* (see Chapter 7), *globalization* is a term that is both familiar and vague to most people (Bartelson 2000). There have been numerous attempts to define the term, some of which are outlined in Table 8.1. Part of the confusion is that globalization is driven by, and affects, so many things. The economic globalization that is encouraged by governments and transnational corporations (TNCs), for example, is itself grounded in political globalization (trade agreements and global institutions), cultural globalization (the spread of consumer tastes and symbols), and the globalization of information and communications technologies. Another issue is that we all seem to be agents of globalization—from the TNC with operations in dozens of countries around the world to the individual citizen browsing the web or sending emails effortlessly across borders. At the same time, however, the term *globalization* masks deep inequalities. According to the World Bank, only 33 per cent of the world's population has access to the Internet —at home, work, or other public venues (ranging from 80 per cent in North American countries to under 10 per cent in South Asian countries such as India and Bangladesh). The same inequalities are evident in levels of Foreign Direct Investment (FDI), which are seen by economists as one of the key benefits of globalization. While China attracted $220 billion US in FDI in 2011 (compared to the United States' $257 billion), Bangladesh attracted $0.80 billion; Kenya, $0.34 billion; and Nepal, a paltry $0.09 billion. In other words, globalization is still in its infancy—it is *an unfolding process* rather than a *fait accompli*. Whatever definition one prefers in Table 8.1, we must recognize three things: (1) globalization is dynamic, meaning that it expresses itself differently in different contexts; (2) it is multidimensional, meaning that it has multiple

Table 8.1 Some Academic Definitions of *Globalization*

Definition	Source
"The intensification of worldwide social relations which link distant localities in such a way that local happenings are shaped by events happening many miles away and vice versa."	Giddens (1990: 64)
"A process (or set of processes) which embodies a transformation in the spatial organization of social relations and transactions—assessed in terms of their extensity, intensity, velocity and impact—generating transcontinental or interregional flows and networks of activity, interaction and the exercise of power."	Held et al. (1999: 16)
"The recomposition of time and space [through] displacement, compression, distanciation, and even dissolution."	Burawoy (2000: 4)
"A process leading to greater interdependence and mutual awareness (reflexivity) among economic, political, and social units in the world, and among actors in general."	(Guillén 2010: 4)
"A multidimensional process, broadly restructuring and integrating the world's economies, institutions, and civil societies. It is a dynamic, ongoing, and accelerating process that is increasing the links among actors, as well as the structures within which they operate, both within states and across borders."	Clapp and Dauvergne (2011: 20)
"A prophecy in quest for self-fulfillment."	Bartelson (2000: 193)

drivers and forms of expression; and (3) it is uneven, meaning that it proceeds at different speeds in different contexts, and can even be reversed under certain circumstances.[2]

Why Globalization Matters to the Environment

For better or worse, the fate of the world's natural environment is increasingly tied to the (for now uncertain) outcomes of globalization. This is the case for several reasons. First, as mentioned in Chapter 3, environmentalism has itself been a major contributor to constructing a popular "global consciousness." While earlier movements, such as preservationism, focused on protecting particular landscapes from development or exploitation, post-1960s environmentalism was born global—focusing on the long-term and large-scale consequences of nuclear weapons testing, resource depletion, and (later) degradation of the ozone layer and climate change. In other words, environmentalism—with its metaphors of Spaceship Earth, One World, and sustainable development—has both helped to legitimize globalization (by encouraging people to see the world as a borderless place) and to establish a critique of globalization (that reckless behaviour in one place affects us all). This double narrative is evident in current debates over the environmental effects of globalization that we will consider later in the chapter.

The second reason why globalization matters to the environment is because we have reached the point where environmental problems are so serious and challenging that they require a coordinated global response. One of the great difficulties in environmental politics, however, is that while the most severe problems are global in scale—such as the depletion of the oceans, the alarming rate of global extinctions, and climate change—most political institutions are national (Elliott 2004: 109). As is painfully evident in current international negotiations over climate change policy, national institutions are often more dedicated to defending national interests than tackling global problems (Harrison and Sundstrom 2010). Given that politics occurs primarily at the level of the nation-state, the strength of international law depends primarily on inter-state agreements or treaties. These generally fall into two categories: agreements that directly address environmental issues or problems (see Table 8.2), and those that address other issues but have environmental dimensions or consequences, such as the North American Free Trade Agreement (NAFTA) and the World Trade Organization (WTO). To put it mildly, the environmental effectiveness of both types has been mixed. Among the most successful environmental treaties are the International Convention for the Regulation of Whaling, which has effectively barred commercial whaling despite the efforts of certain nations such as Japan to continue the practice, and the Montreal Protocol, which has phased out production of ozone-layer depleting CFCs. On the

Table 8.2 Major International Environmental Agreements

Agreement or Treaty	Date	Issue Addressed
International Convention for the Regulation of Whaling	1946	Commercial whale hunting
Nuclear Test Ban Treaty	1962	Atmospheric nuclear weapons testing
Biological and Toxic Weapons Treaty	1972	Chemical and biological weapons
London Convention	1972	Ocean pollution
Convention on the International Trade in Endangered Species	1973	Trade involving endangered species or products derived therefrom
Montreal Protocol	1987	Ozone-layer depletion
Basel Convention	1989	International transport of hazardous wastes
Convention on Biological Diversity	1992	Extinction and biodiversity loss
Kyoto Protocol	1997	Mandatory reduction of carbon emissions
Copenhagen Accord	2009	Voluntary reduction of carbon emissions

Sources: Based on Boyce (2004: 109) and Elliott (2004)

other side of the ledger, treaties such as the Basel Convention, regulating the transport of hazardous wastes, and the Kyoto Protocol, which sought to limit greenhouse gas emissions, have been far less successful, largely because of problems with enforcement (Elliott 2004: 62). The effectiveness of non-environmental agreements such as NAFTA and the WTO is hotly contested, and we will consider them in greater detail below.

Third, and most importantly, globalization matters because it is currently driving a remarkable extension and reorganization of global capitalism. As late as the 1980s, it made sense to consider the economies of highly developed countries such as the United States and Britain as being nationally bound, relying strongly on both internal production and consumption (Lash and Urry 1987). Since the beginnings of trade liberalization in the late 1980s and early 1990s, however, the scale of global trade has become truly staggering. According to WTO statistics, the volume of world exports has tripled from 1990 to 2011, and will likely more than quadruple by the year 2020 (WTO 2012). Numbers such as these, however, fail to capture the extent of the changes underway. In his influential book *The World Is Flat*, for instance, journalist Thomas Friedman (2007) outlines in great detail how manufacturing has been fundamentally reorganized in recent years. In the past, it was reasonable to assume that manufacturing occurred "in a given place," namely a factory or a series of factories owned or controlled by a given company that processed inputs in the form of raw materials into outputs in the form of finished goods. Three developments that took hold in the 1980s and 1990s began to change this: the removal of barriers to trade, the continued expansion of cheap global transportation networks, and the maturation of digital communications technologies such as the Internet. These changes have allowed manufacturing to "splinter." Rather than being manufactured in a single place, the smartphone in your pocket or the computer on your desk has been manufactured by *dozens* of companies located in places all over the world—the microprocessor, in Costa Rica; the memory card, in Korea; the touchscreen, in China; the battery, in Malaysia; and so on—a process coordinated via Internet and made possible by fossil-fuel-powered transport (Friedman 2007: 583). One of the side-effects of this process is that the recognized manufacturer of many products—such as Apple Inc.'s status as the "maker" of MacBooks, iPhones, and iPads—does not in fact do much manufacturing anymore. Instead, companies like Apple now focus predominantly on product design, coordinating its global network of suppliers/assemblers, brand management, and retailing (Dauvergne and Lister 2012). Another side-effect is that this system requires tremendous amounts of energy to function. World oil consumption has almost doubled since 1980, with nearly all of that growth occurring in developing countries. The global circulation of parts and products is also eating up a growing share of the world's energy, such that one-tenth of global oil production "is now consumed by just moving goods around the world" (Newell 2012: 66).

Simply put, globalization raises the ecological stakes by accelerating economic processes. The ultimate outcome of this acceleration is subject to considerable debate. On the one hand, optimists argue that global integration encourages the diffusion of cleaner technology and better management practices to formerly closed economic spaces (Schofer and Granados 2006). On the other hand, more critical observers argue that as the global economy becomes more integrated, we are locking ourselves into a system that might be *economically* efficient but that, in the words of Dauvergne (2008: xi), "casts long ecological shadows" that are unsustainable over the long term. The following sections look closely at these competing arguments.

The Optimistic View: Globalization as an Opportunity to Improve Environmental Performance

Optimistic observers of globalization argue that it is having a generally positive impact on environmental performance, particularly in poorer or less developed countries. This argument is based on the notion of **environmental convergence**, whereby globalization creates the incentives and means for developing countries to adopt the "greener" standards, technologies, and production techniques found in developed nations (Boyce 2004). The convergence argument is itself based on a series of assumptions. The first assumption is grounded in neo-classical economics (discussed in Chapter 7), specifically the idea that the competitive pressures in a globally integrated economy function to stamp out inefficiencies. For example, pro-globalizers argue that global agricultural production is currently distorted by subsidies and trade barriers in places such as Europe, the United States, and Canada. These subsidies, it is argued, prop up farming activities in developed nations that are not otherwise economically viable—meaning that there is a fair degree of *economically unnecessary* production and inefficient duplication (Newell 2012: 61). If subsidies were to be removed, lower cost regions would likely outcompete much First World agriculture, thus lowering farming's overall ecological burden and freeing up the excess land for other uses (including conservation). In turn, a free global market in agriculture would spur investment in low-cost countries, thus "rationalizing" agriculture in these regions—consolidating small inefficient farms into larger ones that require fewer inputs of labour and land. In this idealized example, undistorted free trade in agriculture would improve its environmental efficiency in both developed and developing countries by allowing freer flow of both goods and investment (this, of course, says nothing about the social and economic disruption that would occur alongside such a restructuring).

The second assumption anchoring the optimistic view of globalization is rooted in the **modernization theory of development**. This theory suggests that less developed countries are poor because they are "further behind" more developed countries in terms of access to capital, skills, domestic wealth, institutional capacity, and infrastructure development (Escobar 2012). What is implied here is that poorer nations would benefit from emulating or otherwise following the Western lead. With respect to the environment, optimists argue that when TNCs set up shop in a new region, they import new technologies, practices, and advanced management techniques that were previously unavailable. Many domestic firms in developing countries have poor environment track records due not only to a lack of technology, but also to cronyism, poor transparency, and forgiving governments willing to overlook environmental damage and pollution (Clapp and Dauvergne 2011: 169). In comparison, many TNCs demonstrate what's called a "home country effect." Given that most TNCs are based in countries with more advanced corporate and environmental regulations, they typically (but not in all cases) have better governance and accountability mechanisms, "greener" corporate cultures, and more sophisticated environmental planning and waste management practices (Boyce 2004). While critics of globalization frequently argue that TNCs flee jurisdictions with strong environmental regulations and seek out "pollution havens" where they are freer to behave badly, there is in fact little evidence of this happening on a broad scale (but see Box 8.1). As Newell (2012: 64) notes, "the costs of meeting environmental standards constitute a fraction of the overall costs faced by industry and pale in comparison to other factors such as labour costs, the skills base, and available infrastructure." Some empirical studies even suggest that regions with a high number of TNCs benefit from a "pollution halo"—becoming islands of relatively clean production in countries that have struggled with long-term environmental degradation (Cole et al. 2008).

Finally, some scholars are optimistic about globalization because of the broad institutional changes that come with it (Frank et al. 2000). This perspective, which is sometimes called the **"world polity school in sociology"** (Dick 2010: 196), argues that globalization is a vehicle for spreading strong environmental norms and expectations. According to Schofer and Hironaka (2005: 25), the rise of global institutions like the United Nations Environment Programme (founded in 1972) and the United Nations Framework Convention on Climate Change (1992), has "helped to establish a world society (or world polity) that influences national agendas, providing policy prescriptions and exerting pressure on a wide range of environmental issues." Environmental treaties such as those described in Table 8.2 act as a means of exerting international "peer pressure," and environmental groups such as Greenpeace and celebrity scientists such as

Box 8.1

The Darkest Side of Globalization—Union Carbide and the Bhopal Disaster

While optimists argue that TNCs usually improve the environmental efficiency of production in developing countries, in some cases they clearly do the opposite—using lax environmental regulations as an excuse to cut corners. The case of Union Carbide and the Bhopal disaster serves as a stark warning of what can happen when TNCs choose to go down this road. Union Carbide was a US-based chemicals manufacturer that operated a pesticides plant in the central Indian city of Bhopal. In the middle of the night of 3 December 1984, a massive leak from the plant spread poisonous gas over the city. Within hours, over 8,000 people had been killed—making this the worst industrial accident in human history. Thousands more died in the weeks and months that followed, as the world digested horrifying images of corpse-strewn streets and disfigured survivors. Union Carbide originally claimed sabotage, but documents released in 2002 indicated that the company had failed to install safety systems that were mandatory for similar plants in the United States, and that the limited system that did exist (a single flare tower) was offline for repair the night of the accident (Mackenzie 2002). The documents also revealed that the Bhopal plant failed to treat wastes, and routinely poured spent chemicals into open lagoons (while unrelated to the leak, this has permanently contaminated soil and groundwater adjacent to the site). Union Carbide paid $470 million into a compensation fund for victims in 1989, and was bought out by fellow TNC Dow Chemical in 2001. Victims groups continue to press for the prosecution of senior executives at the company—something that so far has not happened.

David Suzuki and James Hansen work tirelessly to keep environmental issues in the public eye. Using a logic that is reminiscent of ecological modernization theory (see Chapter 7), world polity theorists argue that these developments create strong incentives for nations and corporations to clean up their acts (Schofer and Granados 2006). At a more fundamental level, world polity theory suggests that access to the most lucrative consumer markets—specifically North America, Europe, and Japan—increasingly depends on environmental performance. As we saw in Chapter 7, big retailers such as Walmart, Home Depot, Nike, and Eddie Bauer are working hard to cultivate a green image in their home markets, and in doing so force environmental reforms back through their supply chains (Dauvergne and Lister 2012). Optimists argue that these changes are increasingly squeezing dirty producers out of the mainstream global economy (Vogel 1997).

The Critical View: Globalization as a Major Environmental Problem

While optimists are hopeful that globalization can stamp out inefficiencies and raise environmental standards worldwide, critics argue that it is doing far more environmental harm than good. First, many critics argue that the economic acceleration associated with globalization is irreparably harming the planet. The globalization of production has driven down the cost of many consumer goods in developed countries, encouraging the already-wealthy to consume even more (Dauvergne 2008). At the same time, a rising capitalist class in countries such as China and India is proving just as dedicated to conspicuous consumption as their Western counterparts. Markets in specialty products like shark fin soup, bear gall bladders, and elephant ivory are booming, wiping out much of the hard-won progress made over the last 30 years to conserve endangered species (see Box 8.2). Even the rise of a more modest middle-class of factory workers places a high demand on the planet. One of the first changes that newly prosperous households make is to increase their consumption of meat, which requires more land, water, and energy inputs than vegetarian calories. While development is surely a desirable outcome of globalization, many environmentalists fear that "lifestyle convergence" between developing and developed nations would be ecologically disastrous. Instead of assuming that developed nations are paragons of environmental cleanliness that ought to be emulated by developing nations, Boyce (2005) suggests that many common practices in poorer countries—such as eating locally-sourced food and commuting by bicycle—would greatly benefit the global environment if they were "imported" to wealthier ones.

Second, critics argue that the new institutions of global governance anchoring globalization promote rather than restrict environmental degradation. While the environmental treaties outlined in Table 8.2 are important, many of them lack resources and rely on individual states to enforce them. This institutional weakness contrasts with the strong disciplinary and enforcement powers possessed by trade agreements such as the North American Free Trade Agreement (NAFTA) and the World Trade Organization (WTO), as well as by global organizations like the World Bank (WB) and the International Monetary Fund (IMF). These are unabashedly *economic* institutions that prioritize trade, development, and free markets. While optimists point out that NAFTA and the WTO have environmental provisions that allow nations to restrict trade in cases where human, animal or plant life is directly threatened, critics argue that these are ineffective precisely because they are embedded in economic agreements (Charnovitz 2008). For example, in a landmark 1990 case, the US attempted to restrict imports of tuna from Mexico, Venezuela, and Vanuatu because of concerns

Box 8.2   The Rise of "Third World" Consumers

One of the biggest environmental dilemmas associated with globalization is the rise of a new consumer class in developing countries. Companies are targeting the "newly comfortable" with a range of products that are essentially low-cost versions of Western consumer staples. For example, Tata Motors, an Indian company, attracted international attention in 2009 by announcing that it would sell its "Nano" brand cars for under $2,000 US. Other car makers such as Hyundai are following suit, developing ultra-low-cost cars for consumers in the developing world. China's fleet of vehicles grew by an astonishing 27.5 per cent from 2010 to 2011, and will soon exceed 130 million. Based on current trends, the OECD expects there will be 2.5 *billion* cars on the road worldwide by 2050. Tencer (2011) rightly asks, "Can the world handle this many wheels?" It's hard to imagine how it could.

These changes are accompanied by growth in high-end consumer markets. Newly wealthy Chinese consumers, for instance, have taken a shining to elephant ivory, driving renewed poaching in Eastern and Southern Africa. Large-scale seizures of illegal ivory are commonplace again, after decades of decline. In December 2012, Malaysian officials found 1,500 tusks hidden in a container ship bound from Togo to China. Another high-end consumer market involves shark fins. While the shark fin market is global, most fins are consumed in China, where they are believed to have medicinal properties and where shark fin soup is considered an essential wedding-day delicacy for wealthy Chinese. Shark finning is particularly brutal, as the sharks typically

that fishers in these countries were using nets that also trapped and killed dolphins. Mexico protested to the General Agreement on Tariffs and Trade (GATT, the precursor to the WTO) that the US was unfairly restricting trade by projecting its own laws and regulations to other countries. When the GATT panel ruled in Mexico's favour, environmentalists were outraged, and saw this as a clear indication that environmental concerns would always be secondary to the push for freer trade (Newell 2012: 75). Similar criticisms have been levelled at the WB and IMF, particularly around their practice of tying lending and debt relief in poorer countries to **structural adjustment programs** (SAPs) that often involve liberalization, deregulation, and privatization of natural resources. While advocates of neoliberalism argue that this can enhance conservation (see Chapter 7), critics see it as further proof of the prioritization of corporate interests over environmental protection (Shandra et al. 2011).

have their fins cut off while still alive and are dumped back overboard to die of suffocation or infection. Conservation groups estimate that over 70 million sharks are killed each year, many of them for the shark fin market (Qin 2013).

In his book *The Shadows of Consumption*, Peter Dauvergne (2008) argues that the rise of the Third World consumer is one of the most important environmental challenges of the early twenty-first century. While much of the world is still mired in poverty, the newly prosperous middle and upper classes in countries such as China, India, and Brazil are proving just as eager to consume as their counterparts in developed nations. This puts Western-based environmental groups in a difficult position. On the one hand, it is brazenly hypocritical for Western voices to criticize consumption in poorer countries, given our own seemingly insatiable appetite for both low- and high-end goods. On the other hand, environmental activists have learned from experience that consumer education matters. Campaigns against fur clothing, animal testing, and elephant ivory have hinged on convincing consumers to boycott these products. The rise of non-Western consumers means that many of these battles will likely have to be fought again in new "cultural battlegrounds." Again drawing on experiences in the West, some groups are turning to national celebrities for assistance. Anti-shark-finning groups, for example, have enlisted Chinese basketball superstar Yao Ming as a spokesperson to get their message across to consumers. In India, the World Wildlife Fund has featured Bollywood star Rana Daggubati in campaigns to discourage the poaching of endangered Bengal tigers. It remains to be seen whether these efforts will pay off, or if the rise of Third World consumers will ratchet up the environmental crisis to new heights.

Third, some critics argue that globalization is unlikely to contribute to the long-term development of poorer countries at all. According to this view, globalization is a means for richer countries to boost their own prosperity while parasitically drawing on the human and natural capital found in other parts of the world. This perspective is common among sociologists and political scientists working in the **world systems theory** (WST) tradition. WST is a neo-Marxist perspective that "evolved out of efforts to explain how and why some countries in the world economy have been able to grow in power and wealth while others remain trapped in apparent stagnation" (Roberts and Grimes 2002: 172). WST theorists argue that these imbalances are historical—at different points in time a set of "core nations" has dominated the "world system" or global economy, drawing wealth away from "peripheral nations" that have little choice but to trade with the more powerful core (Wallerstein 1974). Because wealthy nations dominate global economic institutions, they are able to set the "terms of trade" that reflect their own interests (Jorgenson and Clark 2009a: 628). Institutions such as the WB, WTO, and IMF were established by core nations, and have become key vehicles for spreading Western policy preferences around the world (Chase-Dunn et al. 2000). Moreover, TNCs based in core countries control the world's supply of private capital, which leaves lesser-developed countries to compete for investment. According to WST, this encourages a "race to the bottom," where countries try to lower costs as much as possible to attract and retain foreign capital. Peripheral countries that try to enhance social services by raising corporate taxes or implementing a minimum wage can simply be bypassed by TNCs that can easily find lower taxes and labour costs elsewhere (Malm 2012). In practice, this means that poor countries are being drawn into a globalization process that they have little hope of controlling or influencing.

While most WST scholarship focuses on issues of labour and development, these inequalities extend to the environment as well. Recently, environmental sociologists have sought to "ecologize" WST via the concept of **ecologically unequal exchange** (EUE). EUE looks at how core nations not only benefit economically from globalization, but also environmentally. To fully appreciate this, we need to get a sense of how the environmental "goods and bads" generated by production and consumption are distributed across the globe (Buttel 2006). This in turn means looking at the entire life-cycle of products, most of which is hidden from Western consumers (see Figure 8.1). This life-cycle is closely linked to the **global division of labour**. Most consumer products are designed in rich countries, but manufactured in poor ones. The "brain work," which typically involves high-paying jobs, occurs in wealthy regions while the "hands work" occurs in poorer ones. Apple Inc. even plays this up, labelling their products as "Designed in California and Made in China." Economy-wide, the vast majority of everyday consumer products are now manufactured in poorer countries and shipped to richer ones for consumption. When I was a child, most toys, articles of clothing, electronics, and appliances carried the label "Made in Canada" or (more frequently) "Made in the U.S.A." That era is long past. Everything from dollar store wares to high-end electronics are now manufactured elsewhere, "drawing on raw materials extracted mostly from peripheral places and concentrating them in the mostly urban spaces [of developed countries]" (Buttel 2006: 159). What is equally important is what happens *after* consumption. While a lot of consumer waste ends up in local landfills, a significant amount is exported back to peripheral countries as waste. This is particularly true of electronics—computers, smartphones, cameras, tablets, batteries and the like. Electronic waste or "e-waste" is valuable because of the rare minerals and elements it contains. Unfortunately, recovering or recycling these elements is frequently done by villagers and other labourers who are not given protective gear and who are paid by the pound of recovered material. This encourages them to work quickly, using hammers to break apart circuit boards and open fires to melt away plastics and collect metals (Lubick 2012). While export of e-waste is regulated by the Basel Convention, weak enforcement means that the vast majority of e-waste movements are unrecorded (UNEP 2009). Recent estimates suggest that more than 12 million used computers are exported from the United States each year for overseas recycling (Kahhat and Williams 2012). More broadly, it is estimated that up to 10 per cent of global maritime freight is composed of hazardous waste being moved legally and illegally around the world (Boudier and Bensebaa 2011).

Western consumers are thus increasingly insulated from the environmental consequences of either production or disposal—allowing our economy to appear greener than it actually is. In biological terms, we enjoy consumer products in their "fixed" state—when they are neither being assembled (requiring inputs) nor breaking down (producing outputs). The inverse is true in developing countries, which experience consumer goods in their transient state—expending resources and energy to *build* the products as well as to *disassemble* them at the end of their life-cycle (Rice 2009: 221). It is therefore useful to think of consumer products as embedded in **environmental flows** that *begin and end* in poorer countries to the economic and environmental benefit of Western companies and consumers (see Figure 8.1).

Finally, EUE theory suggests that this ecological burden has the long-term effect of suppressing development in poor countries. A series of large-scale comparative studies have suggested that countries that export more goods to developed countries have *lower* domestic consumption levels than countries that export less (Rice 2007; Jorgenson et al. 2009; Jorgenson and Clark 2009). This seems counter-intuitive, given the experiences of

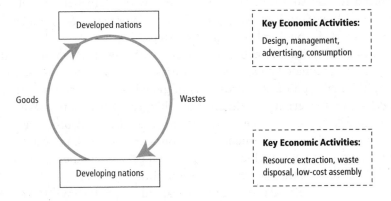

Figure 8.1 Environmental Flows at the Heart of Ecologically Unequal Exchange

export-heavy countries such as China that have levered globalization into strong domestic growth and growing middle classes. These studies show, however, that China is the exception rather than the rule. On the one hand, China fits the description of a "peripheral nation" because it suffers a great deal of environmental degradation and pollution in order to build goods for the West (Malm 2012). On the other hand, China is an emerging superpower that is now "outsourcing part of its environmental costs to [even] lesser-developed countries" (Jorgenson et al. 2009: 226). As discussed in Chapter 1, for example, China has become a major investor throughout Africa—using state-controlled companies to secure rights and buy up land for agriculture, mining, and oil and gas exploration (French 2010). This is not a model that most other peripheral nations can follow. More ominously, it suggests that China's long-term development may depend on passing environmental costs further down the economic food chain, leaving an impoverished environment for Africans who would face an even steeper climb toward sustainable prosperity (Mol 2011).

Which Kind of Globalization?

Thus far, we have seen that globalization is a complex and multi-dimensional phenomenon that produces contradictory effects—some positive and some negative. This suggests that globalization is not a "take it or leave it" package, but something that is flexible and manipulable. In other words, the globalization we see today is just one possibility among many—the product of particular values, priorities, and choices that have been made by powerful actors over the last several decades. According to Newell (2012), this means that the question before us is not "Is globalization good or bad?" but "Which kind of globalization do we want?" Answers to this question will vary, but it's fair to assume that most people would prefer an environmentally sustainable globalization that treats everyone fairly and enhances prosperity for all. So, if a more equitable, fairer, and "greener" globalization is possible, how could we get there? This discussion is far broader than these pages allow, but here are some first steps.

One of the most overwhelming problems with globalization-as-we-know-it is that it is dominated by *economic* priorities and institutions. As mentioned earlier, the major political instruments of globalization—trade treaties such as NAFTA and international institutions like the WB and the IMF—exist to promote and enforce free markets and free trade. All other priorities, be they cultural or environmental, are considered secondary. While many newer trade agreements include environmental provisions, their purpose is to amend or qualify economic agreements and thus *cannot* serve as the basis for a more sustainable global economy. To paraphrase Karl Polanyi (1944), these agreements and institutions insist that society (and the natural environment) adapt to the needs of the economy, not the other way around. This leaves little room for nations to act on environmental priorities. For example, trade agreements like the WTO forbid nations from restricting trade with another country that they believe is recklessly degrading their environment. Trade discrimination based on "production methods and standards" is explicitly barred, making it extremely difficult to ban imports from countries that encourage or turn a blind eye to such things as deforestation, overfishing, poaching, or pollution as part of the production process.

Remedying this means, at the very least, rebalancing international agreements and institutions so that environmental standards and protections play a more dominant role. This change needs to go beyond the rules-on-paper. At the moment, international economic agreements are enforced by quasi-judicial panels with real disciplinary powers. As we saw earlier, the dispute between the United States and Mexico over tuna imports was judged by a tribunal whose decisions were considered binding. Most environmental treaties, in contrast, lack this supra-national authority and rely on national governments to enforce them. For example, the Basel Convention on the international transport of hazardous waste is only enforced if national governments choose to build a case against suspected violators and prosecute them in their own courts. Many countries lack the funding and capacity to do this consistently, and companies involved in the international waste trade know this. The horrific case of toxic dumping in Abidjan, Côte d'Ivoire, that we encountered at the outset is simply an extreme episode of what happens every day, as companies move hazardous wastes to poorer and less-regulated parts of the world without much fear of prosecution (Clapp 2001). Another example is the Kyoto Protocol to reduce emissions of greenhouse gases. Kyoto was meant to be a treaty with teeth, requiring signatories to meet mandatory reduction targets or suffer stiff monetary penalties. Unfortunately, it too depended on national governments to play by the rules—something that the Canadian government has refused to do. While the Liberal Party government of Jean Chrétien ratified Kyoto in 2002, it failed to enact meaningful policies to curb carbon emissions. The subsequent Conservative Party government of Stephen Harper, after its election in 2006, did its best to ignore the Kyoto Protocol (Young and Coutinho 2013), and in 2012 used its majority to pass legislation repealing its ratification—thus exempting Canada from any penalties. Closing these loopholes will take real political effort, but it can be done. International trade agreements are effective because of their strong enforcement. Countries monitor one another for violations and have recourse to tribunals and panels whose judgments are backed by institutional authority. More often than not, countries choose to "discipline themselves" and adjust domestic policy rather than risk being hauled in front of a WTO, NAFTA, or EU panel. This disciplinary power is utterly absent from the current global environmental governance system. Nations need to fear violating international norms, not be free to simply ignore them when they become inconvenient.

Whatever form these strengthened international institutions take (either within trade agreements or parallel to them), they must address the unequal environmental flows discussed previously. Globalization has allowed developed countries to consume more while offshoring many of the environmental problems associated with producing goods and disposing of wastes. Distressingly, this offshoring is often perceived in Western countries as evidence of environmental improvements and progress. For example, fossil fuel consumption has recently fallen in many developed countries (including Canada and the United States), mostly because energy-intensive manufacturing has relocated to lesser-developed countries. While Western governments are quick to claim this as evidence of success, these emissions have simply been shifted to the Third World. As shown in Figure 8.2, for instance, emissions in China have skyrocketed in recent years as it has become the "world's factory." According to one estimate, nearly *half* of all Chinese emissions can be linked to the export sector, leading Malm (2012) to argue that China has become "the world's chimney"—emitting far more carbon dioxide and air pollution than justified by domestic consumption levels.

This ecological imbalance is intentionally ignored by the governments of wealthy nations. According to Roberts and Parks (2009), the first step towards remedying the situation would be for Western governments and consumers to recognize the substantial ecological debt we owe to poorer countries that have suffered environmental damage on our behalf. Unfortunately, Western politicians usually argue the opposite. The Canadian government under Stephen Harper has repeatedly stated, for instance, that it will not sign on to a new global climate change agreement unless it includes strict obligations for developing countries like China and India. This argument intentionally ignores the fact that a substantial fraction of Chinese and Indian emissions are simply *displaced* from wealthy countries. It is highly hypocritical to insist that this pollution belongs to the Third World when it is so closely tied to Western consumption.

Paying down our ecological debt could take several forms. As we saw earlier, pro-globalizers point out that TNCs frequently transfer cleaner technologies to developing countries as they set up shop. While this is true, the fact that TNCs bring cleaner technologies with them does not necessarily mean they share them with local domestic firms. What is needed are "technology transfer" or "technology collaboration" agreements to ensure that developing countries have broad access to the greenest technologies. This has been done before, as when pharmaceutical companies decided in the early 2000s to cut the price of HIV/AIDS medications in developing countries by up to 90 per cent. The price cut was done in the name of access, but was also a response to threats from some developing countries, particularly South Africa, to invalidate their patents and open the door for generic drug makers to provide supply. The transfer of green technologies would benefit everyone in the long run, as it would help manufacturers to grab a larger global market share and ensure future demand. Some technology transfer does occur through existing programs like the Clean Development Mechanism (negotiated in the Kyoto Protocol) and the Global Environment Facility (affiliated with the World Bank), but these are limited programs whose long-term effectiveness is uncertain (Newell 2012: 129).

Finally, developed nations need to be open to the "transfer back" of green technologies. The trade disputes over Chinese solar panels discussed at the outset help to illustrate this. One of the great boons of globalization is

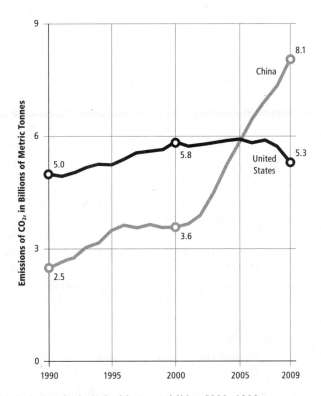

Figure 8.2 CO_2 Emissions in the United States and China, 1990–2009

Source: The Heritage Foundation. www.heritage.org/multimedia/infographic/2010/07/china-and-us-co2-emissions. Data source: Olivier and Peters, J. (2010).

that it greatly expands the pool of human innovation. The wealth generated by globalization is helping to expand education systems in countries such as China and India, which will allow the world to draw on the talents and creativity of millions of erstwhile excluded or ignored people. Wealthy nations need to be open to this, and encourage the importing of green technologies even if they threaten home-grown industries.

The suggestions I have made in this section are neither radical nor exhaustive. None would fundamentally alter globalization-as-we-know-it, but neither are they enough to guarantee a more sustainable globalization. Instead I see them as a bare minimum—a starting point for deeper reforms to address the problems discussed in this chapter. To date, globalization has been uneven and unequal—both environmentally and economically— but it doesn't have to be that way. An "economy first" globalization risks collapse under the weight of its social and environmental consequences (Curtis 2009), but global integration can take many forms—some of them quite positive. It's time to look beyond the narrower vision of globalization that has dominated the process so far.

Conclusion

The fate of the natural environment is now intimately tied to the future outcomes of human globalization. Globalization is both "speeding up and spreading out" human relations (Massey 1994: 146) and this is raising the stakes on key environmental issues and problems. Scholars are divided on the odds that this gamble will pay off. Optimists argue that globalization will help to spread good ideas and technologies, allowing "best practices" to disseminate more evenly around the world and raise environmental performance across the board. They expect that global rules and norms will continue to evolve and strengthen, creating both an imperative and a roadmap to reform. Most compellingly, optimists suggest that a prosperous and educated global population will allow for a green revolution driven as much by the Third World as by the First, bringing new innovations to market and driving down the cost of green technologies. Critics, on the other hand, have a different interpretation. Thus far, globalization has meant higher energy use, more consumption in both the developed and developing world, and a highly unequal global distribution of environmental costs. For many critics, globalization is an extension of Western power rather than its abdication. Having set the rules for global trade, developed countries are able to strengthen their economic and environmental position by expropriating the ecosystems of poorer countries, many of which do not dare pass new environmental laws for fear of scaring off foreign investment. For critics, globalization-as-we-know-it is like the spending spree at last call—maximizing the buyers' short-term pleasure with no thought to the inevitable hangover that follows the binge.

While these two arguments are in many ways diametrically opposed, reforms could be undertaken today to "ecologize" globalization. The institutions that anchor and promote globalization are today too focused on the economic dimension. A re-balancing must occur that includes strengthening the enforcement of environmental treaties and agreements. Rich nations must also acknowledge the ecological debt that they owe developing countries that are saddled with "displaced" extraction, pollution, and waste from the global economy. Redress could take many forms, but should build on the strengths identified by optimists—specifically the transfer of clean technologies, sponsorship of clean development projects, and openness to trade in green technologies. These first steps are just that—but they would help to improve the odds on the "globalization gamble" that we are collectively undertaking.

Questions for Critical Thought

1. Who do you think is more responsible for the environmental problems associated with globalization—producers who manufacture and promote goods, or consumers who seek out and buy them?

2. Is it possible to have an "environmentally friendly" globalization? How would we get there?

3. What role do you think cultural globalization plays in environmental issues? Do global media and the Internet help or hinder environmental progress?

Suggested Readings

Dauvergne, Peter. (2008). *The Shadows of Consumption: Consequences for the Global Environment*. Cambridge: MIT Press. A highly accessible volume that empirically demonstrates the ecological consequences of rampant consumerism, this book uses case studies, in which Dauvergne brilliantly links everyday consumer products to their often-distant ecological costs.

Newell, Peter. (2012). *Globalization and the Environment: Capitalism, Ecology and Power*. Malden: Polity. This succinct book provides a thorough analysis of how globalization affects the natural environment. It pays particular attention to production, trade, and the role of finance in maintaining global inequalities.

Rice, James. (2009). "The transnational organization of production and uneven environmental degradation and change in the world economy," *International Journal of Comparative Sociology* 50 (3–4): 215–236. This is a good review article that describes ecologically unequal exchange theory and the uneven global flow of environmental goods and wastes.

Suggested Websites

The Basel Action Network (BAN)
www.ban.org
> BAN is a US-based organization dedicated to ending the illegal trade in hazardous wastes. The site contains a wealth of information, research, and petitions on the subject.

The United Nations Environment Programme (UNEP)
www.unep.org
> The UNEP promotes global sustainable development under the auspices of the United Nations. Its website is vast, containing information on global trade, industry, green technology, and global environmental governance.

9 Science and Knowledge

Key Points

◎ Science occupies a privileged place in Western culture as a special path to knowledge and truth, which makes it a valuable political tool in environmental conflicts.

◎ Over-reliance on science can be problematic, especially when it is used to pre-empt or close down democratic debate.

◎ Many observers believe that science is becoming increasingly "politicized" by interest groups that have stakes in particular environmental outcomes.

◎ Science is neither perfect nor fatally flawed; therefore, a major societal challenge is to find the right role for science in a more inclusive approach to environmental decision-making that also makes room for local, traditional, and experiential forms of knowledge.

Introduction

How do we come to know about environmental problems? How do we know how serious they are? What has caused them? How to solve them? The answers to these questions vary case by case. In some instances, people come to know about environmental problems because they experience them directly. Living next to a landfill or an industrial brownfield, for instance, makes environmental degradation difficult to ignore. People living in the Arctic region can literally see the effects of climate change as the permafrost melts and the sea ice retreats. But as we saw in Chapter 3, most urban and middle-class people are insulated from such experiences. In most cases, our understanding of environmental issues is predominantly based on *claims* made by other people—scientists, activists, politicians, or celebrities—looking to communicate a message either directly or through intermediaries such as the mass media. In other words, we know about environmental problems because we are *told about them* rather than experiencing them directly. The human senses are unable to tell us that ozone depletion is linked to the manufacture of CFCs, that acid rain is caused by SO_2 emissions, and climate change by the special heat-retaining qualities of greenhouse gases like CO_2 and CH_4. We know about these connections not because we have experienced or witnessed them, but because we have been informed by people who "know more" than we do. In each of these cases, moreover, powerful interests with a lot to lose from environmental regulations have challenged these links, arguing that we can't be sure, that nothing is proven, and that these problems might have other causes that haven't been adequately researched or even discovered yet. Faced with these competing claims, people have to choose whom to believe—what type of claimant and what type of knowledge they judge to be more credible on a given issue.

This chapter argues that environmental conflicts are increasingly embroiled in knowledge conflicts, specifically struggles over *what* we know, *how* we know it, and what this knowledge *means* for policy and political action (Grundmann and Stehr 2003). Given that most environmental problems are "discovered" through the natural sciences, much of this struggle occurs over scientific facts and their meanings (Yearley 2010). Scientists have achieved a high level of legitimacy in Western societies as (supposedly) impartial investigators and interpreters of the world—capable of unveiling Nature's secrets and "seeing further and more clearly" than the human senses allow. At the same time, however, the authority of science is being challenged on multiple levels. On the one hand, science is being challenged "laterally" or horizontally by the multiplication of voices using scientific facts and claims to advance political agendas. Environmental groups, industry associations, think tanks, charities, private foundations, and political parties have all become adept at mobilizing scientific arguments in public debates and discussions over environmental issues. According to Pielke (2007: 10), "increasingly, science has come to be viewed as simply a resource for enhancing the ability of groups in society to bargain, negotiate, and compromise in pursuit of their special interest [with] the result that political battles are played out in the language of science, resulting in policy gridlock and the diminishment of science as a resource for policy-making." On the other hand, science is also being challenged "from below" by the political rise of "other ways of knowing" that Western society has long considered less valid than scientific knowledge. These ways of knowing, which include local knowledge, traditional knowledge, and experiential knowledge, are gaining legal and public recognition as legitimate sources of environmental facts and claims. Overall, these trends point to a *pluralization* of voices claiming special authority on environmental issues—resulting in less certainty about "what to do" to solve environmental problems.

In this chapter I argue that we need new tools for evaluating, accommodating, and dealing with plural (and often contradictory) knowledge claims about the environment. At the moment, many of our institutions are still based on the idea that scientific certainty is achievable and can guide us to the right decision about how to treat the natural environment. The pluralization of knowledge claims is exposing this as a false hope. Instead, we need to admit that all knowledge is deeply political, and find ways to end the paralysis that often results from knowledge conflicts.

Why Science Matters to the Environment

There are two main reasons why science matters to environmental issues and problems. The first is, quite simply, because "it works" (Hacking 1999: 67). Science plays a significant role in the history of nearly every major environmental issue, typically as either the discoverer or the confirmer of a problem. Issues such as acid rain, ozone depletion, and global warming were all recognized as *potential* problems and debated within the scientific community long before they were recognized as *real world* issues. For example, the heat-retaining properties of greenhouse gases such as CO_2 were discovered by chemist John Tyndall in 1859, over a century before global warming became a major political issue. In other words, science is critical for anticipating, understanding, and resolving environmental problems (even if politicians aren't always listening). It has a well-earned reputation for providing valid and reliable advice on issues of great importance to the planet.

The second reason why science matters is because of the privileged status of scientific knowledge in contemporary Western culture and society. Authorities, including the media and government, are rarely spurred into action by ordinary people's everyday observations of the natural environment. Science is seen as the only way to be sure that an environmental problem exists, to judge its severity, and to evaluate possible solutions. According to Hannigan (2006: 94), this gives scientists a substantial amount of power as "gatekeepers, screening potential claims for credibility" and endorsing some while disqualifying others. For example, the First Nation community of Aamjiwnaang, near the city of Sarnia in southwestern Ontario, has complained for decades about health problems that community leaders believe are caused by air and water pollution from nearby chemical plants. Aamjiwnaang is located in the midst of what some call Canada's "Chemical Valley"—an industrial park housing giant chemical and petrochemical companies such as Dow Chemical, Suncor, Imperial Oil, and Shell. Neither the provincial nor federal ministries of health would acknowledge the community's complaints, however, citing a lack of evidence and an unwillingness to launch new policies based on "anecdote." In 2005, however, a study published in the academic journal *Environmental Health Perspectives* (Mackenzie et al. 2005) seemed to validate community concerns, finding that far fewer boys were being born in the community relative to the number of number of girls—a "gender bending" pattern that is sometimes found in birds, fish, amphibians, and reptiles exposed to endocrine-disrupting chemicals (Webster 2006). The article brought

Box 9.1   Is Western Society Really Uncritical of Science?

In his excellent book *The Scientific Revolution* (1996), Steven Shapin argues that the cultural authority of science is flimsier than it first appears. At the time when Galileo was measuring the movements of the heavenly bodies, and Francis Bacon was developing his inductive method for extrapolating real-world observations to "natural laws," the vast majority Europe's population were illiterate peasants who were far more influenced by religious teachings than those of fledgling science (Shapin 1996: 8). In fact, European society was far more conservative at the time than Middle Eastern and Asian cultures. The Chinese were known as great innovators, having invented technologies such as gunpowder, the compass, and modern pulp-based paper hundreds of years before the European Scientific Revolution. Muslim scholars similarly developed advanced knowledge in chemistry, mathematics, and biology in the period 800–1200 AD, when Europe was mired in the Dark Ages, dominated by conservative religious interpretations of the world (Dallal 2010). These conservative views did not evaporate overnight at the dawn of the Scientific Revolution in Europe—it took hundreds of years before science gained the broad public legitimacy that it enjoys today in Western culture. Even then, however, science has never gone unquestioned. The notion that science can be immoral and even dangerous dates back hundreds of years, and is evident in early masterpieces of science fiction such as Mary Shelley's *Frankenstein* (1818) and H.G. Wells' *The Island of Dr. Moreau* (1896). In these works, science's technical capabilities (what it can do) lead to highly unethical and terrifying creations that ultimately "strike back" at their creators.

further academic attention to Aamjiwnaang, and prompted Health Canada to provide funding for a conference bringing together international experts in endocrinology and human reproduction. While officials continue to drag their feet, this case illustrates the gatekeeping power of science to get an issue into the media and onto the political map.

Where Does the Cultural Authority of Science Come From?

The cultural authority of science in Western society has important historical roots. According to the historian and sociologist of science Steven Shapin (2010: 47), "there has always been an intimate connection between how people recognize good knowledge and how they conceive a good society." This suggests that knowledge is primarily evaluated according to *cultural*

The twentieth century saw its fair share of real-world scientific horrors. The early part of the century saw the rise of **eugenic** science, which sought to improve public morals and health by restricting the reproduction of the mentally ill, racial and ethnic minorities, and the poor. While eugenic science was popular across Europe and North America (including Canada—see McLaren 1990) it took its full horrifying turn in Nazi Germany. The Nazis were deeply committed to the biological and physical sciences, and encouraged scientists to experiment directly on human beings in prisons and concentration camps (Grundmann and Stehr 2012). The detonation of atomic bombs over the Japanese cities of Hiroshima and Nagasaki in 1945 also spurred public fear and revulsion. While public criticism was muted at first (because the bombs effectively ended the Second World War), the idea that science had unleashed an evil and unnatural power into the world was commonly held in the 1950s and 1960s (Gamson and Modigliani 1989).

Shapin also argues that the special status of the scientist in society has been overstated by historians eager to recast the rise of modern science as a heroic undertaking (Shapin 2008b). He argues that most histories of the Scientific Revolution (a term that was actually coined in the 1920s) were written at a time when science was under threat of becoming "more ordinary" as it was progressively institutionalized in universities, government agencies, and private industry. This mainstreaming of science gradually eroded the myth that scientists were special people with high morals and exceptional talents (Shapin 2008a). By mid-century, science had become a job like any other, and no longer a mythical calling spurring exceptional people to achieve superhuman intellectual feats. Scientists were now just "ordinary men"— coming to neighbourhood barbecues, playing on the local softball team, and serving on the PTA just like anybody else. In other words, they were now fallible people open to the same critiques of political bias, poor judgment, and professional incompetence as anyone else (Shapin 2008a: 73).

criteria rather than its utility, generalizability, or applicability to specific issues and problems. People tend to privilege knowledge that reflects their values. More traditional societies, for instance, often grant special status to religious or spiritual knowledge over the more mechanistic and reductionist knowledge produced by the natural sciences.

As we saw in Chapter 6, Western societies are deeply committed to the modernist values of progress, reason, and order. Sociologist Donna Haraway (1988) argues that the cultural authority of science in Western societies derives in large part from its fit with these values, particularly the notions of "objectivity" and **"value neutrality."** During the Scientific Revolution, scientists (many of whom were wealthy hobbyists who funded their own research) defended their actions against traditionalists by arguing that they had no political agenda and were merely investigating the "laws of nature."[1] Francis Bacon (1561–1626), a pioneer of modern science, saw science as a sacred calling—arguing that scientists had a religious duty to study Nature, because "curiosity about the workings of the world was a natural outcome of God's endowing humans with the capacity to explore and reason" (Hird 2012: 15). According to this view, a scientist's task was to follow cues in the natural world and ignore the vagaries and petty politics of the human world. Knowledge existed, out there, waiting to be found, and it was the scientist's duty to discover it and deliver this knowledge to others so that they might better understand. If a scientist descended to the level of politics, it was in the role of a disinterested "honest broker" who could help rulers understand the problems they dealt with and the potential contribution science could make to solving them (Pielke 2007; Shapin 2008a: 57). This notion that science is a "pure" pursuit untainted by human politics is still widely held today, despite the efforts of historians to dispel the myth and present a more nuanced portrait of early scientists as "struggling to establish credibility and authority" in a political environment still deeply influenced by religious and traditional worldviews (Shapin 2010: 18).

The special status afforded to science and scientists in Western society means that we frequently turn to science to help solve environmental problems. This reliance on science, however, is not without consequences. In the next two sections, I address two problems in particular that have emerged directly from our over-reliance on science to tell us what to do: the democratic-deficit problem, and the problem of "politicized" science.

The Democratic-Deficit Problem

While science is an extremely useful tool, some scholars argue that we have become *too* reliant on scientific knowledge to solve problems that are essentially political in nature (e.g., Fischer 2000; Callon et al. 2009; Brown 2009). According to this view, scientists and experts are frequently granted too much influence over decision-making processes that ought to be undertaken democratically. For example, Leiss (2001) traces the process through which genetically modified (GM) seeds were approved for use in Canadian agriculture. The decision to use GM technology has far-reaching economic and ecological implications—affecting farmers, land owners, consumers, and potentially whole ecosystems (if some GM crops were to "go wild" and propagate without human involvement). But instead of consulting with these groups and inviting them into the decision-making process, the Government of Canada chose to base its decision on narrow technical assurances of the GM technology's safety as evaluated by government and industry scientists. This is an example of what Fischer (2000: 20) calls **technocratic governance**: policy-making or decision-making based on the inputs and opinions of scientists, experts, and other knowledge elites to the exclusion of citizens and stakeholders.

Critics see technocratic governance as deeply undemocratic (Wynne 2011). First of all, they point out that science is ill-equipped to answer moral and ethical questions. Early scientists were keenly aware of the distinction between "is" and "ought" (just because something *is* possible, doesn't mean that it *ought* to be)—and saw the latter as being the domain of politics (Shapin 2008a: 11). Technocratic governance blends the two without providing any means for outside moral and ethical input. Second, critics argue that technocratic governance is a thinly disguised way of granting the private sector special access to policy- and decision-making. Returning to the case of GM technology, industry scientists were invited to collaborate with regulators in assessing the safety of their technology and determining whether special policies were needed to regulate it (Leiss 2001: 21). From the government's point of view, "working with industry" makes sense, because industry scientists know more about the product in question and their involvement can save time and money. On the other hand, inviting industry to participate in closed-door decision-making beyond the view of stakeholders and the general public is a morally questionable practice, and invites accusations that government and industry have colluded to make decisions against the public interest.

Critics therefore argue that the authority of science is frequently used as a way of suppressing democracy by closing down debates on contentious issues and problems before they begin. By claiming that an issue is settled on technical grounds, powerful actors create a **democratic deficit** or gap that makes it extremely difficult for citizens and activists to participate in decision-making. Interestingly, Canada has a long tradition of technocratic decision-making that compares poorly to the United States and Europe, where there are more opportunities for citizen inputs and debates (Leiss 2000; Cox 2004). Canada has only recently become more open to direct stakeholder participation in the evaluation of new technologies, industries, and developments (see the section on "Other Ways of Knowing" below). Even when stakeholders are involved, however, experts and politicians often have difficulty accepting their views, no matter how sophisticated they may be (see Box 9.2).

The Politicization Problem

The second problem stemming from our over-reliance on science involves its use in the political arena. The cultural authority of science means that it is highly sought after by "issue advocates" who are looking to marshal political power and public attention to their cause (Pielke 2007). Science, with its veneer of objectivity and value-neutrality, is a great way to make an argument. If the "facts speak for themselves," then having the facts on

Box 9.2   The Citizen-Expert vs. Technocracy

Governments now routinely try to legitimize their decisions about controversial developments and industries by holding public forums, consultations, and hearings that are meant to show that they are listening to concerned citizens (Brown 2009). While some of these forums offer real opportunities for citizen engagement, often they are empty exercises that have little impact on the final decision-making that occurs behind closed doors (Cox 2004: 313). Recently, however, citizens have begun using these venues as an opportunity to challenge technocratic decision-making on its own turf. The rise of the Internet and other communications technologies has facilitated public access to scientific publications, technical reports, and news media from around the world. This has contributed to the rise of a new class of self-informed **citizen-expert** who is well versed in scientific arguments and findings. According to Callon et al. (2009) citizen-experts have become powerful players in public struggles over environmental issues because they are able to directly challenge the "official" science put forward by government and industry. To use an example from my own research, in 2006 I attended several public meetings and hearings of the Government of British Columbia's *Special Committee on Sustainable Aquaculture*, which was convened in an attempt to defuse the controversy over fish farming and table recommendations on how to "responsibly" expand the industry. Aquaculture is a contentious issue in both the Pacific and Atlantic regions of Canada, and each session went over time to accommodate the number of speakers who showed up. Many of those who spoke were ordinary citizens who had serious concerns about how salmon aquaculture in particular was being conducted in the province. While the testimony was often emotional, many speakers demonstrated a deep technical understanding of aquaculture practices that often exceeded those of the panel members (who were politicians). This frequently put the "authorities" on the defensive, as they didn't quite know how

one's side is a formidable advantage in any political debate. This, in and of itself, is nothing new. But one of the most commonly heard complaints in both scientific and advocacy circles is that science is becoming increasingly politicized and therefore less trustworthy as a neutral and impartial guide for action (Young and Matthews 2010: 138).

Sometimes, complaints about **politicized science** refer to the dishonest or selective use of scientific data or findings by politically motivated non-scientists. This type of politicization is largely outside the individual scientist's control. For example, Canadian climatologist Andrew Weaver co-authored an article in 2012 that compared the potential effect of major to respond to these claims. The following exchange was typical (from a hearing in the community of Tofino on Vancouver Island):

> *Citizen*: I am not a scientist [but] there needs to be acknowledgment that there are other points of view out there [than that] of the industry. . . . Salmon farmers use a wide range of substances, including synthetic pigments to artificially colour their fish, antibiotics to treat disease, chemicals to treat sea lice and other parasites and disinfectants to wash nets. The waste from feed and feces has been linked to increased mercury levels in rockfish, a main component in the diets of many coastal people. Rockfish sampled in Clayoquot Sound were found to have the highest levels of mercury. That's from farm feed and feces. Colourants, chemicals, antibiotics, herbicides and pesticides. All of these contaminants make their way into the marine environment, into the food chain and into our food. Again, there's different science out there. Let's bring it [all] together and look at it. This is a serious issue.

> *Panelist 1:* There are a lot of gaps in information, and science has got both sides of the fence. Your position is noted.

> *Panelist 2:* I respect that you're not a scientist, and you didn't claim to be. You did mention a fact [though] that doesn't coincide with what I've been informed from a scientist. I'd like to know what your source is. Could you quote the source so we could look at that, examine that as a fact? I can't take it from you as a fact, since you admit you're not a scientist.

In this case, as with so many others, officials are unsure how to respond to citizens who are challenging them on matters of science and fact. While the panelists' responses are not dismissive, they are certainly condescending—reasserting the division between citizens (amateurs) and true experts (scientists) as the real authorities on environmental problems.

energy sources on future greenhouse gas emissions (Swart and Weaver 2012). The article found that coal was the biggest potential contributor to global warming. Based on current known reserves, burning all the coal in the world would cause global temperatures to rise by an estimated 15°C, while burning all the known natural gas in the world would cause it to rise by an estimated 3°C; and burning all the oil in the Alberta oil sands would raise global temperatures by 0.36°C. Following publication of the article, former Canadian minister of natural resources Joe Oliver began referring to it in speeches as definitive scientific proof that development of the Alberta oil sands would have a negligible effect on global climate change.

Weaver responded that this was not the intent nor the main conclusion of the article, and wrote an opinion column in the *Toronto Star* explaining his position that "the tar sands remain the largest source of greenhouse gas emission growth in Canada and are the single largest reason Canada is failing to meet its international climate commitments and failing to be a climate leader" (quoted in Munson 2012). Some academics suggested that Weaver should not have published the article at all knowing that it would be misused in this way (e.g., Jaccard 2012). The article continues to be cited by Oliver and other oil sands advocates, despite Weaver's objections, as proof that restricting development in the name of mitigating climate change would be pointless (e.g., Koring 2013).

In other cases, complaints about politicized science refer to the actions of scientists themselves. This is a more serious accusation that implies that a scientist or scientific organization is being dishonest—for instance by choosing research questions and methods that are likely to lead to pre-determined answers. In the natural sciences, however, there are strong incentives against falsifying data ("cooking the books" as it's called), using slippery methods, and skewing discussions of findings. Norms of honesty and objectivity are enforced by mechanisms like peer review of manuscripts, applications for research grants, and career rewards for tenure and promotion at universities. These mechanisms are intended to protect the integrity of science by weeding out cheats and fraudsters. Assuming that they work, why do people inside and outside the scientific community have the impression that science is more politicized today than in the past?

The answer is twofold. First of all, we need to recognize that *there is no such thing as science*. We tend to think about science as being a unified thing or a grand project that, despite being carried out in different fields and laboratories around the world, is propelling human knowledge forward in a linear manner. According to this view, science is a cumulative endeavour—a "great edifice" built brick by brick by scientists toiling on their own particular problems (Shapin 2008a: 7). But science is not a single thing, method, technique, or worldview. Each branch or discipline has its own way of achieving valid and reliable knowledge, its own traditions of peer review, and its own way of distributing rewards and recognition. The sociologist Karin Knorr Cetina demonstrated this in her 1999 book *Epistemic Cultures*, which compared how "knowledge is made" in two distinct disciplines: molecular biology and particle physics. Knorr Cetina found that the two disciplines approach the natural world and the process of experimentation in radically different ways. Particle physicists, who do much of their work using huge multi-billion-dollar equipment such as high energy particle colliders, engage in large-scale collaborations involving hundreds of researchers looking for "anomalies" in the massive amounts of data spewed out by the colliders. Microbiologists, on the other hand, typically work in small labs that are dominated by a single "Principal Investigator" and spend much of their time doing "bench work"—taking samples from plants and animals and looking for consistencies across specimens (rather than anomalies) as their basis for generalization. There is in fact very little common ground between these two disciplines in how they conduct scientific investigation, and even less common ground if we broaden our focus to include all disciplines of the natural sciences. This leads Knorr Cetina to conclude that there is no such thing as a unified "Science with a capital *s*." While different disciplines clearly influence one another, scholars "are now much more dubious of claims that there is anything like a 'scientific method'—a coherent, universal, and efficacious set of procedures for making scientific knowledge" (Shapin 1996: 4). In practice, this means that scientists from different disciplinary backgrounds approach problems and issues differently—using different starting points and research methods—that can lead them to diametrically opposed conclusions that are nonetheless considered scientifically valid by their community of peers.

Moreover, the natural sciences are today undergoing a fresh round of *pluralization* that is further straining the illusion of unity. Traditional disciplines like biology, chemistry, and physics have been joined by new fields like ecology, nuclear science, genomics, bioinformatics, neuroscience, and nanotechnology—each of which are developing their own traditions for producing and evaluating knowledge. Another important change has been the "institutional diffusion" of science that has occurred due to both an increasing supply of science graduates and greater demand for scientific authority in non-traditional organizations (Young and Matthews 2010: 82). Canadian universities are now churning out 14 times more PhD degrees each year than in 1960, while American schools are graduating 7 times more (Chiswick et al. 2010). Needless to say, only a fraction of these graduates end up with regular university appointments. Graduates increasingly end up working for government agencies, corporations, environmental groups, think-tanks, industry associations, lobbyists, consulting companies, and communications firms, all which have come to see scientific knowledge as an important tool in broader political struggles (Stehr and Grundmann 2012).

The second reason why science appears to be more politicized today is because of a recent shift in environmental politics. As discussed in Chapter 3, the anti-environmentalist movement has largely abandoned arguments about the economic benefits of environmental degradation, and adopted a new strategy of attacking the scientific credentials and veracity of their critics. This technique has proven effective in part because mainstream scientists are poor defenders of their work. According to Freudenburg et al. (2008), anti-environmentalist groups have become adept at exploiting scientists' reluctance to attach "claims of certainty" to their work. Science is governed by a series of **norms**—or behavioural expectations—that are instilled in the socialization process (a scientist's training) and enforced by other scientists (in the form of peer pressure and peer review). One of the most important scientific norms is that scientists refrain from overstating or having too much confidence in their findings. In technical terms, this relates to the distinction between **Type I** and **Type II errors**. Freudenburg et al. (2008: 7) summarize it thusly:

> There are basically just two ways in which a scientist can reach a false conclusion: Type I errors are created by accepting hypotheses that are ultimately shown to be wrong, whereas Type II errors are created by rejecting hypotheses that are ultimately shown to be true.

According to Kleinman (2005: 105), scientists live in mortal fear of Type I errors (accepting something as true that is really false), because they can brand them as being careless, biased, or incompetent: "Whereas a false negative can lead a scientist to miss an important discovery, a false positive can hurt an investigator's professional reputation, possibly suggesting that her work in not sufficiently careful." For this reason, scientists avoid saying that *anything* is certain—instead using the language of statistics and probabilities to state that a finding is "suggestive" or "promising" rather than certain.

Anti-environmentalists exploit this by arguing that scientists' lack of certainty is indicative of *uncertainty*, which is definitely not the same thing. If a scientist is 99 per cent confident that exposure to a given chemical is associated with a higher risk of cancer (in statistical terms, $p < .01$), this is a significant finding even if it is not 100 per cent certain. Oreskes and Conway (2011) argue that the technique of sowing doubt through claims of uncertainty was pioneered by the tobacco industry in the 1950s and 1960s, when studies began piling up showing a link between smoking and lung diseases such as cancer and emphysema. In response, the tobacco industry established the neutral-sounding "Council for Tobacco Research" (CTR) in 1958 as a supposedly independent research institute that was entirely funded by tobacco companies. According to documents leaked many years later, the industry saw CTR as a way of keeping anti-smoking findings under wraps while publicizing data that questioned the link between smoking and illness.

> If CTR research were to show high risks from cigarette smoking, the tobacco companies could maintain plausible deniability about their aware-ness of findings that would never be finalized and disseminated [beyond the walls of the institute]. On the other hand, any findings that might undermine the growing scientific consensus about the risks of cigarette

smoking . . . could of course be published and publicized with considerable fanfare. (Freudenburg et al. 2008: 19)

The purpose of CTR science was not to convince people that tobacco
was harmless, but to sow enough doubt about the health effects of smoking that new laws or regulations would seem premature, unnecessary, or
even "irrational." Freudenburg et al. (2008) call this tactic "**Scientific
Certainty Argumentation Methods**" or SCAMs. SCAMs can take on
various forms, but they usually involve highlighting uncertainties about
existing data, pointing out counterfactual or exceptional examples or cases,
proposing alternative interpretations of causation, arguing against the generalizability of a given study, and/or suggesting that more research is needed
before coming to definitive conclusions. These claims rarely appear in credible scientific sources—such as peer reviewed academic journals—but this
doesn't matter because SCAMs aren't targeting the scientific community as
much as journalists, policy-makers, and the general public. In this sense,
there is little cost to eschewing academic journals that are usually only read
by specialists. Instead, SCAM claims are widely disseminated via reports,
press releases, blogs, websites, and listserves hosted by think-tanks, industry
associations, environmentalist groups, and political parties. Their explicit
aim is to confuse and unsettle—to create the impression of uncertainty and
thus block political responses to authentically peer-reviewed scientific findings (Hoggan 2008).

Overall, the apparent politicization of science is having a corrosive
effect on public confidence in science. When scientific-sounding claims
contradict one another in this way, people are forced to decide which voice
is more credible or trustworthy—a distinctively "unscientific" decision that
is based on an evaluation of the *claims-maker* more than the claim itself
(Hannigan 2006: 65). Surveys are showing that the general public is less
and less confident in the ability of science to solve environmental and health
problems, particularly among people who self-identify as being politically
conservative (Gauchat 2012).

Other Ways of Knowing

Despite its cultural dominance, science is not the only way of knowing
about the natural environment. Colonial explorers knew that local people had a special knowledge of the territories they inhabited, and relied
on them to find food, shelter, and resources. Many early anthropologists
also marvelled at the sophisticated knowledge and classification systems
developed by so-called "primitive" or "non-scientific" cultures that allowed
them to simultaneously explain, exploit, and conserve the natural environment (Berkes 2008: 10). For years, however, the stereotype persisted that

while scientific knowledge was "universal"—applicable in all circumstances and able to explain all natural phenomena—local and traditional knowledge was "limited" or "contextual"—applicable only to the specific circumstances in which it is embedded. Recently, however, scholars have become far more aware of the depth and breadth of local and traditional knowledges, seeing them as "different but equal" to Western science in many ways (Frideres 2011: 52).

First, it is now widely recognized that traditional knowledge is empirical (based on observation and experimentation) and not simply anecdotal. According to Fikret Berkes, a Canadian ecologist and one of the world's most respected researchers of local and traditional knowledge, "there is now a great deal of evidence that traditional people do possess a scientific curiosity [that prompts them] to develop knowledge beyond matters of immediate practical interest" (Berkes 2008: 10). Berkes therefore sees a great deal of overlap between Western science and traditional knowledge systems—arguing that both are curiosity-driven, have internal logics and methods, and rules for assessing data and generalizing from observations. The main difference between science and traditional knowledge, therefore, has to do with morals and ethics rather than accuracy and reliability (Frideres 2011: 52). As we saw earlier, Western science tries to separate knowledge from ethics, making a distinction between "is" and "ought." The "is" refers to an (objective) reality found out there, in nature, while "ought" is a political question that belongs to the (subjective) human world. Most traditional knowledge systems make no such distinction, and "tend to have a large moral and ethical context [that stresses] the importance of community, the lack of separation between nature and culture, and commitment or attachment to the local environment as a unique and irreplaceable place" (Berkes 2008: 11).

Second, scholars now recognize that traditional knowledge systems are not as tied to their particular context or environment as once thought. While traditional knowledge is based predominantly on (shared) experiences, they also include broad **cosmologies** that seek to explain "how the world works" at a fundamental level (Frideres 2011: 53). For example, the anthropologists Scott Atran and Douglas Medin (1997) outline the cosmology of indigenous Mayans living on the Yucatan peninsula in Northern Guatemala. The Maya live in a specific environment—a tropical jungle with rich biodiversity and vegetation but poor soils that are easily eroded—and they have an intimate knowledge of how to harvest and farm the jungle responsibly (for instance, by clearing small plots of land, leaving them to fallow for long periods, and leaving hilltops forested to avoid erosion). Behind this knowledge, however, is a cosmology that is *not* restricted to the jungle. The Mayan cosmology conceives of the natural world as a "household," in which humans, animals, and plants co-exist and co-habit, sometimes uneasily (Atran and Medin 1997: 188). Households are not always conflict-free, nor are they egalitarian (the Maya see humans and jaguars as leaders of the household, with other plants and animals playing less important roles). What matters in a household, however, is mutual respect—if one member of the household is angry, disrespected, or abused, everyone suffers. This cosmology serves as a specific guide for Mayan people farming in the jungle. At the same time, however, it is not limited to jungle environments. The Mayan vision of nature as a "household" would apply equally to a temperate forest, a desert, a coastal environment, a city, or wherever else a Mayan person might find themselves. The members of the household might change, but the household cosmology is just as universal and transportable as any metaphor based in Western science (such as "ecosystem," "food web," and "ecological footprint").

In recent years, there has been a movement in Canada and elsewhere to recognize the validity of local, traditional, and experiential knowledges and include them in environmental management and decision-making. This movement has not been entirely voluntary. In 1997, the Supreme Court of Canada accepted the validity of First Nation oral histories as accurate accounts of traditional activities and conditions in the natural world prior to European contact. The *Delgamuukw* decision, as it is known, also required Canadian governments to "meaningfully consult" with First Nations prior to approving development projects that potentially affected Aboriginal rights and title (although the court failed to define what exactly constituted meaningful consultation, thus leaving the door open to future litigation that continues to this day). This provided governments with an incentive to acknowledge local and traditional knowledge and launch several pilot projects involving the **co-management** of territories, natural resources, and ecosystems (Armitage et al. 2007).

Experiences in co-management have been mixed. In theory, co-management implies that governments share responsibility with local communities in the drafting, implementation, and assessment of environmental management plans. Many observers have welcomed co-management as way of getting around the "technocracy problem" discussed earlier and involving local people in environmental decision-making (Brunner et al. 2005). Co-management also involves an implicit recognition of the limits of science in addressing complex problems—by involving non-scientists in decision-making, governments are acknowledging that "science alone" is a limited tool that can only offer partial answers (see Box 9.3).

But co-management has also been criticized for not going far enough in recognizing local and traditional knowledge. In an influential article, Agrawal (1995) argues that efforts to include traditional knowledge in processes already dominated by Western science and bureaucracy usually mean subjugating the former to the latter. Nadasdy (1999; 2005) makes a similar

Box 9.3   "Wicked Problems" and the Limits of Science

In a now-classic article, Rittel and Webber (1973) made a distinction between "tame problems" and "wicked problems." A tame problem is a problem that is relatively straightforward, well-defined, and has a quick and easy technical solution. Unfortunately, many environmental problems are instead wicked problems that resist quick fixes (Murphy 2012). According to Jentoft and Chuenpagdee (2009: 553),

> Problems are wicked when they are difficult to define and delineate from other and bigger problems and when they are not solved once and for all but tend to reappear. . . . Wicked problems have no technical solution, it is not clear when they are solved, and they have no right or wrong solution that can be determined scientifically.

Wicked problems tend to occur at the intersection of nature and society. Jentoft and Chuenpagdee (2009) use fisheries as a key example. The scientific goal of "protecting fisheries" means simultaneously monitoring complex *natural* phenomena (the number of fish in a given population, the vitality of fish habitat, relationships to predators and food sources, and marine pollution levels) and complex *social* phenomena (the behaviour of fishers, poachers, boaters, and tourist operators, as well as the decisions made by municipalities, industries, and landowners regarding sewage, waste management, land use, and port facilities). With this many variables and competing interests in play, it is never clear if and when the problem is "solved," or what "solving it" even means. Instead, wicked problems tend to grind on, generating constant controversy and trying the patience of everyone involved. Jentoft and Chuenpagdee argue that a wicked problem cannot be solved by science alone. Instead, what is needed are flexible, transparent, and inclusive *political* processes that involve stakeholders in all stages of decision-making, from data collection and analysis to enforcement (Jentoft and Chuenpagdee 2009: 555).

point based on years of observing co-management committees and boards in Canada's Yukon territory. He argues that traditional biologists (most of whom work for the federal or territorial government) have real difficulty accepting the validity of traditional knowledge claims that they cannot "verify" using standard scientific methods. In practice, this means that "traditional knowledge is never used as the sole basis for decision-making;

instead, it is used only to confirm the knowledge produced by wildlife biologists and legitimate the decisions made by bureaucratic managers" (Nadasdy 2005: 224).

This is deeply unsatisfactory for holders of traditional knowledge, who are being asked to participate in processes they have little chance of influencing. Occasionally, open conflict breaks out. For example, there has been a long-running dispute between federal scientists and several Inuit communities and organizations in the Canadian Arctic regarding the status of polar bear populations. Polar bears rely on sea ice to hunt, and are therefore highly vulnerable to climate change, which risks cutting their hunting season short and causing "nutritional stress" that can lower a population's reproductive capacity and survival rate (Henri et al. 2010: 276). In 2005, however, Inuit participants in the joint federal–territorial–Inuit co-management board argued that polar bear populations were *increasing* rather than decreasing, and that the annual hunting quota ought to be increased as well (Dowsley and Wenzel 2008). The polar bear hunt is an important Inuit cultural activity, as well as a significant economic resource as many hunters sell polar bear skins and claws to Southern collectors and trophy-hunters. The Inuit members of the co-management board cited testimony from hunters that they were observing more polar bears in their travels and closer to communities. According to Henri et al. (2010: 277), "while Inuit residents have attributed the increase in human–bear encounters around their communities to increases in the polar bear population, scientists suggest that receding ice and longer ice-free summers have concentrated polar bears in areas where humans are more likely to encounter them." Ultimately, the scientists over-ruled the Inuit participants using data from animal-tagging studies that suggested a decline in *some* Arctic populations, and the quota was lowered. This has angered many Inuit, who continue to maintain that polar bear populations in most regions are healthy and increasing (Audla 2012).

Finding the Right Role for Science

Science plays a central role in environmental politics and problem-solving, and this is unlikely to change. All in all, the contributions of the natural sciences to environmentalism should be celebrated. As stated at the outset of this chapter, scientists have helped to discover major environmental problems, encourage the public and policy-makers to take environmental issues seriously, and lend credibility and legitimacy to the environmental movement. But as we've seen throughout this discussion, science is not a perfect guide to a better environmental future. As with any source of authority, scientific knowledge needs to be questioned—both in how it is generated and how it is used. These questions are especially urgent now that scientific claims are increasingly wielded as political weapons—used to establish, legitimize, and discredit political interests masked as environmental "facts."

I argue that one of the major challenges of contemporary environmental politics is to find the right role for science in our collective decision-making about how to treat the natural world. How can we harness the best of science while inoculating ourselves against its worst tendencies and uses? To start, we need to distance ourselves from what Kleinman (2005) calls **scientism**. Scientism refers to the over-glorification of science as the *only* path to knowledge and truth. Scientism encourages technocratic decision-making, as it "leads to the conclusion that only trained scientists—experts at unearthing objective 'facts'—can appropriately participate in decision-making on technical matters" (Kleinman 2005: 4). According to Wynne (2011: 2), scientism permits authorities "to confuse public issues that involve scientific questions with scientific issues [in and of themselves]." At the same time, we have to be careful not to go too far in the other direction—rejecting the legitimacy of science and tipping into relativism. Relativism refers to the idea that all knowledge reflects the values, priorities, and interests of its generators and that all knowledge claims are contextual, incomparable, and by extension equally (in)valid. Considering all scientific claims as equal opens the door for the kind of abuses embodied by professional doubt-sowing and SCAMming that seeks to publicly discredit science that has been validated through peer review. We need tools that help forge a middle ground between scientism and relativism, while allowing non-scientific voices to play as big a role as possible. For reasons of space, I will focus on three suggested ways of achieving this: one that is *attitudinal*, one that is *conceptual*, and one that is *procedural*.

First, sociologist Sheila Jasanoff (2003; 2007) has called for an attitudinal shift among both generators and users of scientific knowledge away from "hubris" and towards "humility." Jasanoff (2003: 239) argues that a hubristic approach to science is based on an "overconfidence in the accuracy and completeness of the pictures it produces." A hubristic attitude sees science as capable of solving all problems and "reassuring a nervous public" that everything is under control. The problem with the hubristic approach is that its inevitable failures create a backlash that diminishes public confidence in science. What is needed is "greater humility about both the limits of scientific knowledge and about when to stop turning to science to solve problems [that require] ethical solutions" (Jasanoff 2007: 33). Jasanoff argues that this attitudinal shift can be facilitated by greater integration of the natural sciences with the humanities, social sciences, and local and traditional ways of knowing: "This call for humility is a plea for policy-makers to cultivate, and for universities to teach, modes of knowing that are often pushed aside in expanding scientific understanding and technological capacity" (Jasanoff 2007: 33). In other words, authorities need to acknowledge what science *does not know* and have the wisdom to allow non-scientific voices to fill these substantial gaps.

Second, Rosa and Clarke (2012) advance a conceptual tool for evaluating competing knowledge claims that they call **epistemological hierarchicalism** (epistemology refers to "ways of knowing"; and hierarchicalism, to ranking or evaluation). The purpose of epistemological hierarchicalism is to suggest a way to distinguish good knowledge claims from bad ones without falling back into scientism:

> Epistemological hierarchicalism sees all knowledge claims as fallible, but denies that all knowledge claims are *equally* fallible. If all knowledge claims were equally fallible (or equally valid), we all would be living behind a veil of ignorance where there would be no knowledge at all. Hierarchicalism allows for variation in the quality of knowledge claims along a continuum, ranging from those characterized by considerable agreement to those characterized by great disagreement. (Rosa and Clarke 2012: 44)

By looking at levels of agreement, we free ourselves from the (artificial) need for certainty or consensus that anti-environmental groups seize on to argue against action. This approach allows us to distinguish between claims that are *honestly* disputed (such as the health of polar bear populations in the Arctic) and those that are *spuriously* disputed (such as the link between smoking and cancer). It puts the onus back on a "weight of evidence" judgment without insisting that this evidence be unanimous or come only from the natural sciences.

Third, Callon et al. (2009) suggest a procedural shift in how environmental science is conducted. Like Jasanoff, Callon and colleagues argue that policy-makers run into trouble when they presume that science can solve problems on its own. To remedy this, they propose that stakeholders be involved in all stages of scientific discovery—from setting research goals to formulating research questions to interpreting the results (similar arguments are also made by Gibbons et al. 1996; Brown 2009; and Wynne 2011). Callon and colleagues argue that the enthusiasm of laypersons or "citizen-experts" (see Box 9.2) means that they are often better informed about an issue than are experts who have only "specialized knowledge" based on their discipline and training:

> It is absurd to contrast lay knowledge and expert knowledge by resorting to terms like rationality and irrationality, objective knowledge and subjective beliefs. In many cases, the opposite is true. Conservatism,

stubbornness, absence of intellectual openness, and the refusal to welcome the unexpected are all found on the side of the experts. Boldness, attention to novelty, and the spirit of innovation are the qualities found in the laypersons' camp. (Callon et al. 2009: 80)

According to this view, the inclusion of non-experts in the scientific process makes science *more creative*, more responsive to societal needs, and ultimately more legitimate. Instead of delivering fully formed and scientifically tested "facts" to the people, Callon et al. argue that universities, funding agencies, governments, and even the private sector should be encouraging what they call "research in the wild" (i.e., research with full public participation) as a way of bridging the gap between different types of knowledge.

Conclusion

Science is an extremely useful tool that helps us to understand environmental problems and identify potential solutions. Science, however, is not a perfect source of knowledge nor is it a perfect guide to action. Science occupies a special place in Western culture as a privileged path to knowledge and truth, which has led to its misuse in the political sphere. On the one hand, government's willingness to harness the authority of science has led to a "democratic deficit" on many important environmental issues. Relying on experts to formulate policy behind closed doors pre-empts important public discussions on new technologies, industries, and developments. On the other hand, the ongoing pluralization of science is broadening the range of credible scientific claims (as disciplines, methods, and data sources grow and diversify) and providing political actors with access to a broad pool of scientific talent. These developments, along with changes in anti-environmentalist strategies such as doubt-sowing and SCAMming, give the impression that science is becoming increasingly "politicized," which in turn lowers public confidence in science to help solve environmental problems.

All of this points to the urgent need to "find the right role" for science in environmental politics. This means de-centring it, to allow more room for local, traditional, and experiential ways of knowing—which are increasingly recognized as valid and valuable forms of knowledge with much to contribute. It also means reorienting how we think about scientific evidence. Rather than insisting on certainty prior to acting—something that scientists are unwilling to give and anti-environmentalists are eager to exploit—we should be basing decisions on the weight of available evidence and democratic input from all sources.

Questions for Critical Thought

1. Can facts and values be separated (as assumed in Western science) or are they inherently joined (as assumed in traditional knowledge cultures)?

2. Do you think that science is becoming more politicized?

3. What is "the right role" for science in environmental decision-making?

Suggested Readings

Berkes, Fikret. (2008). *Sacred Ecology*, 2nd edition. New York: Routledge. This is the best introduction to local and traditional knowledge systems available. Berkes, a Canadian ecologist, draws on his vast experience working with indigenous peoples to outline the similarities and differences between traditional knowledge and Western science. A must-read.

Freudenburg, William, Gramling, Robert, and Davidson, Debra. (2008). "Scientific certainty argumentation methods (SCAMs): Science and the politics of doubt," *Sociological Inquiry* 78 (1), 2–38. Freudenburg and colleagues outline the ways that anti-environmental groups use claims about uncertainty to discredit legitimate scientists.

Pielke Jr., Roger A. (2007). *The Honest Broker: Making Sense of Science in Policy and Politics*. New York: Cambridge University Press. An easy read that outlines the different roles that science takes in decision-making, this volume puts heavy emphasis on the attitudes and interests of both the scientists who produce knowledge and government officials who receive it.

Shapin, Steven. (2010). *Never Pure: Historical Studies of Science as if It Was Produced by People with Bodies, Situated in Time, Space, Culture, and Society, and Struggling for Credibility and Authority*. Baltimore: John's Hopkins University Press. Shapin is a historian and sociologist of science who analyzes both the culture and the structure of science. This myth-shattering book gives fresh perspective on the special authority that science enjoys in today's world, tracing it back to the struggles of real and fallible people trying to establish science as a meaningful source of knowledge in a largely traditional world.

Suggested Websites

American Association for the Advancement of Science (AAAS)
www.aaas.org
An organization that seeks to "advance science and serve society," the AAAS website and annual conference are interesting forums for discussion about the broader impacts of science on policy, people, and the social good.

Inuit Tapiriit Kanatami (ITK)
www.itk.ca
ITK is an organization representing the 55,000 Inuit people living in Canada's Arctic. Its website contains a wealth of information regarding traditional Inuit knowledge of the Arctic.

10   Disaster, Shock, and Resilience

Key Points

◎   Natural disasters have always been with us, but they are becoming more costly in human lives and financial capital, leading some to argue that we are currently living in an unprecedented "age of disasters."

◎   Sociologists argue that the effects of natural disasters are determined more by human decision-making and socio-political structures than by nature itself.

◎   Some people and societies are far more vulnerable to natural disasters than others, and these divisions usually reflect established social inequalities.

◎   As global environmental change accelerates, resilience and adaptation at both the community and societal level become more important.

Introduction

No matter how technologically advanced human societies become, the natural world still has the power to surprise us, overwhelm us, harm us, and turn us into helpless, powerless victims of forces beyond our control. This is the usual media narrative in the immediate aftermath of **natural disasters** such as hurricanes, tornadoes, earthquakes, volcanic eruptions, fires, and floods. When such events happen, readers and viewers are invited to marvel at the raw destructive power of nature, to sympathize with and pity the human victims of such unpredictable "acts of God," and to help in whatever small way they can by donating money, food, blankets, and blood. This narrative has some truth to it. Geological and atmospheric forces are both unpredictable and powerful, and natural disasters have a way of shocking us (however temporarily) out of the modernist assumption that we are masters of nature and in control of our own destinies.

Increasingly, however, sociologists who study natural disasters argue that their scale, severity, and short- and long-term consequences have more to do with *human* decisions and socio-political structures than with the natural world per se. It is human decision-making, for instance, that leads to the building of cities on floodplains (Winnipeg) and river deltas (New Orleans); and it is the overvaluing of ocean-front property that leaves hundreds of millions vulnerable to storm surges and tsunami. As we will see in this chapter, natural disasters are points of intense interaction between nature and society that tell us a lot about ourselves. Disasters tend to be revealing: showing both our better angels (in the form of help, altruism, and community resilience) and our worst mistakes (in the form of system breakdown, conflict, inequality, and corruption). Perhaps most importantly, natural disasters shine a light on possible futures for humanity. For reasons both natural and social, disasters are becoming more frequent, more intense, and more expensive. How we choose to tackle this problem of increasing **vulnerability** will have long-term consequences down the road.

The Age of Disasters

Natural disasters have always been with us. Rapid-onset disasters such as cyclones (hurricanes) have plagued South Asia for millennia, killing hundreds of people each year and occasionally taking thousands and tens of thousands of lives. In the year AD 115, the ancient city of Antioch in modern-day Turkey was hit by a massive earthquake that killed an estimated 260,000 people—a staggering number given the small Eurasian population at the time. Slow-onset disasters such as famines were just as deadly in the Ancient World as they are today, and disease epidemics more so (see Chapter 6).

Despite this, it is plausible to argue that we live in an "age of disasters" today that is unparalleled in human history (Alexander 1997). To be clear, this does *not* mean that the sheer number of natural events is increasing. Various agencies around the world keep track of the number of natural disasters that occur in any given year, and these typically show that 4–5 times more disasters occur today than in 1960 (Smith 2001: 32; Hilhorst and Bankoff 2004). However, much of this increase has to do with improvements in reporting and greater incentives for communities to declare "states of emergencies" in order to access national and international aid. What *is* increasing, however, is the overall impact of natural disasters—both in terms of human lives and financial capital. As global population continues to grow, more people are living in more marginal places. These marginal places—which can be rural or urban (in slums, for instance)—are typically poorly serviced, have little or no "first response" emergency infrastructure, and have homes and workplaces that are poorly constructed using salvaged or second-rate materials. Over 90 per cent of fatalities from natural disasters over the last 100 years have occurred in the developing world, suggesting that there is a significant global imbalance in vulnerability to natural events (Gregg and Houghton 2006: 21). Disasters are also becoming more expensive, eating up a greater share of public and private resources. In this case, however, the most expensive disasters occur in developed, rather than developing nations, where housing and infrastructure is more costly to replace and where citizens expect their governments to underwrite private

Box 10.1

Same Disaster, Different Outcomes:
A Tale of Two Earthquakes

On 17 October 1989, millions people in North America were settling in to watch Game Three of the World Series between the San Francisco Giants and the Oakland Athletics, when the pregame show on ABC television was interrupted by static, shouting, and broadcaster Al Michaels exclaiming "I think we're having an earth—" before the screen went blank. At that moment, an earthquake measuring 7.1 on the Richter scale hit just south of San Francisco, violently shaking one of the most densely populated regions in the United States, home to about 5.5 million people. While the media predictably focused on the damage, including the collapse of a 50-foot section of the San Francisco–Oakland Bay Bridge, the real story was in fact how little damage was done. Stringent building codes ensured that recently built homes and workplaces withstood the tremors, and Candlestick Park (where 60,000 people were about to watch a baseball game) had just been seismically retrofitted the year before. A total of 63 people were killed by the quake, with approximately 4,000 injured and an equal number left homeless.

On 12 January 2010, an almost identical earthquake struck just north of Port-au-Prince, the capital and most populous city in the Caribbean nation of Haiti. The earthquake measured 7.0 on the Richter scale, and struck at almost the exact same time of day (five o'clock in the afternoon). But while the San Francisco earthquake of 1989 killed 63 people, the 2010 Haitian earthquake killed approximately 220,000.[1] A quarter of a million homes collapsed in the shaking, as did tens of thousands of commercial and government buildings. Rescue efforts were hindered by a lack of heavy equipment, and hospitals were overwhelmed by the injured seeking treatment. Looking

insurance and provide total compensation for lost property. Hurricane Katrina, which struck New Orleans in August 2005, cost the public and private sector $149 billion US just to deal with its immediate aftermath (Hallegatte 2008).

The argument that we live in an age of disasters is therefore more about *context* than *frequency*. The same number of major earthquakes are likely happening today as in the past, but their effects are magnified because more people and property are exposed to earthquake hazards than in the past (see Box 10.1). The same is true for storms and floods. The real damage done by Hurricane Katrina was not the high winds but the storm surge that punched holes in the engineered levees that were intended to protect the city, allowing water from the Gulf of Mexico and Lake Pontchartrain to pour into New Orleans. However, Freudenburg et al. (2009) point out at the two examples, another tragic difference stands out. While the cities of the San Francisco Bay Area quickly rebuilt and returned to normal, recovery in Port-au-Prince and in Haiti more generally has been painstakingly slow (Kolbe et al. 2010). Haiti, the poorest country in the Western hemisphere, continues to suffer from the earthquake and will for years to come.

These two cases illustrate what sociologists mean when they argue that natural disasters are "sociological events" shaped by human decisions and structures (Murphy 2009). Sociologist Nicole Youngman (2009) argues that the impact of a natural disaster is determined by three things—the characteristics of the natural environment, the characteristics of the built environment, and human social and political systems. With respect to the natural environment, the two cases are almost identical. Both earthquakes occurred at shallow depths (making them particularly powerful) and very close to densely populated areas. The key differences are therefore in the built environment and socio-political systems. The built environment in Port-au-Prince proved deadly on the day of the earthquake and its immediate aftermath, as many poor people were crushed or buried in homes they either built themselves or were constructed by unregulated contractors. A lack of urban planning also meant that streets that were already narrow and winding became impassable either for rescue vehicles or for people seeking help. Corruption also played a role, as unscrupulous builders skirted regulations over many years by bribing officials—which likely explains the widespread collapse of major commercial and government buildings (Bell 2012: 239). Finally, Wilson (2012: 31) argues that the long dictatorship of the Duvalier family (1957–86) eroded Haiti's economic and institutional capacity to respond to the earthquake. After decades of exclusion and oppression, Haitians lacked the physical tools, services, and wealth to rebound quickly—thus leaving the country dependent on foreign experts and aid.

that the real culprit was decades of reckless development. Historically, New Orleans benefited from protection by natural swamps and wetlands surrounding the city that were destroyed to make way for urban sprawl and the development of offshore oil wells. The loss of these wetlands meant that there was nothing to slow the storm surge down on its way into the city, leaving the levees to bear the full brunt of rapidly moving water (the levees were burst rather than inundated). In other words, Hurricane Katrina as a natural event could have easily happened in 1925 instead of 2005, but it would not have done the damage it did. This mistake is being repeated all over the world, most notably in tropical zones where the destruction of coastal mangroves (aquatic forests) to make room for aquaculture and ocean-front housing is epidemic (Warne 2011). These human decisions are increasing our vulnerability to normally occurring natural events, suggesting that there will be many more Hurricane Katrinas in an age of disasters.

Finally, we need to acknowledge the real possibility that human activities will have a direct impact on the character, frequency, and severity of natural disasters in the future. Climate change is already causing sea levels to rise, and we simply don't know how the oceans and atmosphere will respond to warming temperatures. While scientists are reluctant to draw direct parallels between climate change and specific weather events, one likely outcome is that weather patterns will become more difficult to predict. Hurricane Sandy, which had an unexpectedly strong impact on New York City and devastated Staten Island and the New Jersey shore in October 2012, followed a highly unusual track before making landfall, leading some to speculate that climate change will wreak havoc not only with the weather but our ability to anticipate major events (e.g., Freedman 2013).

Individual and Collective Responses to Disaster

Each disaster is unique, and people react to them in different ways. One of the most consistent findings in disaster research, however, is that people tend to react altruistically to catastrophes, especially those that have a quick or unexpected onset. This contradicts the most prevalent **disaster myth** in popular culture—that people respond selfishly to disasters, taking them as opportunities to steal, loot, and commit violence:

> It has been illustrated time and again that very little panic, looting or other anti-social behaviour takes place during disaster. . . . Instead of reacting in an anti-social manner, individuals and groups typically become more cohesive and unified during situations of collective stress. (Drabek and McEntire 2003: 99)

Simply put, one of the most predictable individual responses to disaster is to help others. Research on large-scale disasters like earthquakes and floods suggest that around 80–85 per cent of the lives saved immediately following a disaster are due to the efforts of ordinary people using their hands to move rubble or pull others to safety (Delicia-Willison and Gaillard 2012). The dramatic professional rescues that occur days and even weeks after an event are rare even though they garner significant media attention. Most people are saved by their neighbours, relatives, and strangers who are the real "first responders" on the scene. According to Drabek and McEntire (2003), people show a remarkable capacity to self-organize during disasters, coordinating their efforts and creating spontaneous systems for communication, rescue, triage, and evacuation (see also Stallings and Quarantelli 1985). This collectivist spirit also extends to non-critical events, such as the massive electrical failure that blacked out a broad swath of central Canada and the Northeastern United States in August of 2003, including the cities of Toronto and New York. As subways failed and traffic lights went out, ordinary people in both cities started directing traffic by hand and offering rides to stranded commuters. As New York City braced for a hot summer night in total darkness, the 24-hour news networks sent helicopters equipped with infrared cameras to circle the city, hoping to record an orgy of looting and crime that never materialized. To the frustration of the media, people overwhelmingly responded to the "disaster" by behaving themselves and being nice to one another.

There are some important exceptions to this tendency. People will usually accept significant danger to themselves to help others, for instance by clambering over unstable rubble. However, some disasters pit people directly against each other for survival—and this leads to very different behaviour. In a famine, for instance, a morsel consumed by you diminishes my own chances of surviving—which unfortunately lessens the chances that I will share or help. Similarly, a fire in a building with a small number of exits (as is often seen in nightclubs, apartment buildings, and factories in many developing countries) frequently leads to panic, competition, and trampling rather than orderly behaviour and mutual help. Research by sociologist Kai Erikson (1976; 1994) highlights another exception—when disasters are caused by humans rather than nature. The key case for Erikson is the Buffalo Creek disaster, which occurred in West Virginia in 1972. A local coal-mining company had built a tailings (waste) pond high in the hills overlooking Buffalo Creek, and after a particularly heavy rainfall the artificial dam burst and 16 villages downstream were washed away by a "terrifying black wall of water" that killed 125 people (Erikson 1994: 12). The mining company refused to accept blame for the accident, claiming that "the dam was simply incapable of holding the water God poured into it" that day (Erikson 1994: 19). Erikson argues that instead of encouraging solidarity, human-caused disasters are corrosive to communities, who have to struggle to secure compensation and are victimized over a long period of time by the legal wrangling and procedural morass that is rarely evoked in a true natural disaster. Communities are also often internally divided; some people go back to work for the responsible party, or accept limited compensation, while others continue to press for redress.

We also have to be careful to distinguish between disasters and their aftermath. While altruism rules in the early hours and days following a disaster, the weeks, months, and years that follow are more difficult to predict. The aim of most disaster relief is a "return to normalcy" in as short a time as possible (Lizarralde et al. 2010). If recovery is delayed, however, social tensions can quickly rise. Access to aid is often highly unequal. Wealthier citizens typically have better resources following a disaster (such as access to cash, transportation, and officials), meaning that they frequently receive preferential access to medical care and disaster relief over poorer people. Women and ethnic minorities also frequently have difficulty accessing services, particularly in traditional societies (Sultana 2010). Disasters that occur in conflict zones can also ratchet up tensions and inequalities. Humanitarian groups often naively assume that the "social solidarity" that arises immediately following a disaster will continue indefinitely. For example, the 2004 Indian Ocean tsunami that killed over 230,000 people caused a momentary lull in the long-running civil war in Sri Lanka. According to Kleinfeld (2007), international aid groups tried to encourage this "silver lining" by flooding the region with money and relief. Unfortunately, the aid itself became a further source of competition between the government and Tamil rebels, causing a re-escalation of the fighting that ultimately hampered civilian recovery.

Tensions can also rise beyond the disaster area. For instance, people who are displaced by a disaster can quickly lose their status as "victims" and become "problems" in the eyes of host communities concerned about squatting, homelessness, and strain on health and welfare services (Wisner et al. 2012: 30). Many people displaced by Hurricane Katrina chose to remain in cities such as Houston and Atlanta—particularly poor black families who lost whatever (often uninsured) property they owned in New Orleans and saw little reason to return (Fussell et al. 2010). These cities, however, offered few legitimate job opportunities for Katrina's refugees. Many displaced people lived in hotel rooms and temporary shelters, hindering their ability to apply for jobs (Crowley 2006). Poor people also typically rely on family and friends for child care, networks that were left behind in the wake of the storm. In the weeks and months after Katrina, the local media in host cities began running stories about crime sprees committed by migrants from New Orleans. While official statistics showed only a small rise in overall crime rates, the victims of Katrina found themselves unfairly stigmatized in their new cities—raising new barriers to their return to normalcy (Varano et al. 2010).

Vulnerability to Disaster

As argued earlier, disasters are revealing—showing both the strengths and the weaknesses of the societies they impact. While no nation or group is immune to disaster, there are vast differences in vulnerability to harm. Generally speaking, wealthier nations have better systems of disaster preparedness and response than poorer countries, although this is not always the case. Following the massive earthquake off the coast of Sendai, Japan (8.9 on the Richter scale), in 2011, the world watched in horror as engineers worked desperately to avert a meltdown at the Fukushima nuclear power plant that had been crippled by the quake and resulting tsunami. While a great deal of radiation was released, it was only the heroism and luck of the nuclear technicians trapped in the plant that stopped an epic catastrophe from unfolding. In this case, the highly developed technology of a wealthy country made the disaster worse (see Box 10.2).

Studies of vulnerability usually highlight differences at the *individual* and *societal* levels. At the individual level, we know that adult males are more likely to survive disasters than women, children, and the elderly (Neumayer and Plumper 2007). Some of this has to do with biology. On average, men have more upper body strength than women, which provides them with greater ability to "self-rescue." In flash-floods, for example, the ability to hold on to structures or to keep one's head above water is directly related to arm and torso strength— meaning that more women and children typically die in these events than men (Cannon 2002). Neumayer

Box 10.2

Have We Become More Helpless? The Loss of Redundancy and General Skills in Wealthy Countries

Perrow (1999) argues that one of the best antidotes to "normal accidents" is redundancy. In engineering, this means designing fail safes and backups that can pick up the slack and prevent problems from cascading throughout the system. It is interesting to speculate if this is true for social systems as well. As sociologist Émile Durkheim noted long ago, one of the hallmarks of a modern society is specialization via the division of labour. Complex societies have many roles that, if properly performed, allow us to increase efficiency and enhance the collective good. But the division of labour is getting more and more refined. The rise of the knowledge economy and globalization means that most Canadians now work in the service economy, far removed from the natural world. My grandparents built their own house, tended an enormous vegetable garden that provided food for much of the year, and fixed their own car. I do none of these things, and neither do most people. Skills that used to be common (i.e., redundant) have become specialized— held by fewer people. This raises the question of how vulnerable we in the developed world are to truly catastrophic events—ones that disrupt systems for a long period of time (Homer-Dixon 2006). How many urbanites really know how to build a fire outdoors? To identify wild plants that are digestible and safe to eat? To repair clothing? These are common skills in the developing world, but they are being stamped out in wealthy countries by our lifestyle choices and economic pressures to develop evermore specialized skills. We are losing our ability to "pick up the slack," and in the process putting an awful lot of faith in our systems to keep working as they should.

and Plumper (2007) also point to socio-cultural reasons for women's high vulnerability. In many traditional societies, girls are not taught to swim or climb, and adult women are encumbered by traditional dress codes that reduce mobility. Women are also more likely to be in or around the home at the time of a disaster strike, which can dramatically increase vulnerability. When the Indian Ocean tsunami of 2004 struck, many of the men living in coastal villages were out at sea fishing. Tsunami waves are often imperceptible in the ocean and only rise as they approach shore and the energy breaks against land. As a result, three to four times more women died in the tsunami than men (Pittaway et al. 2007). In much of the world, women are also the primary caregivers for children and the elderly, and are more likely to be with dependants at the time of a disaster strike—often choosing to remain with them rather than flee. Women are also more vulnerable in the long aftermath of disasters, and suffer much higher post-disaster mortality than men (Neumayer and Plumper 2007). Refugee camps and temporary housing are notorious havens for sexual violence (Fisher 2010). In disasters that cause scarcity in food and water, men are better able to outmuscle others and hoard these resources, leaving women and children in highly precarious situations (Neumayer and Plumper 2007).

Societal-level vulnerability is not quite as clear-cut. As we have seen throughout this chapter, poor nations suffer far more acutely in disasters and take longer to recover than do wealthy ones. Disaster planning, response, and recovery take a tremendous amount of resources. While developed countries usually draw on domestic wealth to rebuild (including their governments' capacity to borrow), developing countries are forced to rely on foreign aid—which is often inadequate, late, and comes with onerous conditions to satisfy foreign governments that their help is not being "squandered" (Berke et al. 2008). But the relationship between vulnerability and development is not linear. Most people who die in earthquakes, for example, are killed by falling debris—usually from the structures they are in or near. An earthquake that hits a so-called "primitive society" is therefore unlikely to cost many lives. While it may sound a bit facile, having a grass hut collapse on your head is preferable to having stone, brick, or concrete do the same. Sociologist Raymond Murphy provides another counter-intuitive example. His book *Leadership in Disaster* (2009) chronicles the unexpectedly severe ice storm that hit Ontario, Quebec, and New York State in January 1998. The storm paralyzed Montreal, Quebec City, Ottawa, and Kingston for days. More critically, the storm knocked out key infrastructure including electricity—anyone who lived through the storm remembers the iconic images of electricity transmission towers crumpling like origami under the weight of the ice. Following the storm the temperature plummeted, and many people were left without the ability to heat their homes. Central air furnaces would not work, and many newer homes were built with gas-burning fireplaces (whose blowers require electricity) rather than wood-burning ones. Gas stations soon ran out of fuel, meaning that even back-up generators went dead. Farms in the region suffered catastrophic losses, as automatic heating, feeding, and milking systems failed. The one population that did not suffer, however, were the Amish (sometimes also referred to as Old Order Mennonites). The Amish belong to a conservative religious order that eschews modern technology, including cars, machines, computers, and even electricity (although there are exceptions to this, such as using battery power on buggy lamps for safety). Amish communities are typically rural and agricultural, using traditional tools and practices. As such, the storm had little impact on their *systems*: homes could still be heated, food could still be prepared, livestock could still be cared for. The disaster simply passed them by. Murphy argues that there are profound lessons in this. In this case, vulnerability was *created by* the technologies and luxuries associated with economic development. Technologies of efficiency and convenience, such as central air, electric ovens, gas fireplaces, and urban sprawl, became big liabilities in this disaster; while the "less developed" lifestyles of the Amish were unaffected.

Murphy's case study raises interesting questions about vulnerability. Generally speaking, developed nations rely on complex systems to reduce vulnerability. For example, emergency responders rely on communications, electricity, and road systems to help others; while citizens do the same to learn about threats, stock up on supplies, or evacuate. But what if these complex modern systems are themselves vulnerable? In 1984, sociologist Charles Perrow published a book entitled *Normal Accidents*, which had a significant impact on the field of disaster studies (Perrow 1999). Perrow argues that as systems become more complex, they become more vulnerable to failure. To take an everyday example, cars have been made more "functional" compared to 30 years ago by the addition of computers, circuit boards, cameras, and mechanical functions like automatic door locks and windows. At the same time, however, these additions mean that a car can break down in more ways than it used to. In the past, an electrical problem in a car could usually fixed by buying a new fuse and inserting it by hand; now, it requires a complex diagnostic by specialists who may prescribe new hardware, software, or a combination of the two. More complexity means more opportunity to fail—accidents (i.e., failures) become a "normal" event in the operation of the system. Additionally, Perrow argues that failure is more likely in systems that are "**tightly coupled**"—where a problem in one part of the system quickly cascades through others (Perrow 1999: 90). Again, consider the example of electricity. In recent years, electricity has become far more important than it used to be for the functioning of other systems. An electrical failure no longer just affects household appliances, but also computing—which in turn affects everything from aircraft control to communications to finance. Think about how electricity affects banking via computing. Before computers were widespread (as late as the 1980s), account balances were kept on paper ledgers, and people typically lined up at the local branch with deposit/withdrawal slips and paper bankbooks in hand. In an extended blackout, banks could conceivably use their paper records to keep taking deposits and processing withdrawals so long as they had money in the vaults. Today, they absolutely cannot. Banking has become embedded in computing systems which are in turn embeddeded in electrical systems. Failure at any one of these levels cascades through the overall system—ATMs would go dead, tellers would have no idea how much money is in what account, and Internet-enabled debit and credit cards would be rendered useless. Electricity and computing have made banking more convenient, efficient, and profitable—but arguably a lot more vulnerable as well. How much cash do you have in your pocket right now? Is it enough to ride out even a short-term failure in any of these systems?

In summary, vulnerability is easier to assess at the individual than at the societal level. Individual vulnerability tends to follow established patterns of inequality in a given society, meaning that the poor, ethnic minorities, women, children, and the elderly are the most vulnerable during and after a disaster. This was dramatically demonstrated in the Indian Ocean tsunami and in Hurricane Katrina, when wealthy people abandoned New Orleans before the storm hit while poorer people, many of whom were black and did not have access to private vehicles, stayed behind (Haney et al. 2010). Assessing vulnerability at the societal level, however, is not so clear-cut. On the one hand, wealthy societies are better able to protect themselves and recover from *predictable* disasters. As we saw in Box 10.1, far fewer people died in the San Francisco earthquake of 1989 than the near-identical 2010 earthquake in Port-au-Prince, due in large part to better infrastructure, preparedness, and emergency response. On the other hand, wealthy societies rely on increasingly complex and tightly coupled systems to perform everyday social and economic tasks—systems that are highly vulnerable to *unpredictable* events such as the 1998 ice storm and the 2011 nuclear crisis in Japan. The bare fact of the matter is that all societies are vulnerable to shocks and disasters of one kind or another, and are likely to become more vulnerable as global population continues to rise and environmental problems like deforestation, coastal degradation, and climate change worsen. This has led many scholars to broaden their perspective on vulnerability and look at **resilience**, or the ability of social and natural systems to respond to changes without breaking down. That's what we'll consider next.

Resilience and Adaptation

Discussions of social resilience borrow heavily from recent developments in ecology and ecosystem science. In the early days of ecology, scientists assumed that ecosystems were stable phenomena that developed linearly towards a state of balance or equilibrium (Folke 2006). The classic example, which is still used in some textbooks, is that of a forest that has been disturbed by fire. The forest recovers in stages—first the grasses regenerate, which eventually give way to bushes and fast-growing trees, which eventually give way to the mature canopy of tall trees that anchor the nutrient and water cycles of the whole forest and *voilà*, the ecosystem has recovered. This kind of linear thinking has proven problematic. As we saw in Chapter 7, the Canadian government assumed that the Atlantic cod fishery could be managed this way—that huge amounts of cod could be removed from the Grand Banks ecosystem, and that the stocks would rebound if given enough time. Instead of returning to its earlier state, however, the ecosystem appears to have qualitatively changed, leaving less room for Atlantic cod (Finlayson and McCay 1999). The shock was too much, and the ecosystem *transformed* rather than *recovered* (Gunderson and Holling 2002).

Cases such as this one have led ecologists to rethink their assumptions, and to see ecosystems as more dynamic and variable than before (Davidson 2010). Ecosystems are now thought to have *multiple possible equilibriums* rather than just one. This is illustrated schematically in Figure 10.1. The circle in the two images in Figure 10.1 can be thought of as a ball resting in a groove. Under the older assumption, it was thought that pressure could be brought to bear on an ecosystem (that the ball could be rolled up either side of the groove) and if the pressure was not so great that it destroyed the ecosystem, it would recover (the ball would roll back to the bottom). The new assumption, however, is that ecosystems can recover from certain

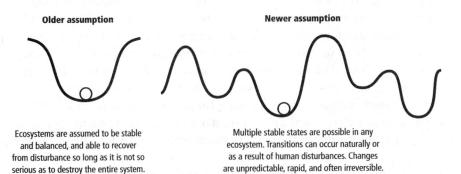

Older assumption	Newer assumption
Ecosystems are assumed to be stable and balanced, and able to recover from disturbance so long as it is not so serious as to destroy the entire system.	Multiple stable states are possible in any ecosystem. Transitions can occur naturally or as a result of human disturbances. Changes are unpredictable, rapid, and often irreversible.

Figure 10.1 Older and Newer Assumptions about the Reaction of Ecosystems to Disturbances
Source: Based on Gunderson and Holling (2002: 11–13)

disturbances, but that at some point there is a qualitative switch-over—the ball is pushed to the point that it leaves the groove and comes to rest in another. The original stable state is lost, and a new reality emerges.

These ideas have been picked up by social scientists interested in knowing how individuals, communities, and societies respond to big environmental changes—be they sudden disasters or slow-onset transformations such as droughts, famines, or climate change (Magis 2010; Wilson 2012). "Resilience," therefore, is not just about "returning to normal," but adapting to changes that may be permanent (Adger 2000). Most social scientists therefore conceptualize resilience as "the capacity of a system to absorb disturbance while undergoing change to retain essentially the same function" (Wilson 2012: 15). In other words, a community is resilient if it retains its function (as a cohesive, peaceful, prosperous home to its residents) despite shocks or changes. Sometimes this will mean "recovering" to its original state, and sometimes adapting or even *transforming* itself to reflect new realities (Engle 2011).

The application of ecological notions of resiliency to human populations is controversial. Davidson (2010), for instance, points out that humans have special capacities for learning, anticipation, and collective action that plants and animals do not. More fundamentally, studies of resilience sometimes seem to imply that it is *up to* communities to drag themselves out of trouble, thus ignoring the role that governments and private industry have played in causing environmental changes and thus increasing vulnerability. These critiques are valid, but they don't negate the fact that local resilience is critically important in an age of disasters and broad environmental change. With this in mind, let's review what resiliency research has found.

The work of geographer W. Neil Adger has probably had the broadest impact on the study of resiliency in human communities. Adger argues that communities and regions with a broad diversity of social, economic, and ecological assets are better equipped to deal with environmental changes than those that are dependent on a narrow range of assets. For example, a single-industry town dependent on forestry is much more vulnerable to climate shifts than one that has a variety of occupations and sectors (Adger 2000: 351). The same is true for governance. Societies with authoritarian governments usually do poorly in disasters, because the government forbids community and civil society groups from forming and excludes the citizenry from political decision-making—which hampers the ability of people to self-organize in response to shock or change (Adger 2003). Adger (2006: 274) also argues that traditional knowledge or "social memory" is a significant resource for adaptation and resilience, because it provides a guide for dealing with change and variability. Traditional knowledge and social memory help to keep skills alive—such as hunting, foraging, and farming—that can become critical in an emergency (see Box 10.2).

Political scientist Arun Agrawal (2010) has performed one of the most comprehensive studies to date of adaptation to environmental change. Agrawal used the United Nations' "Coping Strategies Database," which has archived 118 cases of severe community disruptions due to environmental changes, such as drought and crop failure, to identify several key variables in successful adaptations to these events. According to this research, successful adaptation usually involves one or more of the following responses: mobility (moving away from disaster regions and troublespots), storage (conserving and sheltering essential resources like food and water from the crisis), diversification (having a range of food sources, occupations, and skills in the community), communal pooling (sharing of available resources), and access to external markets (the ability to buy or receive supplies from unaffected areas). Of all these options, mobility is likely the least desirable, because it uproots communities and creates **environmental refugees** who must be resettled elsewhere. Unfortunately, Agrawal found that migration was frequently used as a coping strategy by the poor, while wealthier communities were more likely to rely on storage and access to external markets.

Resiliency scholars also pay attention to what Magis (2010) refers to as "**community capitals**." Capital refers to an asset that can be drawn upon to achieve a goal. The most obvious form is financial capital (money), but there is also human capital, social capital, and natural capital. Human capital refers to the skills, knowledge, and credentials that exist within a community; social capital, to the relations of trust and solidarity that facilitate collective action; and natural capital, to the biological and physical resources that exist in or near a community. High levels of community capital allow residents more choices and flexibility in how they respond to change (Magis 2010: 404). For example, communities with high levels of human capital are able to imagine what alternative futures might look like, and use social capital as a means of collectively articulating and pursuing these goals (Young 2012). Alternatively, communities with significant stores of financial and natural capital might be able to fund a transition from an economy based on fishing to one based on tourism, as is being attempted in many communities in the Maritimes and British Columbia (George et al. 2009).

Resiliency, however, is not a given even under ideal circumstances. Communities and regions that are subject to multiple shocks or a series of dramatic environmental changes may never recover (Wisner et al. 2012). For example, each year an estimated 12 million hectares of productive farmland is lost worldwide due to erosion, desertization, and urban development (Montgomery 2007: 174). This loss is permanent, and it is difficult to imagine how farming communities can viably adapt to such a radical transformation. Examples such as this illustrate the importance of mitigation in adaptation—that the best way to adapt to change is to minimize its impact. This shifts the focus away from communities and puts the onus squarely back on senior governments and their ability to effectively manage the natural environment over the long term.

Preparing for the Future

While natural disasters and environmental change are part of life on Earth, there are things we can do to minimize their cost in lives and treasure, as well as their existential threat to the systems that anchor our high quality of life. The first thing to do is stop ratcheting up vulnerability. At a global level, this means taking climate change seriously and moving towards meaningful and equitable reductions in greenhouse gas emissions (see Chapter 8). The world is warming, and we have already committed ourselves to broad environmental changes that will have an impact on both the severity of natural disasters and the resilience of key global systems, including agriculture and food (Nelson 2009). Since 1995, major droughts have hit the world's most important grain-producing regions, including Canada, Australia, Russia, and the United States. The 2012 drought in the US was particularly severe and indicative of the potential costs of climate change. The winter of 2011–12 saw the lowest levels of snowfall in US history, leaving very little moisture in the soil. This was followed by an extended heat wave throughout the summer months that destroyed most of the corn, soybean, and wheat crop across the central United States—causing world food prices to jump by about 10 per cent (Chavez and Wailes 2013). We need to get emissions under control in the name of economic stability if nothing else.

The second thing we need to do is recognize that vulnerability is a social as well as a physical phenomenon. There is no question that good governance helps people to survive disasters, while poor governance costs lives. In 2008, an earthquake measuring 8.0 on the Richter scale struck Sichuan province in central China, killing approximately 85,000 people. What is particularly tragic about this disaster, however, was the high number of children killed. The quake struck in mid-afternoon, when most children were in school. Later investigations revealed that many of these schools had been built by corrupt companies connected to local political leaders. This led to significant (but brief) political turmoil in the province, as bereaved parents demanded prosecutions which have yet to materialize. Examples such as this show that environmental vulnerability is a human rights issue, and ought to be a major priority for the international community. Wealthy democratic nations aren't off the hook either. Images from Hurricane Katrina shattered the illusion that all people are "equally safe" in a natural disaster. As we saw in Chapter 6, Canadian Aboriginal communities are far more vulnerable to disasters such as flooding and storms than other communities, and the barriers to reconstruction are higher. Seeing vulnerability as both a social and an environmental issue encourages us to tackle both simultaneously. Environmental and economic security go hand-in-hand, and improvements in one help to establish and reinforce the other.

The third thing we can do is start taking the issue of adaptation seriously. There is a deep reluctance among local political leaders to talk about adaptation (Youngman 2009: 177). Municipal leaders are expected to be "civic boosters," and many refuse to talk about vulnerability or environmental change for fear that it will chase away business and investment. This is unfortunate, because research shows that small changes at the local level can have a big impact on **adaptive capacity**—or the ability of a community to absorb shocks and adapt to long-term changes (Cutter et al. 2008; Agrawal 2010). Second, national governments seem content to rely on what Adger and Barnett (2009) call an **"adaptation myth,"** which is the assumption that we will be able to "muddle our way through" coming changes without making difficult decisions or engaging in comprehensive planning now. The adaptation myth puts a great deal of faith in the ability of future citizens and leaders to respond to change, while forgiving destructive behaviours now. For example, governments around the world continue to allow fragile coastal ecosystems to be destroyed for housing and industrial development. In the United States, for instance, the government offers free flood insurance through the National Flood Insurance Program for people living in high-risk areas. While the program was intended to help people recover from disasters, it has had the unintended consequence of encouraging reckless development of ecologically vulnerable areas (Youngman 2009: 187). Paradoxically, disasters thus frequently lead to *more* development in vulnerable areas rather than less, as the costs of rebuilding are covered by government and the economic boost associated with reconstruction draws new people in. Finally, environmentalists are also sometimes reluctant to talk about adaptation because it implies that the battle to mitigate or reduce environmental harm has been lost. This needs to change. Even if all environmental problems were solved tomorrow, human societies would still have to deal with environmental changes and extreme events. Environmentalists potentially have a lot to contribute to planning for a more adaptable future, and their participation in this discussion would help demonstrate the movement's ongoing relevance.

One of the major challenges of preparing for the future is that we're not very good at it. As we saw in Chapter 2, humans are remarkably good at solving problems in the here and now, but are less willing or able to address long-term problems before they reach a crisis level. What was true in the past is true in the present. Well before Hurricane Katrina, it was common knowledge among government officials and academics that the levees protecting New Orleans were too weak to withstand a major storm (Perrow 2006). Similarly, governments knew that the tsunami alert system in the Indian Ocean was inadequate years before the murderous 2004 wave caught thousands of communities across South East Asia unawares (Jasanoff 2006). Total safety is an impossible goal in an age of disasters, but the eventuality of these two disasters was entirely predictable. Infrastructure investments, while expensive, could have helped and have since been made. It takes real far-sighted leadership to pursue costly mitigation and adaptation measures, but this is exactly what we need in a changing and environmentally volatile world.

Managing *unpredictable* disasters is even more daunting, because by definition they are difficult to anticipate. One of the ways to deal with them is to learn from them, but this has its limits. The design of electrical transmission towers in Ontario and Quebec has been adjusted following the 1998 ice storm, but our overall reliance on electricity is greater than ever before. Some scholars therefore argue that we need to prepare for generic "unknown" disasters by, for example, providing funding to community-level groups to come up with locally tailored disaster response plans (Pandey and Okazaki 2005). This approach has been widely adopted in Japan, which has a long history of natural disasters (Yamamura 2010). Rather than relying exclusively on a top-down response, community volunteers are assigned specific tasks in advance should a range of different emergencies arise, and local schools are pre-designated as hubs for emergency response—to serve as centres for communication, medical triage, and aid distribution (Ishiwatari 2012). This highly flexible system is credited with saving countless lives during the 2011 Japanese earthquake and tsunami, when citizens had mere minutes to respond. Canada, however, is far behind countries like Japan, preferring to rely on professional responders while instructing its citizens to prepare emergency kits to temporarily care for their families during an emergency (Haque and Etkin 2012). Canada has the largest coastline in the world. Several of its major cities are coastal or located in flood-prone regions. The cities of Vancouver and Victoria are located in one of the most geologically active regions of the world. Disasters will happen, and we need better and more flexible systems to deal with them when they do occur.

Conclusion

Natural disasters have always been with us, but they are becoming more costly in human lives and financial capital. This is because, in the words of Hartman and Squires (2006), "there is no such thing as a natural disaster." Natural geological and atmospheric events become disasters when they interact with human systems. As such, disasters expose a society's strengths and weaknesses. Our homes and cities can either protect us or harm us in the event of a disaster, as can our social and political structures. It is no accident that the vast majority of deaths from natural disasters occur in poor countries, where infrastructure is less developed, governments have fewer resources, and traditional inequalities (particularly among men and women) are strongest.

This doesn't mean, however, that wealthy countries are immune to natural disasters. The costs of disasters in developed countries are extraordinarily high, because citizens expect rapid recovery and high levels of compensation, which usually get underwritten by government. Inequality is also an issue within wealthy nations. Hurricane Katrina, which is by far the most-studied natural disaster in history, shattered the illusion that people are equally vulnerable or equally safe in a disaster. In Canada, Aboriginal communities are far more vulnerable to flooding and storms than their civic counterparts. Finally, wealthy societies are subject to a vulnerability paradox. Our high standard of living is based in large part on complex technological systems that allow us to perform tasks with ever-greater efficiency and convenience. Unpredictable events, however, such as the 2011 nuclear crisis in Japan and the 1998 ice storm in North America, show that these systems can be a source of vulnerability. A failure of the electrical system, for example, quickly cascades through other "tightly coupled" systems such as computing, finance, transportation, communication, and even house heating and agriculture (Murphy 2009). While banks used to be able to operate without power, now they cannot; while we used to be able to heat our homes without electricity, central air furnaces won't run without it, and nor will the fans on modern gas fireplaces. Our drive for greater efficiency and convenience is eliminating many of the redundancies that act as a safety net to system failure. This points to the non-linear nature of vulnerability and raises the question of how prepared we actually are for the unpredictable.

Studies of community resilience and adaptation suggest that there are ways we can reduce our vulnerability. Economic diversification is one way, as is the encouragement of "community capital" development by providing funding and training to community-level groups and volunteers. Research has shown that the most effective responses to disasters are those that mobilize both local and national resources. Unfortunately, Canada lags behind countries like Japan in encouraging the kind of flexible, community-level mobilization that proved so effective in the 2011 earthquake and tsunami. Ultimately, however, the best way to adapt to the new reality of increasingly costly disasters is to learn from our mistakes and stop ratcheting up vulnerability. This means taking real steps to reduce greenhouse gas emissions. It also means reforming destructive practices like mangrove removal, deforestation, and the destruction of wetlands and coral reefs. These are natural defences against disasters, and their removal in the name of development is extremely short-sighted. Natural disasters are humbling, and show us how powerful the natural world can be. There is much that we can do as humans, however, to minimize their impacts and enhance the environment at the same time.

Questions for Critical Thought

1. Should governments be responsible for compensating people who choose to live in vulnerable areas, like floodplains and earthquake zones, in the event of a disaster?

2. Do you think that Canada and Canadians are more vulnerable to disasters today than thirty years ago? One hundred years ago?

3. Why do you think it is so hard for a poor country like Haiti to recover from a natural disaster, while wealthy countries seem to bounce back so quickly?

4. How prepared are you personally for a natural disaster?

Suggested Readings

Freudenburg, W. R., Gramling, R., Laska, S., & Erikson, K. T. (2009). *Catastrophe in the Making: The Engineering of Katrina and the Disasters of Tomorrow.* Washington DC: Island Press. This is one of the most comprehensive analyses of the historical roots of the New Orleans disaster. It describes how poor decision-making concerning coastal development and urban planning quietly increased vulnerability over decades. A potent lesson for all of us moderns.

Neumayer, E., & Plumper, T. (2007). "The gendered nature of natural disasters: The impact of catastrophic events on the gender gap in life expectancy, 1981–2002," *Annals of the Association of American Geographers 97*(3), 551–566. This reading is an eye-opening study that demonstrates the particularly precarious position of women during and after a disaster. Among the main findings is that women and girls have a greater chance of surviving a disaster in societies with greater overall gender equality.

Stallings, R. A., & Quarantelli, E. L. (1985). "Emergent citizen groups and emergency management," *Public Administration Review 45*, 93–100. Enrico Quarantelli is one of the founders of disaster studies in sociology, and this article is one of his most influential. It argues that community response to disasters is critical, particularly people's ability to self-organize.

Wilson, G. A. (2012). *Community Resilience and Environmental Transitions.* New York: Routledge. The book contains an excellent overview of current thinking about resilience, and makes a laudable effort to bring it all together into a comprehensive theory of social-ecological change.

Suggested Websites

Canadian Red Cross
www.redcross.ca
> The Red Cross/Red Crescent network of organizations is one of the oldest international disaster responders in the world. Its website has numerous case studies

of specific disasters and publications about such things as violence prevention in the aftermath of disasters.

Climate Change Adaptation—United Nations Environment Programme
www.unep.org/climatechange/adaptation/

This website describes research into climate change adaptation, as well as programs to enhance resiliency currently in place around the world.

11 Putting Humans and Nature Back Together

Key Points

◎ Environmental sociologists are still unsure of how to put the human and natural worlds together into a single coherent theory. Three possibilities are political ecology, panarchy theory, and theories of co-construction.

◎ Political ecology sees nature as being profoundly shaped by human politics, particularly imbalances in power and social inequalities.

◎ Panarchy theory examines how human activities fit in with the deep rhythms and cycles of the natural world.

◎ Theories of co-construction argue that the human and natural worlds are intertwined, with each acting upon and "producing" the other.

◎ While each theory has potential, the real theoretical innovations in environmental sociology are likely still to come.

Introduction

We are a young species, but one that has had a profound impact on the planet. As discussed in earlier chapters, humans are an exceptional animal due to our ability to purposely shape and re-shape our natural environment to suit our needs and desires. Our fingerprints are all over this Earth, from the deep seas to the high stratosphere. We are the builders and shapers of things.

This does not mean, however, that humans are masters of nature. As we have seen throughout this book, that conceit has led to some dark outcomes—including the over-exploitation of resources, the manufacture of large-scale risks, and the ongoing degradation of ecosystems big and small. Human society and physical nature are intertwined, even if this close relationship is masked from the ever-increasing number of us who live in urban environments far removed from the production of food, fuel, and waste that underwrites our high standard of living.

The challenge for environmental sociology is to provide ways of explaining and analyzing this relationship. In Chapter 1, I argued that sociology is both handicapped and privileged in this endeavour. It is handicapped because mainstream sociology has mostly ignored the biophysical world, pretending it doesn't exist and that everything we need to know about society can be learned by looking only at humans and their political, economic, and cultural constructs. On the other hand, sociology is privileged because it possesses battle-tested concepts and methodological tools for understanding human behaviour. Its emphasis on both individual and collective phenomena, macro and micro, symbolic and structural, means that sociology can provide unique insights into the complex origins and impacts of environmental problems.

This final chapter picks up the gauntlet that was thrown down in Chapter 1—to find a way to theorize the relationship between the human and natural worlds without falling back on the "environmental determinism" that sociology has rightly rejected. The aim here is not to provide a definitive answer, but rather a roadmap towards possible answers. Specifically, this chapter considers three recent theoretical attempts to bridge the human–nature divide—**political ecology**, **panarchy theory**, and theories of **co-construction**. While these theories differ in their ideas and emphasis, each views the human and natural worlds as intertwined rather than separate.

Three Perspectives on Humans and Nature

Writing about current thinking on nature–society relations is like jumping onto a moving train. To put it diplomatically, the ideas discussed in this chapter are under development, meaning that they are still being advanced, debated, refined, and contradicted—both by the key authors themselves and by critics. These are signs of a healthy academic conversation, but it also means that my commentary on these theories ought to be taken with a few grains of salt. First of all, these three theories do not represent the full range of thinking on human–nature relations. In the interests of space and brevity, I've left a lot out, including interesting work on the notion of societal "metabolism" or balance (Foster et al. 2010; Baerlocher and Burger 2010), the role that animals play in bridging and patterning human–nature relations (Tovey 2003; Benton 2010), and how natural and built environments affect everyday human perceptions and practices (Ingold 2000; 2011). Readers should seek out these sources for a more comprehensive view of these issues than I am able to provide here. Second, the three theories vary in their popularity and maturity. Political ecology, for instance, is now a vast field of inquiry populated not only by sociologists but by anthropologists, geographers, and (to a lesser extent) political scientists. This contrasts with panarchy theory, which emerged primarily out of ecology and is still being developed and incorporated into the social sciences. Finally, the lines around and between the theories are not always clearly drawn. What I label "theories of co-construction," for instance, are in fact a loose amalgam of ideas that I see as having much in common even though they sometimes compete and contradict one another. I freely admit that others may have different interpretations of which ideas are distinct and which belong together.

In short, the point of this chapter is to outline some possible future directions for environmental sociology, using the imperfect, incomplete, but extremely interesting building blocks of a work in progress. It is meant to be an inspirational exercise rather than a definitive one. Such are the challenges of trying to hit a moving target.

Political Ecology

The term "political ecology" is sometimes confusing to casual observers. First of all, political ecology is terminologically close to several other perspectives—namely human ecology and social ecology—that have longer histories. Political ecology is distinct from these other theories, although they do overlap in some ways (see Box 11.1). Second, political ecology confuses because it is an extremely broad perspective that lacks a single widely accepted definition. Rather than being a tightly focused theory, political ecology has become a label of convenience for many scholars across multiple disciplines looking to understand human–nature relations (Zimmerman and Bassett 2003). Rather than trying to summarize the range of thinking on political ecology, I will focus on its main principles.

Generally speaking, political ecology starts with the premise that nearly all aspects of the natural environment bear the indelible stamp of human politics, and that no analysis of "natural phenomena" is complete without considering the role that human political decisions have played in shaping them. This position contains an implicit critique of mainstream environmental science (Biersack 2006: 4). As discussed in Chapter 3, the rise of ecology or "ecosystem science" stands as a major landmark in modern environmentalism and the history of science more generally, because it provides a way for us to evaluate the human impact on the natural environment. Ecology is therefore a powerful tool for understanding the human footprint on the world. Robbins (2012), however, argues that standard or mainstream ecology can in fact be highly misleading, laying blame in the wrong places. Specifically, Robbins argues that most ecology as it is currently practised is in fact "apolitical ecology," meaning that it is wilfully ignorant of the role that politics plays in structuring the natural world. Apolitical ecology encourages us to think about the human impact on the environment *only* in ecological terms.

To illustrate, Robbins points to a comparison between the two bordering nations of Kenya and Tanzania in East Africa. Both countries are home to large but threatened populations of savannah-dwelling animals such as elephants, wildebeest, rhinoceros, and lions. In Kenya, however,

Box 11.1 Too Many Ecologies? Human Ecology, Social Ecology, Political Ecology

"Human ecology" and "social ecology" are terms that pre-date "political ecology," and it is not always clear how these three concepts relate to one another. Human ecology refers predominantly to the thinking of sociologists Robert E. Park and Ernest W. Burgess, both of whom worked at the University of Chicago in the 1920s and 1930s. Park and Burgess were interested in urban issues, and used terms from ecology (which was itself just emerging as a credible academic science) to conceptualize cities as ecosystems, using metaphors like succession, dominance, invasion, and symbiosis to explain changing patterns of settlement and migration within Chicago. This type of analysis has largely fallen out of favour, although the term "human ecology" carries on in academic journals such as *Human Ecology* and *Human Ecology Review*. These publications look at "the place of humans in the living world" (Borden 2008: 95)—an orientation that is more consistent with modern political ecology than Park and Burgess's original take on human ecology.

Social ecology is sometimes used synonymously with human ecology, but the term is most often used to describe an intellectual movement advocating a more egalitarian and ecologically just society by, among other things, abolishing private corporations and social hierarchies. This form of social ecology is closely associated with the work of Murray Bookchin (1921–2006), a philosopher and activist who wrote extensively about the links between social and ecological problems (Bookchin 2007). In this way, social ecology overlaps with political ecology, although the latter has developed into a major field in environmental sociology and beyond, while Bookchin's work—which has been influential within the environmentalist movement—is generally considered too programmatic and prescriptive to be broadly useful as a sociological theory.

the decline of these animals has been rapid and acute, while in Tanzania the decline has been more gradual and halting. Looking at this problem through the lens of apolitical ecology is downright confusing:

> Looking at the two countries, we can observe [that] the decline in habitat and wildlife in Kenya is far higher than in Tanzania. Why? Rainfall, human population, and livestock numbers do not differ significantly. . . . [Nor] is the presence or absence of people to blame. The Masai people and their ancestors have inhabited the Central Rift Valley [that bridges both countries] for thousands of years without appreciably impacting wildlife populations. (Robbins 2012: 12)

Instead, the difference is political. Kenya was one of the first African countries to encourage international investment in private agriculture, in the hopes of boosting exports and participating in the global agriculture markets. Tanzania, in contrast, adopted a more nationalist and collectivist approach to agriculture that, despite market reforms in the 1980s and 1990s, continues to influence farmer behaviour (see Cooksey 2011). According to Robbins (2012: 12),

> Private holdings and investment in export-oriented agriculture on the Kenyan side of the border have led to intensive cropping and the decline of habitat. . . . Less developed agricultural markets and less fully privatized land tenure systems in Tanzania mean less pressure on wildlife. The wildlife crisis in East Africa is therefore more political and economic than demographic.

The alarming decline of wildlife in Kenya is therefore not just a question of human encroachment, but the encroachment of a certain type of activity: specifically, **cash-cropping** for export, which encourages farmers to farm more intensively, acquire more land, and reduce fallowing times to better compete in the global marketplace. Nor can we simply blame the locals. The pastoral Masai, who are sometimes vilified as the cause of the problem, have sustainably worked the land for generations and are largely excluded from private agriculture on both sides of the border. Even Kenyan farmers, who are more directly to blame, are only responding to intentional government policies encouraging this behaviour. The difference between a *political* and an *apolitical* ecology is, therefore,

> The difference between identifying broader systems rather than blaming proximate and local forces; between viewing ecological systems as power-laden rather than politically inert; and between taking an explicitly normative approach rather than one that claims the objectivity of [scientific] disinterest. (Robbins 2012: 13)

Political ecology, therefore, is consistent with classical sociological concepts and theories that pay strong attention to issues of power, inequality, and economic interests. Political ecology's main innovation is to extend these classic concepts to a direct analysis of human impacts on the biophysical sphere. It rejects the notion that environmental destruction is driven exclusively by ecological variables (such as human population growth) or by the moral failings of local people trying to earn a living on the land (Peet et al. 2011: 15). Instead, political ecologists argue that environmental problems are the product of political failures and shortsightedness that typically affect people and the natural environment simultaneously. Figure 11.1

illustrates this logic in schematic form. In the Kenyan case, the political decision to privatize farmland has had social and ecological consequences that are clearly linked. Wealthier farmers have been able to acquire land and engage in cash-cropping, while traditional users such as the Masai have been marginalized and pushed into smaller and more ecologically sensitive areas.

Importantly, Figure 11.1 shows that influence can flow in multiple directions. While most political ecologists look at the flow from the political and social spheres towards biophysical nature (Zimmerman 2003), the reverse is equally plausible. For example, Peluso (1992) has written extensively about how the presence of valuable natural resources affects the way that governments treat indigenous people. Focusing on Indonesia in particular, Peluso documents how the government, eager to capitalize on global interest in forest resources (including expensive teak wood), redefined traditional inhabitants of the forest as "pests, squatters, and encroachers" and redrew maps to redefine "long-inhabited land as uninhabited forest for the benefit of state actors and global corporate interests" (quoted in Robbins 2012: 190). Resource development has in turn severely impacted local people who rely on the forest for sustenance, pitching them into a long-term struggle to maintain access to the local environment (Peluso and Vandergeest 2011).

Strengths and Weaknesses of Political Ecology

Political ecology is well within sociologists' comfort zone. The logic of its analysis is familiar, even if the objects of analysis are novel. The link drawn by political ecology between social inequality and environmental degradation is highly compatible with the new activist and academic interest in environmental justice (see Chapter 3). Political ecology is also highly amenable to case studies and comparative research (Peet et al. 2011). It allows analysts to investigate why environmental outcomes differ across ostensibly similar regions and nations, with many studies suggesting that local control over resources and landscapes is key to their conservation (Biersack

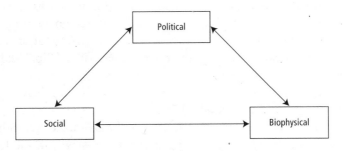

Figure 11.1 Relationship between Political, Social, and Biophysical Spheres in Political Ecology

2006). Perhaps the greatest strength of political ecology, however, is its rejection of shallow explanations of environmental problems. Rather than accepting that environmental problems are caused by blanket conditions like "overpopulation," political ecology prompts researchers to probe for deeper explanations, such as who controls the resource, how it is used, and what impact it has on other potential users. This leads to detailed and context-sensitive explanations of environmental phenomena that recognize the prominent role played by human political structures and decision-making.

Critics of political ecology argue that, despite its attempt to bridge the gap between the human and natural worlds, it remains a very human-focused perspective (Latour 2004). According to this view, the main weakness of political ecology is that it sees nature more as a "setting" for human politics than as a dynamic actor (Walker 2005). Political ecology argues that we can read politics through nature—that the different political structures of Kenya and Tanzania, for instance, are imprinted on their natural environments. This is an important insight, but critics argue that it renders nature too passive—*reflecting* us rather than playing an active role in *shaping* us. Humans do the acting, while nature is the thing that is acted upon. This contrasts with the other two theories—panarchy and co-construction—which afford a much more active role for nature and natural dynamics.

Panarchy Theory

While political ecology is a mostly human-centred theory, panarchy comes from the other direction, looking to bring human variables into a predominantly nature-centred interpretation of the world. Panarchy theory is rooted directly in ecology, specifically the thinking of ecologists C.S. Holling and Lance Gunderson (the term *panarchy* refers to Pan, the Greek god of nature). Holling and Gunderson were early advocates of the paradigm shift within ecology described in Chapter 10. To recap, ecology traditionally viewed ecosystems as being linear and stable. When a disturbance occurred, such as a forest fire or a flood, ecosystems would regenerate in a predictable way, with early colonizers (such as insects, grasses, and bushes) eventually giving way to a stable state dominated by a canopy of mature trees and larger fauna. Holling and Gunderson (among others) instead argued that while ecosystems can easily regenerate after some disturbances, others can cause ecosystems to irreversibly "flip" into one of several possible stable states.

Panarchy refers to their theory of how these different ecological changes (regeneration versus flips) happen (Gunderson and Holling 2002). The easiest way to describe panarchy theory is with an image, reproduced in Figure 11.2. The lopsided figure eight presents the stages in the life cycle of a typical ecosystem. The best place to begin is at the bottom left in the

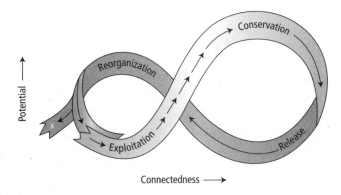

Figure 11.2 The Panarchy Cycle
Source: Based on Gunderson and Holling (2002)

"exploitation" stage, when a new ecosystem is just emerging (either for the first time or following a disturbance). At this stage, the natural environment has little biomass (or what Holling and Gunderson call "potential"), and is not very complex (or "connected"). As early species exploit this new environment, however, both biomass and complexity increase. In Holling and Gunderson's view, however, this increase cannot continue forever, nor does it lead to a "stable state." For example, as a forest reaches maturity the canopy becomes denser (more connected) while fallen trees and leaf litter accumulate as biomass (more potential). At this mature or "conservation" stage, change slows down and there is more stability and continuity in the ecosystem. This stability however, cannot last. The build-up of potential and connectedness has the paradoxical impact of *increasing* the system's overall vulnerability to disturbances such as fire—as there is more fuel available to burn and more opportunity for a fire to jump from tree to tree. According to this view, disturbance is inevitable and healthy, leading to a "release" in both potential and complexity (lower right of the figure eight). The key moment is the "reorganization" phase, where the ecosystem may "regenerate" or else "exit" and flip into something new.

Whether or not an ecosystem will regenerate or flip is a complicated question, but Holling and Gunderson argue that it has to do with *time* and *scale*. Some natural systems are small, and go through the cycle very quickly, while others are large and experience the build-up and release of potential and connectedness over centuries or even tens of thousands of years. For instance, grasslands are far more vulnerable to short-term natural disruptions (such as drought) than forests, which are in turn more vulnerable than watersheds, lakes, and oceans. Holling and Gunderson therefore conceptualize smaller and faster panarchy cycles as being "nested" in larger and slower ones (see Figure 11.3). In the natural environment, each cycle moves

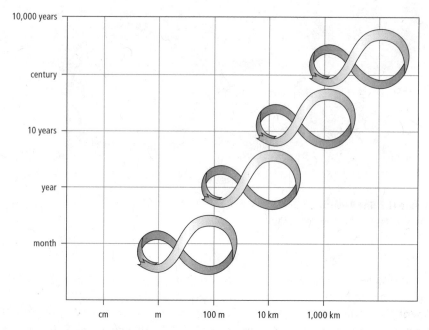

Figure 11.3 Cycles within Cycles across Space and Time
Source: Based on Gunderson and Holling (2002)

at a different speed, meaning that each scale hits the critical "release" and "reorganization" stages at different times. This system of nesting acts as a buffer that contains the sometimes-violent effects of release, thus encouraging regeneration and minimizing flipping.

So where do people come in? Holling and Gunderson make two main arguments about panarchy and human affairs. The first argument is that panarchy cycles are evident in human societies as well. In particular, Gunderson and Holling (2002: 55) argue that economies and organizations go through the same cycle of growth, ossification, collapse, and reorganization (or "exit") as can be seen in the natural world. It is even suggested that whole countries and regions go through the panarchic cycle. For example, Holling (2004) argues that the history of the Soviet Union can be read this way. The Soviet Union was born out of the Bolshevik Revolution in 1917 (itself a "flip" away from monarchism), and grew into a vast empire over the next 70 years as it accumulated wealth, territory, and influence. The empire, however, became unsustainable due to a lack of economic and political flexibility, ultimately leading to a period of collapse and reorganization. While arguments such as these are compelling, they also make some social scientists uncomfortable (Davidson 2010). Sociologists in particular usually reject simple explanations for complex phenomena, and the direct application of panarchy to society is reminiscent of the environmental determinism the discipline rejects.

Holling and Gunderson's second argument is that humans are directly interfering with the system of nested cycles that govern environmental change. The scale of human activities means that we are now affecting even the slowest and largest cycles. Consider the oceans, for example. The rise of industrial-scale fishing means that the oceans are being depleted with breathtaking speed and scope. Some studies suggest that if current trends continue, nearly every major commercial fishery in the world will collapse by the year 2050 (Worm et al. 2006). More than this, however, humans are altering the very chemical composition of the oceans. Widespread emissions of carbon dioxide are contributing to **ocean acidification**, or the lowering of ocean pH levels. As the level of carbon dioxide in the atmosphere increases, the oceans absorb more as well. Upon entering the water, some carbon dioxide dissolves and recombines with water to form carbonic acid (H_2CO_3). A more acidic ocean has widespread consequences for marine life, particularly exoskeletal animals that require hard shells to live, as these are harder to build in acidic water. This is a case where we are causing the cycles to line up—depleting both individual fish stocks and altering the long and slow rhythms of the ocean—creating vulnerability at an unprecedented scale.

One of the most interesting social science takes on panarchy comes from the Canadian scholar and popular writer Thomas Homer-Dixon (2006). Homer-Dixon accepts that human societies go through panarchic cycles, but argues that the "release and reorganization" phases of the cycle can have significant upside, allowing us to rethink our dependency on fossil fuels, for instance, and pursue innovative new technologies and social systems. As with Holling and Gunderson, Homer-Dixon argues that the key is to contain these breakdowns—allowing them to happen in a controlled fashion that does not cause a complete reorganization of the whole system. Homer-Dixon (2006: 232) is particularly concerned that modern societies are hell-bent on stretching the growth phase of the figure eight to the point that the (inevitable) fall will be dramatic. This is reminiscent of the arguments raised by peak theory (see Chapter 5)—where society is ultimately constrained by hard ecological limits. Homer-Dixon argues that we are already on the march towards unseen "tipping points" that will quickly alter natural and social systems together (Carmack et al 2012). Humans, however, have the unique ability to anticipate problems and thus control or at least manage the cycle—assuming that we are able to overcome our modernist assumption that progress is linear and irreversible (Davidson 2010).

Strengths and Weaknesses of Panarchy Theory

One of the main strengths of panarchy theory is that it provides a way of qualitatively analyzing the impact of human activities on natural rhythms and processes. Panarchy theory suggests that human interventions in the natural world are not problematic *in and of themselves*. Nature is always changing, and these changes are neither good nor bad. Human activities become problematic, however, when they alter the quality or character of these changes—making them speed up or align in ways they otherwise wouldn't in the absence of human disturbances. Panarchy theory also shows how local and global issues are directly linked. The notion of "nested cycles" demonstrates how local issues such as overfishing or land degradation interact with (and worsen) the effects of larger-scale changes such as ocean acidification and shifts in climate. Finally, panarchy theory puts nature firmly in the driver's seat. Natural systems function with or without us, and it is up to people to match their behaviours to a dynamic and non-linear nature. Panarchy suggests that the challenge for humanity is not to dominate or control nature, but to "roll with it," minimizing our interference in natural systems but remaining flexible enough to adapt to (inevitable) changes.

Panarchy theory also has substantial weaknesses that hinder its incorporation into environmental sociology and the social sciences more generally. Panarchy theory advances a rather narrow understanding of human society that does not give much consideration to politics, culture, or economic inequality. As mentioned, many sociologists are uncomfortable with the notion that social systems follow pre-determined cycles, and see panarchy as an overly simplistic explanation of complex social and political phenomena. More generally, the notion of panarchic cycles is reminiscent of an unrestrained free market ideology that most environmental sociologists reject. Free market ideology also argues that economies go through cycles that involve the removal of inefficient and inflexible companies (and workers) through a process of "creative destruction" that opens up new room for small start-ups and entrepreneurs. This implication in panarchy theory that such processes are "natural" raises red flags among social scientists accustomed to seeing this as an ideological position rather than a statement of fact.

Finally, panarchy theory has (unintentionally) provided an intellectual boost for the anti-environmental movement that seeks to downplay environmental problems and avoid new environmental rules and regulations (see Chapter 3). The notion that the natural environment is "always changing" allows anti-environmentalists to argue that evidence of change is not necessarily evidence of human impact. Panarchy itself does not provide a reliable method for distinguishing between "natural change," which is morally acceptable and even beneficial, and "human-induced change," which is morally troubling and often damaging. Gunderson and Holling (2002: 31) themselves point out that, prior to the last Ice Age, the Florida everglades were a savannah rather than a marshland. If our own society had existed at the time, they argue, we would have likely seen the loss of this savannah as an ecological tragedy and fought to preserve it. Many equivalent changes are underway today—are they natural or human-caused? More broadly, what is good change and what is bad change? These are legitimate questions, but opponents of environmentalism have seized on them as part of their tactics to delay environmental action.

Theories of Co-construction

Co-constructionism is an imperfect label for a collection of different concepts and ideas that—I freely admit—are not always consistent or complementary. Generally speaking, however, theories of co-construction argue that the human and natural worlds are so closely intertwined that they ought to be considered as "co-constitutive," or producing of one another (Goldman and Schurman 2000: 565). Co-constructionists start from the premise that humans and nature are in constant interaction, engaged in long-term and multi-dimensional "negotiations" that affect and pattern both parties. The notion that nature can negotiate may be counter-intuitive, but it is critical to understanding co-constructionist ideas.

To begin, let's consider the thinking of sociologist Bruno Latour, one of the most influential co-constructionists and one of the founders of **actor-network theory**, which is a particular type of co-constructionism that has been highly influential in both environmental sociology and the sociology of science (Murdoch 2001). Actor-network theory argues that non-humans, which include technologies, objects, and natural phenomena, possess an "agency" that is independent of humans. In other words, they *act* even if they lack consciousness. (Latour uses the term "actants" for these actors-without-consciousness.) The agency of things is evident in their frequent tendency to resist human efforts to define or control them (Latour 2004: 23). For example, consider the example of lead. Lead is a natural substance (a soft metal) that has a long history with human beings extending back at least 5,000 years. Lead possesses certain properties that made it very attractive to early manufacturers, specifically its low melting point, pliability, and resistance to wear and breakage, which made it an ideal substance for making pipes and containers. The Ancient Romans were particularly fond of the substance, and the word *plumbing*, for instance, comes from *plumbum*, the Latin word for *lead*. In the twentieth century, gasoline manufacturers added lead to their products to reduce engine "knocking" caused by over-combustion. It was also used in household products such as paint, solder, and plastics. Lead, in other words, was a miracle substance that helped manufacturers to improve their products and consumers to enjoy them. Lead, however, has refused to remain "stable" over the course of its relationship with humans. Beginning in the 1880s, experts started to question whether there was a link between lead and certain illnesses, particularly in children. Lead is now known to cause neurological impairment, anemia, kidney failure, and heart disease, and has been banned from most consumer products. In this transition from miracle substance to health problem, lead itself changed. Lead was no longer simply a soft metal, but a particle in the air (emitted by the burning of leaded gasoline), a contaminant in drinking water, a household hazard, and a measurable risk in the human bloodstream (having been absorbed by the lungs or stomach). In this way, the changing properties of lead forced major social transformations, not only by spurring new technologies (such as unleaded gasoline), but by creating whole systems for monitoring lead exposure and medically diagnosing lead-related illness. Each time lead changed, it forced society to change with it. Society constructed lead by pulling it out of the ground and giving it "uses," and lead constructed society in return by behaving in an unruly and unpredictable way.

Actor-network theory has proven very useful in examining the careers of different environmental problems. Getting nature to "behave" is in fact very difficult, even for environmentalists who claim to speak for the natural world (Magnani 2012). For example, the environmentalist movement has long been critical of the use of genetically modified organisms (GMOs) in agriculture, arguing (in part) that they may pose a health risk to human consumers. While this remains a possibility over the long term, the GMOs themselves have not (yet) co-operated with activists by making people sick or showing up in epidemiological statistics. In turn, the lack of evidence of GMO-related illness has damaged the credibility of anti-GMO activists—moving an issue that was highly salient in the early 2000s onto the political backburner. In short, defining something as an environmental problem depends on activists' ability to "enrol" human and non-human actors into a "network" arrangement (hence the term actor-network theory) that will co-operate and stay stable over time (Lockie 2004). This is not easily done, precisely because of the agency possessed by non-humans.

While actor-network theory tends to focus on specific cases, other co-constructionists take a more macro-level view of human–nature interactions. Woodgate and Redclift (1998), for instance, argue that nature and society are engaged in a process of **"coevolution"** (see also Noorgard 1984). The notion of coevolution suggests that human societies and nature are continuously pushing one another to adapt. Humans push nature to adapt by using, harvesting, enhancing, and degrading environments, which alters habitats, species mixes, and even local climates. In turn, nature pushes humans to adapt by allowing certain activities and constraining others. Abundant natural resources, for example, encourage different behaviours than scarce resources (as we saw in Chapter 2). Therefore, the coevolution process is driven by "the action capabilities of subjects [i.e., people] and the possibilities of action offered by objects [nature]" (Woodgate and Redclift 1998: 11). Canadian sociologist Raymond Murphy (2004; 2009) uses the metaphor of a dance to capture this back-and-forth relationship. When two people dance together (at least in formal settings), one person takes the role of the "lead" and the other person follows. Sometimes, humans take the lead and nature changes or adapts in response. This is the case, for instance, when land is cleared for a new housing development and the plants and animals that formerly lived there are displaced or destroyed. A human activity prompts a reorganization and adaptation in the natural world. Sometimes, though, nature takes the lead and forces us to adapt and improvise. This is what happens in natural disasters (see Chapter 10), but also when a resource is exhausted or an ecosystem flips into a different state. These changes in lead are often rapid and unforeseen. Moreover, the metaphor of the dance also shows how the two partners can spiral out of control. Global climate change, for instance, is an environmental response to human activities. As the environment changes, however, we are likely to increase rather than decrease our emissions of greenhouse gases, by, for instance, increasing our reliance on air conditioning, using more fuel and fertilizer in agriculture, and turning to energy-intensive desalination to pull drinking water out of the oceans. In cases such as these, the dance becomes a vicious circle, with each partner pulling the other off balance until one or the other can no longer keep up (Murphy 2009: 43).

Strengths and Weaknesses of Co-constructionism

The main strength of co-constructionism is that it lays bare the role that non-humans play in structuring human societies. It exposes the myth that people are the sole architects of society as false, and illustrates how nature "pushes back" against human attempts to define, control, and use it. Co-constructionism also prompts us to rethink key sociological assumptions, such as the idea that only humans possess agency. Accepting that nature can act even without consciousness raises important new questions for sociological analysis. Why do certain natural phenomena "co-operate" with social actors? Why do others "misbehave," resist, and strike back? Answering these questions can give us new insights into the limits of human agency and politics.

Co-constructionism also offers a way around the constructionist-realist debate described in Chapter 4. By conceptualizing the natural and human worlds as intertwined, co-constructionists see "nature in the social, and the social in nature." In Freudenburg et al.'s words (1995: 361),

> The challenge for sociology is not just to recognize the importance of both the physical and the social, and certainly not to argue over the relative importance of the two, but to recognize the extent to which what we take to be "physical" and "social" factors can be conjointly constituted. . . . What we take to be "physical facts" are likely to be strongly shaped by social construction processes, and at the same time, what we take to be "strictly social" will often have been shaped in part by taken-for-granted realities of the physical world.

Critics of co-constructionism usually take exception to the idea of equivalence between nature and humans. Carolan (2005: 394), for instance, argues that nature and society are not equal because "while the biophysical can exist without the social, the converse is categorically impossible." This suggests that nature is independent of human society, and that the argument that they co-construct one another is true in only a limited number of cases. While landscapes can be "co-constructed," for instance, natural laws such as gravity and thermodynamics are completely independent of society (Carolan 2005: 401). Other critics are skeptical of the claim that non-humans are capable of agency and action on par with humans (Murdoch 2001). While most critics accept that nature does indeed act, they argue that action-without-consciousness is fundamentally different from the purposeful and reflective action by humans (Hacking 1999). Because humans think, we are able to anticipate the consequences of their actions and make meaningful choices—something that nature cannot do. This suggests that co-constructionism is too focused on symmetry between the human and natural worlds, and thus downplays the responsibilities that humans have as the *key actors* in the relationship who ultimately cause it to succeed or fail.

Conclusion

The main theoretical challenge for environmental sociology is to find ways of understanding the human and natural worlds together. This chapter has identified and discussed three recent attempts to do just that. The three perspectives discussed here—political ecology, panarchy theory, and theories of co-construction—are not the only theories out there, but they are among the best-known. Each theory approaches the nature–society relationship differently. Political ecology tends to take a human-centred approach; panarchy, a predominantly nature-centred view; and co-construction, a "symmetrical" approach that attempts to put human society and non-human nature on equal footing.

Each theory has significant strengths and weaknesses, which suggests that there is much more work to be done. While sociology and ecology have come closer together, "a new ecological paradigm for sociology that adequately recognizes human–ecosystem interdependence is still in the making" (Manuel-Navarette and Buzinde 2010: 136). The answer, then, may be that we need multiple theories rather than one over-arching paradigm or perspective. Each of the theories discussed here addresses a different aspect of the human–nature relationship. Political ecology exposes the link between social and environmental inequalities, as well as the deeply political nature of landscapes, natural resources, and economic decision-making. Panarchy theory exposes the impacts that humans have on natural systems large and small, and points to cumulating vulnerabilities that mutually threaten ecology and society. Finally, co-construction prompts us to rethink apparent divisions between people and the non-human objects and environments in which we live—to see humans and non-humans as intimates rather than strangers. Each makes an original (if incomplete) contribution to our understanding of nature–society relations.

I can't help but think, however, that the real innovations in environmental sociology are yet to come. As we have seen throughout this book, our relationship with the natural environment is in constant flux. The global economy has reached an unprecedented scale that is putting tremendous pressures on the planet, and we simply don't know the ecological consequences of this level of growth, consumption, and waste. Chances are, however, that the most serious environmental challenges are still in our collective future. Responding to them will take foresight, creativity, and no small measure of will. Sociology can contribute by focusing on both sides of the story—the origins of environmental degradation, as well as possible solutions to our collective environmental dilemmas (Buttel 2003). At the most general level, we need to know what causes environmental problems and what to do about them. More specifically, we need to know how to effectively promote and enact reforms in an inclusive way, how to ensure that environmental problems are addressed equitably, and which solutions are socially viable and which ones are likely to be rejected by a volatile public. These are all questions that an environmentally conscious sociology is well-equipped to handle. There's lots to be done, so let's get to it!

Questions for Critical Thought

1. Which of the three theories do you find the most convincing? The least convincing?

2. What is the same about the human world and the natural world? What is different?

3. What contribution do you think environmental sociology makes to our understanding of environmental problems and solutions?

Suggested Readings

Gunderson, L. H., & Holling, C. S. (2002). *Panarchy: Understanding Transformations in Human and Natural Systems*. Washington DC: Island Press. This is the most complete and provocative formulation of panarchy theory to date. It includes chapters that focus on the natural world, the social world, and intersections between the two. A fascinating and stimulating read.

Murphy, Raymond. (2004). "Disaster or sustainability: The dance of human agents with nature's actants," *Canadian Review of Sociology and Anthropology* 41(3), 249–267. This article describes Murphy's co-constructionism through the metaphor of the dance. It uses the 1998 ice storm that struck Ontario and Quebec as its key example.

Robbins, P. (2012). *Political Ecology*, 2nd edition. Malden, MA: Wiley-Blackwell. An excellent overview of political ecology, Robbins takes readers through the genesis of the theory and the different ways that it has been applied across the social sciences.

Suggested Websites

Bruno Latour's professional website
www.bruno-latour.fr

Bruno Latour is one of the leading co-constructionists and founder of actor-network theory. His website contains articles, lectures, and book excerpts. The material is often dense, but worthwhile.

Resilience Alliance
www.resalliance.org

The Resilience Alliance is an association of ecologists and social scientists investigating human–nature relations. Gunderson and Holling are founding members, and the association continues to develop panarchy theory. The Resilience Alliance also publishes the journal *Ecology and Society*.

Afterword

This book was written at a curious time. As I sequestered myself in my home office, reading articles and writing chapter drafts, two things were happening in the world outside. First of all, the scope and scale of global environmental problems continued to be exposed. The devastating Russian drought of 2011 was followed by another in the United States and Eastern Canada in the summer of 2012. That year also saw the Arctic ice cap shrink to its smallest size ever recorded, about half of what was typical in the 1970s and 80s. While ice cover varies each year, the downward trend is unmistakable and likely to continue. These are signals that we are entering uncharted waters, environmentally speaking. To paraphrase Ulrich Beck, the past is losing its ability to predict the future. We don't know what comes next for the planet, but it is likely to be different from what we've known.

Second, political leaders around the world continued to avoid, delay, and shrug off the difficult choices that have to be made. The Obama administration in the United States was deafeningly silent on environmental issues in the lead-up to the 2012 presidential election—clearly afraid of being tarred as anti-business in the midst of a fragile economic recovery. In Canada, the Conservative Government of Stephen Harper has gone "all in" on resource development—pushing for expansion of the Alberta oil sands in particular by removing existing environmental regulations that might hinder the construction of pipelines to British Columbia, the United States, and Eastern Canada.

I'm not sure how future historians will view this time—when environmental challenges are so glaringly obvious but so studiously ignored by many of the world's political leaders. In the spirit of helping out these future scholars, I want to end this book by stressing the difference between debate and denial. Debate is a healthy part of scholarship and policy-making. Much of this book has been organized around debates. Chapter 4, for instance, considered the long-running debate between constructionist and realist views of nature. Chapter 5 outlined the disagreement between adherents of peak theory and those who believe that natural resources are infinitely flexible or substitutable. Chapter 7 did the same for those who see the free market as a tool for environmental reform and those who see it as fundamentally flawed, and Chapter 8 considered the environmental costs and benefits of globalization. These are legitimate debates that reflect the complexity of the issues. I also firmly believe that such debates encourage the kinds of creative thinking we need if we are to lighten the burden of our species on the planet. Debate exposes the strengths and weaknesses of different methods, interpretations, and assumptions. As such, it can be a tool for enhancing reflexivity, or our ability to anticipate and respond to environmental problems effectively and equitably.

Denial is very different from debate. Denial refuses to be convinced, to cede any ground to different or opposing views, to experiment or to learn. Denial is a tactic—it has nothing to do with disagreement and everything to do with strategy. In a legitimate debate, people assess evidence based on its merit, and change their views if that evidence is sufficiently convincing. Debates don't always result in consensus, but they progress and evolve. Denial, in contrast, uses cherry-picked evidence to accommodate pre-determined views. The ultimate goal of denial is to delay—to resist change and maintain the status-quo. It is intentionally counter-productive, and therefore has no place in debate. I fear that future historians will have a far better understanding of this distinction than we do today.

We need our leaders to come off the fence and participate in environmental conversations and debates, rather than using denial as a mask or excuse for inaction. There are real and profound debates to be had. What do we want our future economies to look like? What kind of cities and countrysides do we want to live in? How much environmental change is acceptable in the name of growth? What is the role of nature in human well-being? People, it seems, are far ahead of their governments on many of these questions. Most Canadians agree that environmental problems are serious, and are willing to change their habits and behaviours to help address them. We are rewriting environmental history before it happens, but the clock is ticking. Our leaders need to catch up.

Notes

Chapter 1

1. Paterson in fact uses the term "ecological modernization capitalism" to describe European economies. Ecological modernization is a complex concept and theory that will be explained in Chapter 7. For simplicity's sake, I have replaced it here with "efficiency capitalism."

Chapter 5

1. Only about 10–12 per cent of the gold mined in a given year is used for industrial purposes. The rest is for ornament and investment.
2. Hubbert's model predicted the drop-off in US oil production from the 1960s–2000s with uncanny accuracy. In recent years, however, Hubbert's prediction has been countered by the rapid development of unconventional oil reserves—a point I return to later in Chapter 5.

Chapter 7

1. The largest such group is the Maine-based Acid Rain Retirement Fund, which by 2011 had purchased and permanently retired the equivalent of 211 annual tonnes of SO_2. (See http://www.acidrainretirementfund.org for more information.)
2. Prior to German unification in 1990, research focused on West Germany. Communist East Germany had a much worse environmental track record.

Chapter 8

1. A number of terms are now used to describe countries and regions that are more and less developed (and consequently richer and poorer). In this chapter, I use "developing nations," "less developed nations," "the Third World," and "the Global South" interchangeably; and do the same with "developed nations," "Western nations," "the First World," and "the Global North."
2. This "reversal" of globalization is far more common than is generally recognized. Countries that experience political turbulence, for instance, frequently find that foreign capital and investment quickly dry up, as has recently been the case with Zimbabwe, Pakistan, Egypt, and Syria.

Chapter 9

1. The term "scientist" was first coined in the nineteenth century, long after the Scientific Revolution of the sixteenth to eighteenth centuries. At the time, people with an interest in investigating the natural world were typically called philosophers or "natural philosophers," but in the interest of clarity I use the term "scientists" throughout the chapter.

Chapter 10

1. The total death toll from the Haitian earthquake is disputed, with estimates ranging from 158,000 to 316,000 people (the latter being the official figure put forth by the Haitian government). In any case, the numbers are staggering.

Glossary

absolute scarcity Refers to scarcity based on the ultimate limits of a resource available within a country or across the planet as a whole.

actor-network theory Closely associated with the work of French sociologist Bruno Latour, it is the most influential of the co-construction theories. Actor-network theory argues that non-human things have agency, and can co-operate and resist human attempts to define and use them.

adaptation myth The assumption that communities or societies will adapt to change automatically or as a matter of course without requiring difficult decisions or advance planning.

adaptive capacity The ability of a community to absorb shocks and adapt to long-term changes.

anthropocene A suggested label for the current geological period, literally the "age of humans," in recognition of our profound and observable impact on the planet.

anthropocentrism A worldview that places humans at the centre; an inability to see the world through the eyes of other living things.

anti-environmentalism An evolving counter-movement that seeks to discredit or limit the influence of the environmentalist movement.

biomagnification The tendency of toxins to accumulate in animals higher along the food chain.

cap and trade A system whereby government sets the total allowable pollution levels in an industry or sector (a cap), and then allows actors to trade pollution permits amongst themselves, thus providing a financial incentive to reduce emissions.

carrying capacity The maximum number of organisms that can be sustained by a given ecosystem or production system.

cash-cropping An agricultural term for growing a small number of products exclusively for export into more lucrative markets. It usually involves questionable environmental practices.

citizen-expert A self-educated or self-informed person who acquires deep knowledge about an issue or field because of personal interest or concern.

co-constitutive The idea that two things create and pattern one another, such as nature and society.

co-construction theory A loose collection of theories that argue that the natural and social worlds are intertwined and deeply affect one another in an ongoing and iterative way.

coevolution An idea associated with co-constructionism, the concept suggests that society and nature are continuously pushing one another to change and adapt.

collective action Co-operation among people in pursuit of a common goal or interest.

co-management The co-operative management of a territory, natural resource, and/or ecosystem. It usually involves partnerships between government and local people.

command and control An approach to environmental regulation whereby governments actively dictate how an industry or sector is to respond to environmental problems.

commodification The creation of exclusive and tradeable property rights where they had not existed before.

community capital The assets possessed by a community, which can be monetary, human (skills), social (networks and solidarity), and natural.

conflict theory A contemporary label for sociologists working in the Marxist tradition, which sees society as riven by deep structural conflicts among groups with different material interests.

conservationism An idea popular in the twentieth century that natural resources needed to be rationally managed by the state to conserve their value over time.

cosmology A very broad and collectively held explanation of how the world works at a fundamental level.

counter-movement A social movement that mobilizes to counter or resist the demands of another social movement.

Crown land Land that is controlled by federal or provincial governments in Canada.

cultural consensus A widely shared agreement on key values and social norms. Does not need to be universally held or recognized.

deconstruction A methodological process of "disassembling" social constructions and looking at how they were built using various claims, symbols, and narratives.

democratic deficit The closing off of opportunities for democratic participation or debate.

disaster myth The assumption that people respond selfishly in a disaster, taking it as an opportunity to steal or commit violence.

discourse Ways of representing reality using language and other symbols. Discourse often reflects hidden assumptions and power relations in a society.

ecological footprint An estimate of the impact of a population's resource consumption and waste production, as translated into the amount of productive land required to produce and absorb those impacts.

ecological modernization theory A sociological theory that suggests that political, economic, and cultural forces associated with heightened environmental concern and knowledge are encouraging reforms in how capitalism is practised, making it greener and less energy and resource intensive.

ecologically unequal exchange A concept that captures the tendency of wealthy nations to import consumer goods while exporting the environmental harm, wastes, and resource depletion involved in the production of those goods.

empiricism A philosophy within the natural and social sciences suggesting that theories and explanations should be based on concrete and observable evidence.

enclosure movement The privatization of agricultural land in England that ended the rights of peasants to use common lands, thus encouraging mass migration to the cities in the seventeenth to nineteenth centuries.

energy return on investment The amount of energy gained from an activity (like harvesting oil) compared to the amount of energy expended. It is usually expressed as a ratio.

environmental convergence The notion that economic and political integration creates incentives and means for developing countries to adopt the "greener" standards, technologies, and production techniques found in developed nations.

environmental determinism The assumption that environmental variables are the sole and uniform cause of observed social phenomena, such as culture.

environmental flows Patterns in the regional and international movement of resources, products, and wastes.

environmental justice The notion that environmental degradation and social inequality are linked; the combination of environmental and social activism.

environmental Kuznets curve Refers to the changing relationship that sometimes occurs between levels of national wealth and environmental damage. At first, wealth and environmental damage rise together, but at some point are decoupled and environmental damage diminishes relative to wealth. It is observable in some but not all countries.

environmental racism The intentional shifting of environmental damage and wastes onto visible minority populations.

environmental realism An approach in environmental sociology that stresses the power of environmental conditions or events to pattern society or social responses.

environmental refugees People who have been forced to temporarily or permanently relocate due to an environmental event or change.

epistemological hierarchicalism A conceptual tool for evaluating knowledge claims. It accepts that valid knowledge can come from multiple sources, but argues that the validity of knowledge should be judged by the weight of available evidence.

epistemology The study of knowledge; a particular view or approach to these questions: What can be known? What is reliable knowledge?

epoch A unit of geological time, usually measured by glaciation periods (ice ages).

era A unit of geological time, typically dozens or hundreds of millions of years in length.

eugenics A scientific and social movement to alter the genetic composition of a group or society. Eugenics was popular in Europe and North America, but discredited following the horrors of the Second World War.

experimentation A method in the natural and social sciences that measures responses to different types of stimulus.

externality A term in economics that refers to a cost or benefit not included in an economic model or decision. Air pollution is frequently an externality, because companies emit it for free.

fracking A new technique for accessing oil and natural gas that uses a high pressure mix of water and chemicals to break apart rock formations deep underground. Critics are concerned that it may affect groundwater and cause minor earthquakes.

framing The strategic use of symbols, metaphors, claims, and stories to advance a particular interpretation of an event or thing.

global division of labour The allocation of different tasks and occupations across the globe. For instance, most manufacturing for the global economy now occurs in lesser-developed countries, but product design, marketing, and finance typically occur in wealthy countries.

globalization The increasing economic, social, and political integration of geographically distant localities.

maladaptation Adaptation to environmental change that further degrades the natural environment.

manufactured risks Risks that are a direct result of human actions or technologies. The archetype is nuclear waste, which does not exist in nature.

market fundamentalism The unwavering belief that the free market is the best way to allocate goods and wealth. It also implies that the market is the ultimate expression of collective will.

means of production The way that value is created within an economy. Typically controlled by a small group who use social controls such as property rights to exclude others. The basis of Marxist class analysis.

modernity The current era, characterized by rationalism, industrialism, the nation-state, a faith in secular science and technology, and a strong notion of linear progress.

modernization theory of development An older theory of economic development that suggests that poorer countries need to "catch up" to wealthier ones by emulating their experiences and modernizing their economies and institutions.

natural capital The value of natural resources and/or productive land and ecosystems. This value can be symbolic and cultural as well as economic.

natural disaster A natural event such as a hurricane, tornado, flood, earthquake, or fire that affects human populations.

neoliberalism An economic system that emphasizes free markets, minimal regulation, and the commodification of nature. Neoliberal theory suggests that by extending property rights to nature and creating pseudo-markets for pollutants, we can harness the power of the market to conserve and improve the natural environment.

neo-Malthusianism A revisionist or adapted interpretation of the ideas of Thomas Malthus (1766–1834) who famously argued that the expansion of the human population would ultimately be checked by absolute scarcity of food.

neo-Marxism A revisionist or adapted interpretation of the ideas of Karl Marx (1818–1883), who argued that capitalist society is shaped by ongoing conflict between capitalist and labouring classes.

norms Expectations of behaviour and conduct that are reinforced by peers.

ocean acidification A consequence of the rising concentration of carbon dioxide in the atmosphere. As carbon dioxide is absorbed into the ocean, it forms carbonic acid, thus lowering the pH level of the ocean and making it more difficult for marine animals to form hard shells.

panarchy theory A theory that originated in biology and ecosystem science that is also sometimes applied to social systems. It examines how social actions and structures fit in to the deep temporal and geographic cyclical rhythms that are common in the natural environment.

peak theory The idea that demand for key natural resources is beginning to outstrip the Earth's ability to provide them, implying a decline in their long-term availability.

political ecology A popular theory across the social sciences that looks at the influence of human politics on natural ecosystems, and vice versa.

politicized science The dishonest or selective use of scientific data or findings by politically motivated groups or individuals. Can also refer to dishonest scientific practice, although it usually refers to the use of scientific findings by non-scientists.

positivism A philosophy within the natural and social sciences suggesting that only those things that are measurable or observable are real.

post-materialist values The values that are thought to predominate in affluent societies, where people no longer have to worry about material wants.

pragmatism An approach to governing that stresses rational problem-solving.

preservationism A social movement that crested in the late nineteenth and early twentieth centuries, an antecedent to modern environmentalism that focused on preserving places of particular beauty and majesty.

principle of substitution The notion that if a resource becomes truly scarce, producers and consumers will shift to a similar alternative resource.

reductionism A scientific method that involves breaking down objects and problems to their simplest components in order to better understand "the fundamentals" of what is being observed.

reflexive modernization According to the risk society thesis, reflexive modernization is the core characteristic of the second stage of modernity (which we are now just entering). Ulrich Beck describes reflexive modernization as a state of "self-confrontation," in which society seeks to address the consequences of past actions and develop mechanisms for better anticipating future problems.

relative scarcity A term originating in economics. It refers to the balance of supply and demand, implying that all scarcity is temporary in a free market because producers will adjust production in response to market signals.

relativism The idea that truth and reality are determined by context and will vary according to social and cultural circumstances.

renewable resources Natural resources that will regenerate in perpetuity unless fundamentally disrupted. Also refers to energy sources beyond human influence (winds, solar, tidal).

resilience The ability of social and natural systems to respond to changes without breaking down.

resource capture The process by which a group or company gains exclusive control or access to a natural resource.

risk society thesis A sociological theory closely associated with the thinking of German sociologist Ulrich Beck. The risk society thesis posits that global society is being restructured by the unintended consequences of modern capitalist development, particularly the creation of new environmental hazards. It argues that these problems are forcing both individuals and institutions into a state of "reflexivity" or self-criticism and self-confrontation that is sowing the seeds of deeper social and political change, ultimately leading to a more participative society.

Romantic movement A literary and artistic movement of the nineteenth century that arose in response to the Industrial Revolution, stressing emotion, aesthetics, and nature over the mechanism of industry.

scarcity A condition of lack or want, where demand exceeds supply. See also *relative scarcity* and *absolute scarcity*.

Scientific Certainty Argumentation Methods The intentional highlighting of uncertainty to obfuscate a scientific finding or delay political action to address a scientifically validated problem.

scientism The assumption that science is the only means of creating reliable knowledge.

social class One of the key divisions in society based on access to economic resources and social power. Closely associated with the works of Karl Marx and Max Weber.

social constructionism An approach in environmental sociology that argues that environmental issues and problems are constructed through the mobilization of claims, symbols, narratives, and other resources. It does not necessarily deny that they are also real.

Social Darwinism The application of Charles Darwin's (1809–1882) ideas about evolutionary competition to the understanding of human societies and groups. It has been largely discredited.

social fact The social forces, values, customs, norms, and institutions that pattern and constrain individual behaviours in a particular circumstance. The concept originates in the work of Émile Durkheim.

social movement A mobilization of citizens to pursue or resist specific political, economic, and/or cultural changes.

social status A hierarchy of privilege and prestige within a group or society.

social structure The assemblage of formal and informal rules and constraints that produce and enforce social patterns in society.

sociology of scientific knowledge The sociological analysis of how scientific knowledge is created and accepted.

structural adjustment programs Refers to the conditions that are placed on loans and debt relief from the World Bank and International Monetary Fund. The conditions usually involve opening up key industries to outside competition and/or privatizing natural resources.

subpolitics Politics that takes place outside of traditional political institutions. It is frequently but not necessarily grassroots.

sustainability The idea that resources can be harvested in perpetuity if they are carefully managed. Sustainability also frequently refers to prudent but perpetual economic growth.

symbolic interactionism A school within sociology that analyzes how people interpret the world through shared symbols, rituals, and understandings.

technocracy Governance and decision-making based exclusively on the inputs and opinions of experts, sciences, and other knowledge elites.

tight coupling Refers to the inter-dependency of technological and/or social systems. Sociologist Charles Perrow argues that systems that are closely intertwined are more likely to produce cascading failures.

treadmill theory A sociological theory of capitalism's impact on nature. It argues that social harmony in a capitalist system is made possible by economic growth based on continuous and accelerating environmental damage and exploitation.

Type I error Accepting a hypothesis that is ultimately shown to be wrong.

Type II error Rejecting a hypothesis that is ultimately shown to be correct.

value neutrality The notion that scientists ought to set their personal values and political preferences aside when creating or evaluating scientific knowledge. It is generally seen as a cornerstone of modern scientific practice.

vulnerability The degree of exposure of a population, group, or individual to potential harm.

world polity school in sociology A sociological theory that argues that globalization is a key mechanism for spreading pro-environmental norms and behaviours.

world systems theory A neo-Marxist theory of international relations and development. It argues that a "core" group of nations has achieved and main-tained a high level of wealth by exploiting the labour and natural resources found in "peripheral" countries.

worldview A symbolic framework for interpreting phenomena and events, usually based in existing personal and societal interests and ideology.

References

Adams, C., Murrieta, R., Neves, W., & Harris, M. (2009). *Amazon Peasant Societies in a Changing Environment*. New York: Springer.

Adger, W. N. (2000). Social and ecological resilience: Are they related? *Progress in Human Geography, 24*, 347–364.

Adger, W. N. (2003). Social capital, collective action, and adaptation to climate change. *Economic Geography 79*(4), 387–404.

Adger, W. N. (2006). Vulnerability. *Global Environmental Change 16*, 268–281.

Adger, W. N., & Barnett, J. (2009). Commentary. *Environment and Planning A 41*, 2800–2805.

Agrawal, A. (1995). Dismantling the divide between indigenous and scientific knowledge. *Development and Change 26*, 413–439.

Agrawal, A. (2010). Local institutions and adaptation to climate change. In *Social Dimensions of Climate Change: Equity and Vulnerability in a Warming World* (pp. 173–198). Washington DC: World Bank.

Agyeman, J., Cole, P., Haluza-DeLay, R., O'Riley, P. (Eds.). (2009). *Speaking for Ourselves: Environmental Justice in Canada*. Vancouver: UBC Press.

Alario, M. V. (2012). Freudenburg on technological risks: Transcendent or titanic? *Journal of Environmental Studies and Sciences, 2*, 53–57.

Alario, M. V., & Freudenburg, W. R. (2010). Environmental risks and environmental justice, or how titanic risks are not so titanic after all. *Sociological Inquiry, 80*(3), 500–512.

Alexander, D. (1997). The study of natural disasters, 1977–97: Some reflections on a changing field of knowledge. *Disasters 21*(4), 284–304.

Allen, R. (2002). Agriculture and the origins of the state in Ancient Egypt. *Explorations in Economic History, 34*(2): 135–54.

Amnesty International, & Greenpeace Netherlands. (2012). *The toxic truth: About a company called Trafigura, a ship called the Probo Koala, and the dumping of toxic waste in Cote d'Ivoire* (No. AFR31/002/2012). London, UK.

Retrieved from http://www.amnesty.org/en/library/info/AFR31/002/2012/en.

Anderies, J. (2006). Robustness, institutions, and large-scale change in social-ecological systems: The Hohokam of the Phoenix Basin. *Journal of Institutional Economics, 2*: 133–155.

Anderson, C., & Stephenson L. (2011). Environmentalism and party support in Canada: Recent trends outside Quebec. *Canadian Journal of Political Science, 44*(2): 341–66.

Armitage, D., Berkes, F., & Doubleday, N. (Eds.). (2007). *Adaptive Co-Management*. Vancouver: UBC Press.

Atran, S., & Medin, D. L. (1997). Knowledge and action: Cultural models of nature and resource management in Mesoamerica. In M. Bazerman (Ed.), *Environment, Ethics and Behavior* (pp. 171–208). San Francisco: New Lexington Press.

Attaran, A., Roberts, D. R., Curtis, C. F., & Kilama, W. L. (2000). Balancing risks on the backs of the poor. *Nature Medicine, 6*(7), 729–731.

Audla, T. (2012). *Polar bear ban: A precautionary tale*. Iqaluit: Inuit Tapiriit Kanatami. Retrieved from https://www.itk.ca/about-itk/dept-environment-and-wildlife/polar-bears/polar-bear-ban-precautionary-tale

Backstrand, K. (2003). Civic science for sustainability: reframing the role of experts, policy-makers and citizens in environmental governance. *Global Environmental Politics, 3*(4), 24–41.

Baerlocher, B., & Burger, P. (2010). Ecological regimes: Towards a conceptual integration of biophysical environment into social theory. In M. Gross & H. Heinrichs (Eds.), *Environmental Sociology: European Perspectives and Interdisciplinary Challenges* (pp. 79–93). New York: Springer.

Bakker, K. (2003). A political ecology of water privatization. *Studies in Political Economy, 70*, 35–58.

Bakker, K. (2007). The "commons" versus the "commodity": Alter-globalization, anti-privatization and the human right to water in the Global South. *Antipode*, *39*(3), 430–455.

Baland, J.M., Bardhan, P., Das, S., Mookherjee, D., & Sarkar, R. (2010). The environmental impact of poverty: Evidence from firewood collection in rural Nepal. *Economic Development and Cultural Change*, *59*(1), 23–61.

Bardi, U. (2009). Peak oil: The four stages of a new idea. *Energy*, *34*(3), 323–326.

Barker, G. (2006). *The Agricultural Revolution in Prehistory: Why Did Foragers Become Farmers?* New York: Oxford University Press.

Barnes, W., & Gilman, N. (2011). Green social democracy or barbarism: Climate change and the end of high modernism. In C. Calhoun & G. Derluguian (Eds.), *The Deepening Crisis: Governance Challenges After Neoliberalism* (pp. 43–66). New York: New York University Press.

Barnett, H., & Morse, C. (1963). *Scarcity and Growth: The economics of natural resource availability*. Baltimore: John's Hopkins University Press.

Barr, S. (2003). Strategies for sustainability: Citizens and responsible environmental behaviour. *Area*, *35*(3), 227–240.

Barr, S. (2008). *Environment and Society: Sustainability, Policy and the Citizen*. Aldershot: Ashgate.

Barr, S. (2008). *Environment and Society: Sustainability, Policy and the Citizen*. Burlington, VT: Ashgate.

Bartelson, J. (2000). Three concepts of globalization. *International Sociology*, *15*(2), 180–196.

Baumgartner, S., Becker, C., Faber, M., & Manstetten, R. (2006). Relative and absolute scarcity of nature: Assessing the roles of economics and ecology for biodiversity conservation. *Ecological Economics*. *59*(4): 487–498.

Bavington, D. (2010a). From hunting fish to managing populations: Fisheries science and the destruction of Newfoundland cod fisheries. *Science as Culture 19*(4), 509–528.

Bavington, D. (2010b). *Managed Annihilation: An Unnatural History of the Newfoundland Cod Collapse*. Vancouver: UBC Press.

Beck, U. (1992). *Risk Society: Towards a New Modernity*. London: Sage.

Beck, U. (1996). World risk society as cosmopolitan society? Ecological questions in a framework of manufactured uncertainties. *Theory, Culture and Society*, *13*(4), 1–32.

Beck, U. (1999). *World Risk Society*. Malden, MA: Polity.

Beck, U. (2009). *World at Risk*. Malden, MA: Polity.

Beck, U. (2010). Remapping social inequalities in an age of climate change: For a cosmopolitan renewal of sociology. *Global Networks*, *10*(2), 165–181.

Beck, U., Bonss, W., & Lau, C. (2003). The theory of reflexive modernization: Problematic, hypotheses and research programme. *Theory, Culture and Society*, *20*(2), 1–33.

Beeby, D. (2012, August 26). BPA Study Brings Good News for Consumers, Environmentalists. *Canadian Press*. Ottawa. Retrieved from http://www.theglobeandmail.com/news/national/bpa-study-brings-good-news-for-consumers-environmentalists/article4499966/.

Bell, M. M. (2012). *An Invitation to Environmental Sociology* (4th ed.). Thousand Oaks, CA: Sage.

Benton, T. (2010). Animals and us. In M. R. Redclift & G. Woodgate (Eds.), *The International Handbook of Environmental Sociology* (pp. 197–211). Northhampton MA: Edward Elgar.

Berelowitz, L. (2010). *Dream City: Vancouver and the Global Imagination*. Vancouver: Douglas & McIntyre.

Berke, P. R., Chuenpagdee, R., Juntarashote, K., & Chang, S. (2008). Human-ecological dimensions of disaster resiliency in Thailand: Social capital and aid delivery. *Journal of Environmental Planning and Management*, *51*(2), 303–317.

Berkes, F. (2008). *Sacred Ecology* (2nd ed.). New York: Routledge.

Bernstein, P. L. (1996). *Against the Gods: The Remarkable Story of Risk*. New York: John Wiley & Sons.

Beronius, A., Ruden, C., Hakansson, J., & Hanberg, A. (2010). A risk to all or none? A comparative analysis of controversies in the health risk assessment of Bisphenol A. *Reproductive Toxicology*, *29*(2), 132–146.

Bhagwati, J. (2007). *In Defense of Globalization* (2nd ed.). New York: Oxford University Press.

Biersack, A. (2006). Reimagining political ecology: Culture/power/history/nature. In A. Biersack & J. B. Greenberg (Eds.), *Reimagining Political Ecology* (pp. 3–40). Durham: Duke University Press.

Bird, M. (1995). Fire, prehistoric humanity, and the environment. *Interdisciplinary Science Reviews, 20*(2), 141–154.

Blumer, H. (1969). *Symbolic Interactionism: Perspective and Method.* Berkeley: University of California Press.

Bookchin, M. (2007). *Social Ecology and Communalism.* Oakland: AK Press.

Boudier, F., & Bensebaa, F. (2011). Hazardous waste management and corporate social responsibility: Illegal transport of electrical and electronic waste. *Business and Society Review, 116*(1), 29–53.

Boyce, J. K. (2004). Green and brown? Globalization and the environment. *Oxford Review of Economic Policy, 20*(1), 105–128.

Boykoff, M. (2009). We speak for the trees: Media reporting on the environment. *Annural Review of Environment and Resources,* 34: 431–457.

Brautigam, D. (2009). *The Dragon's Gift: The Real Story of China in Africa.* Oxford: Oxford University Press.

Brown, M. B. (2009). *Science in Democracy: Expertise, Institutions, and Representation.* Cambridge, MA: MIT Press.

Brunner, R., Steelman, T., Coe-Juell, L., Cromley, C., Edwards, C., & Tucker, D. (2005). *Adaptive Governance: Integrating Science, Policy and Decision-Making.* New York: Columbia University Press.

Bryson, B. (2004). *A Short History of Nearly Everything.* New York: Anchor.

Burawoy, M. (2000). *Global Ethnography: Forces, Connections, and Imaginations in a Postmodern World.* Berkeley, CA: University of California Press.

Burmingham, K., & Cooper, G. (1999). Being constructive: Social construction-ism and the environment. *Sociology, 33,* 297–319.

Burney, D., & Flannery, T. (2005). Fifty millennia of catastrophic extinctions after human contact. *Trends in Ecology & Evolution 20*(7), 395–401.

Buttel, F. H. (2010). Social institutions and environmental change. In M. Redclift & G. Woodgate (Eds.), *The International Handbook of Environmental Sociology* (2nd edition) (pp. 33–47). Northampton MA: Edward Elgar.

Buttel, F. H. (2003). Environmental sociology and the exploration of environmental reform. *Organization & Environment, 16*(3), 306–344.

Buttel, F. H. (2006). Globalization, environmental reform, and US hegemony. In G. Spaargaren, A. P. J. Mol, & F. H. Buttel (Eds.), *Governing Environmental Flows: Global Challenges to Social Theory* (pp. 157–184). Cambridge, MA: MIT Press.

Buttel, F. H. (2009). Ecological moderniza-tion as social theory. In A. P. J. Mol, D. A. Sonnenfeld, & G. Spaargaren (Eds.), *The Ecological Modernisation Reader: Environmental Reform in Theory and Practice* (pp. 123–137). New York: Routledge.

Buttel, F.H. (2002). Environmental sociology and the classical tradition. In R. Dunlap, F. Buttel, P. Dickens, & A. Gijswijt (Eds.), *Sociological Theory and the Environment* (pp. 35–50). New York: Rowman & Littlefield.

Buttel, F.H., Dickens, P., Dunlap, R. & Gijswijt, A. (2002). Sociological theory and the environment: An overview and introduction. In R. Dunlap, F. Buttel, P. Dickens, & A. Gijswijt (Eds.), *Sociological Theory and the Environment* (pp. 3–32). New York: Rowman & Littlefield.

Callon, M., Lascoumes,, P., & Barthe, Y. (2009). *Acting in an Uncertain World: An Essay on Technical Democracy.* Cambridge, MA: MIT Press.

Campell, S. K., & Butler, V. L. (2010). Archaeological evidence for resilience of Pacific Northwest salmon populations and the socioecological system over the last ~7,500 years. *Ecology and Society, 15*(1), 1–17.

Canadian Plastics Industry Association. (2012). *Safety of Bisphenol A.* Canadian Plastics Industry Association. Retrieved from http://www.plastics.ca/articles_ merge/safetyfoodwrapbisph.php.

Canadian Press. (2010). Oakville power plant plan cancelled. 7 October. Retrieved from http://www.cbc.ca/ news/canada/toronto/story/2010/10/07/ oakville-plant.html.

Canadian Press. (2012). Oliver considers streamlining environmental review process. Retrieved from http://www.

ctv.ca/CTVNews/Canada/20120111/oliver-pipeline-110111/.

Cannon, T. (2002). Gender and climate hazards in Bangladesh. *Gender & Development, 10*(2), 45–50.

Carmack, E., McLaughlin, F., Whiteman, G., & Homer-Dixon, T. (2012). Detecting and coping with disruptive shocks in Arctic marine systems: A resilience approach to place and people. *Ambio, 41,* 56–65.

Carolan, M. (2008). The bright- and blind-spots of science: Why objective knowledge is not enough to resolve environmental controversies. *Critical Sociology 34*(5), 725–740.

Carolan, M. S. (2005). Society, biology, and ecology: Bringing nature back into sociology's disciplinary narrative through critical realism. *Organization & Environment, 18*(4), 393–421.

Carter, FW, & Turnock, D. (Eds.) (2002). *Environmental Problems of East Central Europe.* London: Routledge.

Castells, M. (2000). *The Rise of the Network Society* (2nd ed.). Cambridge, MA: Blackwell.

Castree, N. (2008). Neoliberalising nature: The logics of deregulation and reregulation. *Environment and Planning A, 40,* 131–152.

Castro, J. E. (2008). Neoliberal water and sanitation policies as a failed development strategy: Lessons from developing countries. *Progress in Development Studies, 8*(1), 63–83.

Catton, W. Jr. (2002). Has the Durkheim legacy misled sociology? In R. Dunlap, F. Buttel, P. Dickens, & A. Gijswijt (Eds.), *Sociological Theory and the Environment* (pp. 90–115). New York: Rowman & Littlefield.

CBC. (2011, 17 June). Tales of the Flood. CBC Winnipeg. Retrieved from http://www.cbc.ca/player/News/Canada/Manitoba/Flood+2011/ID/2008855795/.

Charnovitz, S. (2008). An introduction to the trade and environment debate. In K. Gallagher (Ed.), *Handbook on Trade and the Environment* (pp. 237–246). Northhampton MA: Edward Elgar.

Chase-Dunn, C., Kawano, Y., & Brewer, B. D. (2000). Trade globalization since 1795: Waves of integration in the world-system. *American Sociological Review, 65*(1), 77–95.

Chavez, E. C., & Wailes, E. J. (2013). US drought impacts on the US and international rice economy. Presented at the Southern Agricultural Economics Association, Orlando, FL.

Chew, S. (2001). *World Ecological Degradation.* New York: Rowman & Littlefield.

Chiswick, B. R., Larsen, N., & Pieper, P. (2010). *The production of PhDs in the United States and Canada* (No. 5367). Bonn: Institute for the Study of Labour. Retrieved from http://ftp.iza.org/dp5367.pdf.

Christoff, P. (2009). Ecological modernisation, ecological modernities. In A. P. J. Mol, D. A. Sonnenfeld, & G. Spaargaren (Eds.), *The Ecological Modernisation Reader: Environmental reform in theory and practice* (pp. 101–122). New York: Routledge.

Clapp, J. (2001). *Toxic Exports: The Transfer of Hazardous Wastes from Rich to Poor Countries.* Ithaca, NY: Cornell University Press.

Clapp, J., & Dauvergne, P. (2011). *Paths to a Green World* (2nd ed.). Cambridge, MA: MIT Press.

Cole, M., Elliott, R., & Strobl, E. (2008). The environmental performance of firms: The role of foreign ownership, training, and experience. *Ecological Economics, 65,* 538–546.

Collins, H., & Evans, R. (2002). The third wave of science studies: Studies of expertise and experience. *Social Studies of Science, 32*(2), 235–296.

Conceicao, P. & Mendoza, R. (2009). Anatomy of the global food crisis. *Third World Quarterly, 30*(6): 1159–1182.

Cone, M. (2009). Should DDT be used to combat malaria? *Scientific American.* Retrieved from http://www.scientificamerican.com/article.cfm?id=ddt-use-to-combat-malaria.

Conference Board of Canada. (2011). Water Consumption. Retrieved from http://www.conferenceboard.ca/hcp/details/environment/water-consumption.aspx

Connelly, J., & Smith, G. (2003). *Politics and the Environment: From Theory to Practice* (2nd ed.). New York: Routledge.

Cooksey, B. (2011). Marketing reform? The rise and fall of agricultural liberalisation in Tanzania. *Development Policy Review, 29,* 57–81.

Cox, R. (2004). *Environmental Communication and the Public Sphere.* (2nd ed.) Thousand Oaks: Sage.

Cronon, W. (1995). The trouble with wilderness. In W. Cronon (Ed.), *Uncommon Ground* (pp. 69–90). New York: Norton.

Crowley, S. (2006). Where is home? Housing for low-income people after the 2005 hurricane. In C. W. Hartman & G. D. Squires (Eds.), *There Is No Such Thing as a Natural Disaster* (pp. 121–166). New York: Routledge.

Curran, D. (2013). Risk society and the distribution of bads: Theorizing class in the risk society. *British Journal of Sociology, 64*(1): 44–62.

Curtis, F. (2009). Peak globalization: Climate change, oil depletion and global trade. *Ecological Economics, 69,* 427–434.

Cutter, S. L., Barnes, L., Berry, M., Burton, C., Evans, E., Tate, E., & Webb, J. (2008). A place-based model for understanding community resilience to natural disasters. *Global Environmental Change, 18,* 598–606.

Dadeby, A. (2012). Energy returned on energy invested. In R. DeYoung & T. Princen (Eds.), *The Localization Reader: Adapting to the coming downshift* (pp. 13–26). Cambridge MA: MIT Press.

Dallal, A. (2010). *Islam, Science, and the Challenge of History.* New Haven: Yale University Press.

Dalton, R. (2009). Economics, environmentalism and party alignments: A note on partisan change in advanced industrial democracies. *European Journal of Political Research, 48*(2), 161–175.

Daubs, K. (2010). Oakville brings in Erin Brockovich to fight power plant. *Toronto Star.* 1 October.

Dauvergne, P. (2008). *The Shadows of Consumption: Consequences for the Global Environment.* Cambridge, MA: MIT Press.

Dauvergne, P., & Lister, J. (2012). Big brand sustainability: Governance prospects and environmental limits. *Global Environmental Change, 22*(1), 36–45.

Davidson, D. (2010). The applicability of the concept of resilience to social systems: Some sources of optimism and nagging doubts. *Society and Natural Resources, 23*(12), 1135–1149.

Delicia-Willison, Z., & Gaillard, J. (2012). Community action and disaster. In B. Wisner, J. Gaillard, & I. Kelman (Eds.), *The Routledge Handbook of Hazards and Disaster Risk Reduction* (pp. 711–722). New York: Routledge.

Demeritt, D. (2001). The construction of global warming and the politics of science. *Annals of the Association of American Geographers, 91*(2), 307–337.

Demeritt, D. (2006). Science studies, climate change and the prospects for constructivist critique. *Economy and Society, 35*(3), 453–479.

Depledge, J. (2006). The opposite of learning: Ossification in the climate change regime. *Global Environmental Politics, 6*(1), 1–22.

Dessler, A. & Parson, E. (2006). *The Science and Politics of Global Climate Change: A Guide to the Debate.* New York: Cambridge University Press.

Devall, B. (1992). Deep ecology and radical environmentalism. In R. Dunlap & A. Mertin (Eds.), *American Environmentalism: The US Environmental movement, 1970–1990* (pp. 52–79). New York: Taylor & Francis.

DeYoung, R. & Princen, T. (Eds.). (2012). *The Localization Reader: Adapting to the coming downshift.* Cambridge MA: MIT Press.

Diamond, J. (1997). *Guns, Germs and Steel.* New York: Norton

Diamond, J. (2005). *Collapse: How Societies Choose to Fail or Succeed.* New York: Viking.

Dietz, T., Rosa, E. A., & York, R. (2012). Environmentally efficient well-being: Is there a Kuznets curve? *Applied Geography, 32,* 21–28.

Dietz, T., Rosa, E. A., & York, R. (2007). Driving the ecological footprint. *Frontiers in Ecology and the Environment, 5*(1), 13–18.

Dilworth, C. (2010). *Too Smart for Our Own Good: The Ecological Predicament of Humankind.* New York: Cambridge University Press.

Dobkowski, M., & Wallimann, I. (Eds.). (2002). *On the Edge of Scarcity.* Syracuse NY: Syracuse University Press.

Dowsley, M., & Wenzel, G. (2008). "The time of the most polar bears": A co-management conflict in Nunavut. *Arctic, 61*(2), 177–189.

Doyle, T. (2005). *Environmental Movements in Minority and Majority Worlds: A*

Global Perspective. New Brunskwick NJ: Rutgers University Press.

Drabek, T. E., & McEntire, D. A. (2003). Emergent phenomena and the sociology of disaster: Lessons, trends and opportunities from the research literature. *Disaster Prevention and Management, 12*(2), 97–112.

Dryzek, J. S. (2005). *The Politics of the Earth: Environmental Discourses* (2nd ed.). New York: Oxford University Press.

Dunlap, R. (2002). Paradigms, theories, and environmental sociology. In R. E. Dunlap, F. H. Buttel, P. Dickens, & A. Gijswijt (Eds.), *Sociological Theory and the Environment* (pp. 329–350). Lanham, MD: Rowman & Littlefield.

Dunlap, R. (2010). The maturation and diversification of environmental sociology: From constructivism and realism to agnosticism and pragmatism. In M. Redclift & G. Woodgate (Eds.), *The International Handbook of Environmental Sociology* (2nd ed.) (pp. 15–32). Northampton MA: Edward Elgar.

Dunlap, R. & Catton, W. (1979). Environmental sociology. *Annual Review of Sociology, 5,* 243–273.

Dunlap, R. & Catton, W. (2002). Which function(s) of the environment do we study? A comparison of environmental and natural resource sociology, *Society and Natural Resources, 15,* 239–249.

Dunlap, R. & McCright, A. (2011). Organized climate change denial. In J. Dryzek, R. Norgaard & D. Schlosberg (Eds.), *The Oxford Handbook of Climate Change and Society* (pp. 144–160). New York: Oxford University Press.

Dunlap, R. & York, R. (2008). The globalization of environmental concern and the limits of the postmaterialist values explanation. *Sociological Quarterly, 49,* 529–563.

Dunlap, T. (1999). *Nature and the English Diaspora: Environment and History in the United States, Canada, Australia and New Zealand.* New York: Cambridge University Press.

Dye, T., & Steadman, D. (1990). Polynesian ancestors and their animal world. *American Scientist, 78*(3), 207–215.

Edwards, S. (1998) A history of the US environmental movement. In M. Clifford (Ed.). *Environmental Crime* (pp. 32–56). Galthersburg MD: Aspen.

Ellerman, A. D., Joscow, P. L., Schmalensee, R., Montero, J.-P., & Bailey, E. M. (2000). *Markets for Clean Air: The US Acid Rain Program.* New York: Cambridge University Press.

Ellickson, R., & Thorland, C. (1996). Ancient land law: Mesopotamia, Egypt, Israel. *Chicago-Kent Law Review, 71,* 321–362.

Elliott, A. (2002). Beck's sociology of risk: A critical assessment. *Sociology, 36*(2), 293–315.

Elliott, L. (2004). *The Global Politics of the Environment* (2nd ed.). New York: New York University Press.

Engle, N. L. (2011). Adaptive capacity and its assessment. *Global Environmental Change, 21,* 647–656.

EPA (Environmental Protection Agency). (2012). *Clean Air Interstate Rule, Acid Rain Program, and Former NOx Budget Trading Program 2010 Progress Report: Environmental and Health Results Report.* US Government. Retrieved from http://www.epa.gov/airmarkets/progress/ARPCAIR10_02.html.

EREC. (2012). *Statistics.* European Renewable Energy Council. Retrieved from http://www.erec.org/statistics/res-e-share.html.

Erickson, B. (2008). Bisphenol A under scrutiny. *Chemical & Engineering News, 86*(22), 36–39.

Erickson, C., & Candler, K. (1989). Raised fields and sustainable agriculture in the Lake Titicaca basin of Peru. In J. Browder (Ed.). *Fragile Lands of Lain America* (pp. 230–248). Boulder: Westview.

Ericson, R. V., Doyle, A., & Barry, D. (2003). *Insurance as Governance.* Toronto: University of Toronto Press.

Erikson, K. T. (1976). *Everything in Its Path: Destruction of Community in the Buffalo Creek Flood.* New York: Simon and Schuster.

Erikson, K. T. (1994). *A New Species of Trouble: Explorations in Disaster, Trauma, and Community.* New York: W.W. Norton.

Erler, C., & Novak, J. (2010). Bisphenol A exposure: Human risk and health policy. *Journal of Pediatric Nursing, 25*(5), 400–407.

Escobar, A. (2012). *Encountering Development: The Making and Unmaking of the Third World* (2nd ed.). Princeton NJ: Princeton University Press.

Finlayson, A. C., & McCay, B. J. (1998). Crossing the threshold of ecosystem resilience: The commercial extinction of northern cod. In F. Berkes & C. Folke (Eds.), *Linking Social and Ecological Systems* (pp. 311–337). New York: Cambridge University Press.

Fischer, F. (2000). *Citizens, Experts, and the Environment: The Politics of Local Knowledge*. Durham: Duke University Press.

Fisher, J. A., et al. (2010). Source attribution and interannual variability of Arctic pollution in spring constrained by aircraft (ARCTAS, ARCPAC) and satellite (AIRS) observations of carbon monoxide. *Atmospheric Chemistry and Physics, 10*(3), 977–996.

Fisher, S. (2010). Violence against women and natural disasters: Findings from post-tsunami Sri Lanka. *Violence Against Women, 16*(8), 902–918.

Flannery, T. (2011). *Here on Earth: A Natural History of the Planet*. New York: HarperCollins.

Folke, C. (2006). Resilience: The emergence of a perspective for social-ecological systems analyses. *Global Environmental Change, 16*, 253–267.

Forsyth, T. (2003). *Critical Political Ecology: The Politics of Environmental Science*. New York: Routledge.

Foster, J. (2008). *The Sustainability Mirage: Illusion and Reality in the Coming War on Climate Change*. London: Earthscan.

Foster, J.B. (1999). Marx's theory of metabolic rift: Foundations for environmental sociology. *American Journal of Sociology, 105*(2), 366–405.

Foster, J.B., Clark, B. & York, R. (2010). *The Ecological Rift: Capitalism's War on the Earth*. New York: Monthly Review Press.

Foster, J. B., & Holleman, H. (2012). Weber and the environment: Classical foundations for a postexemptionalist sociology. *American Journal of Sociology, 117*(6), 1625–1673.

Freedman, A. (2013, 24 January). Risks of Hurricane Sandy-like surge events rising. *Climate Central*. Retrieved from http://www.climatecentral.org/news/hurricane-sandy-unprecedented-in-historical-record-study-says-15505.

French, H. (2010). The Next Empire. *The Atlantic*. May 2010. Retrieved from http://www.theatlantic.com/magazine/archive/2010/05/the-next-empire/8018/.

Freudenburg, W. R., Frickel, S., & Gramling, R. (1995). Beyond the nature/society divide: Learning to think about a mountain. *Sociological Forum, 10*(3), 361–392.

Freudenburg, W. R., Gramling, R., & Davidson, D. (2008). Scientific certainty argumentation methods (SCAMs): Science and the politics of doubt. *Sociological Inquiry, 78*(1), 2–38.

Freudenburg, W. R., Gramling, R., Laska, S., & Erikson, K. T. (2009). *Catastrophe in the Making: The Engineering of Katrina and the Disasters of Tomorrow*. Washington DC: Island Press.

Frideres, J. S. (2011). *First Nations in the Twenty-First Century*. Don Mills, ON: Oxford University Press.

Friedman, T. L. (2007). *The World Is Flat* (3rd ed.). Vancouver: Douglas & McIntyre.

Fussell, E., Sastry, N., & VanLandingham, M. (2010). Race, socioeconomic status, and return migration to New Orleans after Hurricane Katrina. *Population & Environment, 31*, 20–42.

Gallagher, R., & Appenzeller, T. (1999). Beyond reductionism. *Science, 284*(5411), 79.

Galloway, G. (2012, 24 November). Flooded out to save Winnipeg, Lake St. Martin residents now feel forgotten. *Globe and Mail*. Retrieved from www.theglobeandmail.com/news/national/flooded-out-to-save-winnipeg-lake-st-martin-residents-now-feel-forgotten/article5621936.

Gamson, W. & Modigliani, A. (1989). Media discourse and public opinion on nuclear power. *American Journal of Sociology, 95*(1), 1–37.

Gardner, D. (2011, 26 April). The age of America ends in 2016: IMF predicts the year China's economy will pass U.S. *Daily Mail Online*. Retrieved from http://www.dailymail.co.uk/news/article-1380486/The-Age-America-ends-2016-IMF-predicts-year-Chinas-economy-surpass-US.html.

Gauchat, G. (2012). Politicization of science in the public sphere: A study of public trust in the United States, 1974 to 2010. *American Sociological Review, 77*(2), 167–187.

George, E. W., Mair, H., & Reid, D. G. (2009). *Rural Tourism Development: Localism and Cultural Change.* Buffalo: Channel View Publications.

Gereffi, G., & Christian, M. (2009). The impacts of Wal-Mart: The rise and consequences of the world's dominant retailer. *Annual Review of Sociology, 35,* 573–591.

Giddens, A. (1990). *The Consequences of Modernity.* Stanford, CA: Stanford University Press.

Gilbertson, T., & Reyes, O. (2009). *Carbon Trading: How It Works and Why It Fails* (No. 7). Uppsala: Dag Hammarskjold Foundation.

Gillespie, R. (2008). Updating Martin's global extinction model. *Quaternary Science Reviews, 27,* 2522–2529.

Goldman, M. (2007). How "Water for All!" policy became hegemonic: The power of the World Bank and its transnational policy networks. *Geoforum, 38*(5), 786–800.

Goldman, M., & Schurman, R. A. (2000). Closing the "great divide": New social theory on society and nature. *Annual Review of Sociology, 26,* 563–584.

Goudie, A. (2006). *The Human Impact on the Natural Environment* (6th ed.). Malden MA: Blackwell.

Gould, K., Pellow, D., & Schnaiberg, A. (2008). *The Treadmill of Production: Injustice and Unsustainability in the Global Economy.* Boulder CO: Paradigm.

Grayson, D., & Meltzer, D. (2002). Clovis hunting and large mammal extinction: A critical review of the evidence. *Journal of World Prehistory, 16*(4), 313–359.

Gregg, C., & Houghton, B. (2006). Natural hazards. In D. Paton & J.D. Moore (Eds.). *Disaster Resilience: An Integrated Approach* (pp. 19–39). Springfield IL: Charles C Thomas.

Gregg, S. (1988). *Foragers and Farmers: Population Interaction and Agricultural Expansion in Prehistoric Europe.* Chicago: University of Chicago Press.

Grundmann, R., & Stehr, N. (2003). Social control and knowledge in democratic societies. *Science and Public Policy, 30*(3), 183–188.

Grundmann, R., & Stehr, N. (2012). *The Power of Scientific Knowledge: From Research to Public Policy.* New York: Cambridge University Press.

Grundmann, R. & Stehr, N. (2010). Climate change: What role for sociology? A response to Constance Lever-Tracy. *Current Sociology, 58,* 897–910.

Guha, R. (2000). *Environmentalism: A Global History.* New York: Longman

Guillén, M. F. (2010). Is globalization civilizing, destructive or feeble? A critique of five key debates in the social science literature. In G. Ritzer & Z. Atalay (Eds.), *Readings in Globalization: Key Concepts and Major Debates* (pp. 4–17). Malden, MA: Wiley-Blackwell.

Gunderson, L. H., & Holling, C. S. (2002). *Panarchy: Understanding Transformations in Human and Natural Systems.* Washington DC: Island Press.

Gunningham, N., Grabosky, P., & Sinclair, D. (1998). *Smart Regulation: Designing Environmental Policy.* Oxford: Clarendon Press.

Hacking, I. (1999). *The Social Construction of What?* Cambridge, MA: Harvard University Press.

Hajer, M. (1995). *The Politics of Environmental Discourse: Ecological Modernisation and the Policy Process.* Oxford: Clarendon Press.

Hajer, M. (2009). Ecological modernisation as cultural politics. In A. P. J. Mol, D. A. Sonnenfeld, & G. Spaargaren (Eds.), *The Ecological Modernisation Reader: Environmental Reform in Theory and Practice* (pp. 80–100). New York: Routledge.

Hallegatte, S. (2008). An adaptive regional input-output model and its application to the assessment of the economic cost of Katrina. *Risk Analysis, 28*(3), 779–799.

Haney, T. J., Elliott, J. R., & Fussell, E. (2010). Families and hurricane response: Risk, roles, resources, race and religion. In D. L. Brunsma, D. Overfelt, & J. S. Picou (Eds.), *The Sociology of Katrina* (2nd ed., pp. 77–102). New York: Rowman & Littlefield.

Hannigan, J. (2006). *Environmental Sociology* (2nd ed.). New York: Routledge.

Haque, C. E., & Etkin, D. (Eds.). (2012). *Disaster Risk and Vulnerability: Mitigation through Mobilizing Communities and Partnerships.* Montreal: McGill-Queen's University Press.

Haraway, D. (1988). Situated knowledges: The science question in feminism and the privilege of partial perspective. *Feminist Studies, 14*(3), 575–599.

Harper, C., & Fletcher, T. (2011). *Environment and Society: Human Perspectives on Environmental Issues, Canadian Edition.* Toronto: Pearson.

Harris, P. (2007). *Europe and Global Climate Change: Politics, Foreign Policy and Regional Cooperation.* Northampton, MA: Edward Elgar.

Harrison, K., & Sundstrom, L. M. (Eds.). (2010). *Global Commons, Domestic Decisions: The Comparative Politics of Climate Change.* Cambridge, MA: MIT Press.

Hartman, C. W., & Squires, G. D. (2006). *There is No Such Thing as a Natural Disaster.* New York: Routledge.

Harvey, D. (2005). *A Brief History of Neoliberalism.* New York: Oxford University Press.

Harvey, D. (2010). *The Enigma of Capital and the Crises of Capitalism.* New York: Oxford University Press.

Hawken, P., Lovins, A. B., & Lovins, H. L. (2000). *Natural Capitalism: Creating the Next Industrial Revolution.* Boston: Little, Brown & Co.

Haynes, G. (2007). A review of some attacks on the overkill hypothesis, with special attention to misrepresentations and doubletalk. *Quaternary International, 169 & 170,* 84–94.

Hayter, R. (2000). *Flexible Crossroads.* Vancouver: UBC Press.

Heinburg, R. (2010). *Peak Everything: Waking Up to the Century of Declines.* Gabriola Island BC: New Society Publishers.

Held, D., McGrew, A., Goldblatt, D., & Perraton, J. (1999). *Global Transformations: Politics, Economics, and Culture.* Stanford, CA: Stanford University Press.

Helvarg, D. (1997). *The War Against the Greens: The" Wise-Use" Movement, the New Right, and the Browning of America.* Madison, WI: Big Earth Publishing.

Henri, D., Gilchrist, H. G., & Peacock, E. (2010). Understanding and managing wildlife in Hudson Bay under a changing climate. In S. H. Ferguson (Ed.), *A Little Less Arctic: Top Predators in the World's Largest Northern Inland Sea, Hudson's Bay* (pp. 267–289). New York: Springer.

Henriques, A., & Richardson, J. (Eds.). (2004). *The Triple Bottom Line: Does It All Add Up?* London: Earthscan.

Hilhorst, D., & Bankoff, G. (2004). Introduction: Mapping vulnerability. In G. Bankoff, G. Frerks, & D. Hilhorst (Eds.), *Mapping Vulnerability: Disasters, Development & People* (pp. 1–9). London: Earthscan.

Hird, M. (2012). *Sociology of Science: A Critical Canadian Introduction.* Don Mills, ON: Oxford University Press.

Hoggan, J. (2008). *Climate Cover Up: The Crusade to Deny Global Warming.* Vancouver: Greystone.

Holling, C. S. (2004). From complex regions to complex worlds. *Ecology and Society, 9*(1), 11–21.

Homer-Dixon, T. (1999). *Scarcity and Violence.* Princeton: Princeton University Press.

Homer-Dixon, T. (2006). *The Upside of Down.* Toronto: Vintage.

Howlett, M. (2003). Canadian environmental policy and the natural resources sector: Paradoxical aspects of the transition to a post-staples political economy. In E. Lee & A. Pearl (Eds.), *The Integrity Gap* (pp. 42–67). Vancouver: UBC Press.

Hubbert, M.K. (1996). Exponential growth as a transient phenomenon in human history. In J. Daly & K. Townsend (Eds.). *Valuing the Earth* (pp. 113–126). Cambridge MA: MIT Press.

Huber, J. (1982). *Die verlorene Unschuld der Okologie: Neue Technologien und superindustrielle Entwicklung.* Frankfurt: Fisher Verlag.

Hughes, J.D. (2009). The energy issue: A more urgent problem than climate change? In T. Homer-Dixon (Ed.). *Carbon Shift* (pp. 59–95). Toronto: Random House Canada.

Hulme, M. (2009). *Why We Disagree About Climate Change.* New York: Cambridge University Press.

Hulme, M., & Mahony, M. (2010). Climate change: What do we know about the IPCC? *Progress in Physical Geography, 34*(5), 705–718.

Hume, M. (2012a, 16 October). Its livelihood gone, fishing village tries scheme to seed a barren sea. *Globe and Mail.* Retrieved from http://www.theglobe andmail.com/news/british-columbia/ its-livelihood-gone-fishing-village- tries-scheme-to-seed-a-barren-sea/ article4617262/.

Hume, M. (2012b, 19 October). Ocean fertilization experiment alarms marine scientists. *Globe and Mail.* Retrieved from http://www.theglobeandmail. com/news/national/ocean-fertilization- experiment-alarms-marine-scientists/ article4625695/.

Illich, I. (1974). *Energy and Equity.* New York: Harper & Row.

Illich, I. (2012). Less energy, more equity, more time. In R. DeYoung and T. Princen (Eds.), *The Localization Reader: Adapting to the Coming Downshift* (pp. 47–54). Cambridge MA: MIT Press.

Inglehart, R. (1997). *Modernization and Postmodernization: Cultural, Economic, and Political Change in 43 Societies.* Princeton NJ: Princeton University Press.

Ingold, T. (2000). *The Perception of the Environment: Essays on Livelihood, Dwelling and Skill.* New York: Routledge.

Ingold, T. (2011). *Being Alive: Essays on Movement, Knowledge and Description.* New York: Routledge.

Irwin, A. (2001). *Sociology and Environment.* Malden, MA: Polity.

Ishiwatari, M. (2012). Government roles in community-based disaster risk reduc- tion. In R. Shaw (Ed.), *Community, Environment and Disaster Risk Management* (pp. 19–33). Bingley UK: Emerald.

Israel, D. (2007). Environmental participa- tion in the US sulfur allowance auctions. *Environmental and Resource Economics, 38,* 373–390.

Jaccard, M. (2012, 28 February). You can't take the tar sands out of the climate equation. *Globe & Mail.* Toronto. Retrieved from http:// www.theglobeandmail.com/ commentary/you-cant-take-the-tar- sands-out-of-the-climate-equation/ article549657/.

Jasanoff, S. (2003). Technologies of humil- ity: Citizen participation in governing science. *Minerva, 41,* 223–244.

Jasanoff, S. (2006). Risk in hindsight. In I. Richter, S. Berking, & R. Muller- Schmid (Eds.), *Risk Society and the Culture of Precaution* (pp. 28–46). New York: Palgrave Macmillan.

Jasanoff, S. (2007). Technologies of humil- ity. *Nature, 450*(November), 33.

Jasanoff, Sheila (2004). Heaven and Earth: The politics of environmental images. In S. Jasanoff & M. Martello (Eds.), *Earthly Politics* (pp. 31–52). Cambridge, MA: MIT Press.

Jenkins, R. N., Russo, J., Carpenter, M., Elthoum, I., Raghuraman, N., & Jenkins, S. (2009). Oral Exposure to Bisphenol A Increases Dimethylbenzanthracene-Induced Mammary Cancer in Rats. *Environmental Health Perspectives, 117*(6), 910–915.

Jentoft, S., & Chuenpagdee, R. (2009). Fisheries and coastal governance as a wicked problem. *Marine Policy, 33,* 553–560.

Johnston, J. (2006). Who cares about the commons? In J. Johnston, M. Gismondi, & J. Goodman (Eds.), *Nature's Revenge: Reclaiming sustainability in an age of corporate globalization* (pp. 39–71). Peterborough, ON: Broadview.

Jorgenson, A. K., & Clark, B. (2009). The economy, military, and ecologically unequal exchange relationships in comparative perspective: A panel study of the ecological footprints of nations, 1975–2000. *Social Problems, 56*(4), 621–646.

Jorgenson, A. K., & Clark, B. (2012). Are the Economy and the Environment Decoupling? A comparative interna- tional study, 1960–2005. *American Journal of Sociology, 118*(1), 1–44.

Jorgenson, A. K., Austin, K., & Dick, C. (2009). Ecologically unequal exchange and the resource consumption/envi- ronmental degradation paradox: A panel study of less-developed countries, 1970–2000. *International Journal of Comparative Sociology, 50*(3–4), 263–284.

Jorgenson, A. K., Clark, B., & Giedraitis, V. R. (2012). The temporal (in)stability of the carbon dioxide emissions/economic development relationship in central and eastern European nations. *Society and Natural Resources, 25*(11), 1182–1193.

Joyce, T. (2012, 23 November). Canadian tribe's ocean fertilization project attempts to boost salmon population. *Fox News*. Retrieved from http://q13 fox.com/2012/11/23/3024/#ixzz2 DBoH3H6t.

Kahhat, R., & Williams, E. (2012). Materials flow analysis of e-waste: Domestic flows and exports of used computers from the United States. *Resources, Conservation and Recycling, 67*, 67–74.

Kaiser, J. (2010). The dirt on ocean garbage patches. *Science, 328*(5985), 1506.

Keith, D. (2009). Dangerous abundance. In T. Homer-Dixon (Ed.), *Carbon Shift* (pp. 27–58). Toronto: Random House Canada.

Kelly, R. (1995). *The Foraging Spectrum*. Washington DC: Smithsonian.

Klein, N. (2007). *The Shock Doctrine: The Rise of Disaster Capitalism*. Toronto: Knopf.

Kleinfeld, M. (2007). Misreading the post-tsunami political landscape in Sri Lanka: the myth of humanitarian space. *Space and Polity*, 11(2), 169–184.

Kleinman, D. L. (2005). *Science and Technology in Society: From Biotechnology to the Internet*. Malden, MA: Blackwell.

Kline, B. (2011). *First Along the River: A Brief History of the US Environmental Movement*, 4th edition. Lanham, MD: Rowman & Littlefield.

Knapp, A. et al. (1999). The keystone role of bison in North American tallgrass prairie. *BioScience, 49*, 39–50.

Knorr Cetina, K. (1999). *Epistemic Cultures*. Cambridge, MA: Harvard University Press.

Kolbe, A. R., Hutson, R. A., Shannon, H., Trzcinski, E., Miles, B., Levitz, N., . . . Muggah, R. (2010). Mortality, crime and access to basic needs before and after the Haiti earhquake: A random survey of Port-au-Prince households. *Medicine, Conflict and Survival, 26*(4), 281–297.

Koring, P. (2013, 5 March). On US tour, minister touts Keystone as the environmentally clean choice. *Globe & Mail*. Toronto. Retrieved from http://www.theglobeandmail.com/news/politics/on-us-tour-minister-touts-keystone-as-the-environmentally-clean-choice/article9306257/.

Kroll-Smith, S., Gunter, V., & Laska, S. (2000). Theoretical stance and environmental debates: Reconciling the physical and the symbolic. *The American Sociologist, Spring 2000*, 44–62.

Kuznets, S. (1955). Economic growth and income inequality. *American Economic Review, 45*(1), 1–28.

Lahsen, M. (2004). Transnational locals: Brazilian experiences of the climate regime. In S. Jasanoff & M. Martello (Eds.), *Earthly Politics* (pp. 151–172). Cambridge MA: MIT Press.

Langhelle, O. (2009). Why ecological modernization and sustainable development should not be conflated. In *The Ecological Modernisation Reader: Environmental Reform in Theory and Practice* (pp. 391–417). New York: Routledge.

Larner, W. (2003). Neoliberalism? *Environment and Planning D, 21*, 509–512.

Lasch, C. (1979). *The Culture of Narcissism*. New York: Norton

Latour, B. (2004). *The Politics of Nature: How to Bring the Sciences into Democracy*. Cambridge, MA: Harvard University Press.

Latour, B. (1987). *Science in Action: How to Follow Scientists and Engineers through Society*. Cambridge MA: Harvard University Press.

Lawton, J. (1992). Are there general laws in ecology? *Oikos, 84*(2), 177–192.

Le Billon, P., & Carter, A. (2012). Securing Alberta's tar sands: Resistance and criminalization on a new energy frontier. In M. Schnurr & L. Swatuk (Eds.), *Natural Resources and Social Conflict: Towards Critical Environmental Security* (pp. 170–192). New York: Palgrave Macmillan.

Leiss, W. (2000). Between expertise and bureaucracy: Trapped at the science-policy interface. In G. B. Doern & T. Reed (Eds.), *Risky Business* (pp. 49–74). Toronto: University of Toronto Press.

Leiss, W. (2001). *In the Chamber of Risks*. Montreal: McGill-Queen's University Press.

Lever-Tracy, C. (2008). Global warming and sociology. *Current Sociology, 56*, 445–466.

Liberatore, A. (1995). The social construction of environmental problems. *Environmental Policy in an International Context, 1*(1), 59–83.

Lidskog, R. (2001). The re-naturalization of society? Environmental challenges for sociology. *Current Sociology, 49,* 113–136.

Lizarralde, G., Johnson, C., & Davidson, C. (Eds.). (2010). *Rebuilding After Disasters: From Emergency to Sustainability.* New York: Spon Press.

Lockie, S. (2004). Collective agency, non-human causality and environmental social movements: A case of the Australian landcare movement. *Sociology, 40*(1), 41–57.

Lockie, S. (2010). Neoliberal regimes of environmental governance: Climate change, biodiversity and agriculture in Australia. In *The International Handbook of Environmental Sociology* (2nd ed., pp. 364–377). Northhampton MA: Edward Elgar.

Lomborg, B. (2001). *The Skeptical Environmentalist: Measuring the Real State of the World.* New York: Cambridge University Press.

Longhofer, W. & Schofer, E. (2010). National and global origins of environmental association. *American Sociological Review, 75*(4), 505–533.

Lovins, A. B., & Burns, C. (2011). *The Essential Amory Lovins: Selected Writings.* New York: Earthscan.

Lubick, N. (2012). Shifting mountains of electronic waste. *Environmental Health Perspectives, 120*(4), 148–149.

Luhmann, N. (1993). *Risk: A Sociological Theory.* New York: A de Gruyter.

Maantay, J. (2002). Zoning law, health, and environmental justice: What's the connection? *Journal of Law, Medicine & Ethics, 30*(4), 572–593.

McAnany, P., & Yoffee, N. (Eds.). (2010). *Questioning Collapse: Human Resilience, Ecological Vulnerability, and the Aftermath of Empire.* New York: Cambridge University Press.

McCormick, J. (1995) *The Global Environmental Movement.* (2nd ed.) Chichester: Wiley.

McCright, A., & Dunlap, R. (2011). The politicization of climate change and polarization in the American public's views of global warming, 2001–2010. *Sociological Quarterly, 52,* 155–194.

Macdonald, D. (2007). *Business and Environmental Politics in Canada.* Peterborough ON: Broadview.

McIntosh, R. (1987). *Pluralism in ecology. Annual Review of Ecological Systems* 18, 321–341.

McKay, J. (2005). Water institutional reforms in Australia. *Water Policy.* 7, 35–52.

Mackenzie, C. A., Lockridge, A., & Keith, M. (2005). Declining sex ration in a First Nation community. *Environmental Health Perspectives, 113*(10), 1295–1298.

MacKenzie, D. (2002). Fresh evidence on Bhopal distaster. *New Scientist, 176*(2372), 6–7.

McKenzie, J. (2002). *Environmental Politics in Canada.* Don Mills, ON: Oxford University Press.

McLaren, A. (1990). *Our Own Master Race: Eugenics in Canada, 1885–1945.* Toronto: McClelland & Stewart.

McMahon, T. (2013, 27 January). How China is going to save the world. *Maclean's.* Retrieved from http://www2. macleans.ca/2013/01/27/business/.

Macnaghten, P. & Urry, J. (1998). *Contested Natures.* London: Sage

MacNeill, J. (2007, 10 October). *Our Common Future: Advance or retreat? Sustainable development: A new urgency.* Institute for Environment, University of Ottawa, University of Ottawa, Canada. Retrieved from http://www. ecolomics-international.org/eops_ 07_3_jim_macneill_uoottawa_ lecture_20_years_our_common _future_advance_or_retreat.pdf.

Maggio, G., & Cacciola, G. (2009). A variant of the Hubbert curve for world oil production forecasts. *Energy Policy 37*(11), 4761–4770.

Magis, K. (2010). Community resilience: An indicator of social sustainability. *Society and Natural Resources, 23*(5), 401–416.

Magnani, N. (2012). Nonhuman actors, hybrid networks, and conflicts over municipal waste incinerators. *Organization & Environment, 25*(2), 131–145.

Malm, A. (2012). China as chimney of the world: The fossil capital hypothesis.

Organization & Environment, 25(2), 146–177.

Manuel, J. (2010) EPA tackles fracking. *Environmental Health Perspectives*. 118(5): 199.

Manuel-Navarette, D., & Buzinde, C. N. (2010). Socio-ecological agency: From "human exemptionalism" to coping with "exceptional" global environmental change. In M. R. Redclift & G. Woodgate (Eds.), *The International Handbook of Environmental Sociology* (pp. 136–149). Northhampton MA: Edward Elgar.

Marchak, P., Aycock, S., & Herbert, D. (1999). *Falldown: Forest Policy in British Columbia*. Vancouver: David Suzuki Foundation.

Marchak, P. (1983). *Green Gold: The Forestry Industry in British Columbia*. Vancouver: UBC Press.

Martin, P.S. (1972) The discovery of America. *Science, 179*, 969–974.

Mason, J. B. (1992). *Acid Rain: Its Causes and Effects on Inland Waters*. Oxford: Clarendon Press.

Massey, D. (1994). *Space, Place and Gender*. Malden, MA: Polity.

Matthews, E. (1983). Global vegetation and land use: New high-resolution data bases for climactic studies. *Journal of Climate and Applied Meteorology 22*, 474–487.

Matus, K., Nam, K., Selin, N., Lamsal, L., Reilly J., & Paltsev, S. (2012). Health damages from air pollution in China. *Global Environmental Change, 22*(1), 55–66.

Maus, H. (1965). *A Short History of Sociology*. London: Routledge.

Meadows, D., Meadows, D., Randers, J., & Behrens, W. (1972). *The Limits to Growth*. New York: Universe Books.

Mehta, L. (Ed.). (2010). *The Limits to Scarcity: Contesting the Politics of Allocation*. Earthscan: London.

Meyer, D., & Staggenborg, S. (1996). Movements, counter-movements, and the structure of political opportunity. *American Journal of Sociology, 101*(6), 1628–1660.

Milberg, P., & Tyrberg, T. (1993). Naive birds and noble savages: A review of man-caused prehistoric extinctions of island birds. *Ecography, 16*(3), 229–250.

Miller, J.W. (2012, 12 June). Meet me at the centre of the Earth. *Globe & Mail*. B10.

Mills, J. H., & Waite, T. A. (2009). Economic prosperity, biodiversity conservation, and the environmental Kuznets curve. *Ecological Economics, 68*(7), 2087–2095.

Mirosa, O. & Harris, L. (2012). Human right to water: Contemporary challenges and contours of a global debate. *Antipode, 44*(3), 932–949.

Mol, A. P. J. (1995). *The Refinement of Production: Ecological Modernization and the Chemical Industry*. Urtech: Van Arkel.

Mol, A. P. J. (2006). Environment and modernity in transitional China: Frontiers of ecological modernization. *Development and Change, 37*(1), 29–56.

Mol, A. P. J. (2011). China's ascent and Africa's environment. *Global Environmental Change, 21*, 785–794.

Mol, A. P. J., & Janicke, M. (2009). The origins and theoretical foundations of ecological modernization theory. In A. P. J. Mol, D. A. Sonnenfeld, & G. Spaargaren (Eds.), *The Ecological Modernisation Reader: Environmental Reform in Theory and Practice* (pp. 17–27). New York: Routledge.

Mong, A. (2012, 24 February). Bathed in smog: Beijing's pollution could cut 5 years off lifespan, expert says. *NBC News*. Retrieved from http://behindthewall.msnbc.msn.com/_news/2012/02/24/10484609-bathed-in-smog-beijings-pollution-could-cut-5-years-off-lifespan-expert-says?lite.

Montgomery, D. (2007). *Dirt: The Erosion of Civilizations*. Berkeley CA: University of California Press.

Mooney, C. (2005). *The Republican War on Science* (2nd ed.). New York: Basic Books.

Mostafa, M. (2011). Wealth, post-materialism and consumer's pro-environmental intentions: A multilevel analysis across 25 nations. *Sustainable Development*, volume to be determined. DOI: 10.1002/sd.517.

Munson, J. (2013, 22 February). Media coverage of oilsands prompts scientists' rebuke. *iPolitics*. Ottawa. Retrieved from http://www.ipolitics.ca/2012/02/22/

media-coverage-of-oilsands-prompts-scientists-rebuke/.

Murdoch, J. (2001). Ecologising sociology: Actor-network theory, co-construction and the problem of human exemptionalism. *Sociology, 35*(1), 111–133.

Murphy, R. (1994). *Rationality and Nature*. Boulder, CO: Westview.

Murphy R. (1997). *Sociology and Nature*. Boulder, CO: Westview.

Murphy, R. (2004). Disaster or sustainability: The dance of human agents with nature's actants. *Canadian Review of Sociology and Anthropology, 41*(3), 249–267.

Murphy, R. (2006). Environmental realism: From apologetics to substance. *Nature and Culture, 1*(2), 181–204.

Murphy, R. (2009). *Leadership in Disaster: Learning for a Future with Global Climate Change*. Montreal: McGill-Queen's University Press.

Murphy, R. (2011). The challenge of anthropogenic climate change for the social sciences. *International Review of Social Research, 1*(3), 167–181.

Murphy, R. (2012). Sustainability: A wicked problem. *Sociologica, 2*(1), 1–23.

Mythen, G. (2007). Reappraising the risk society thesis: Telescopic sight or myopic vision? *Current Sociology, 55*(6), 793–813.

Nadasdy, P. (1999). The politics of TEK: Power and the "integration" of knowledge. *Arctic Anthropology, 36*(1-2), 1–18.

Nadasdy, P. (2005). The anti-politics of TEK: The institutionalization of co-management discourse and practice. *Anthropologica, 47*(2), 215–232.

National Energy Board [NEB] (2011a). Canada's Oil Sands: Opportunities and challenges to 2015: An update. Retrieved from http://www.neb.gc.ca/clf-nsi/rnrgynfmtn/nrgyrprt/lsnd/pprtntsndchllngs20152006/qapprtnt sndchllngs20152006-eng.html.

National Energy Board [NEB] (2011b). Natural gas: How Canadian markets work. Retrieved from http://www.neb-one.gc.ca/clf-nsi/rnrgynfmtn/prcng/ntrlgs/cndnmrk-eng.html.

Nelson, G. C. (2009). *Climate Change: Impact on Agriculture and Costs of Adaptation*. Washington DC: International Food Policy Research Institute.

Neumayer, E., & Plumper, T. (2007). The gendered nature of natural disasters: The impact of catastrophic events on the gender gap in life expectancy, 1981–2002. *Annals of the Association of American Geographers, 97*(3), 551–566.

Newell, P. (2012). *Globalization and the Environment: Capitalism, Ecology and Power*. Malden, MA: Polity.

Newell, P., & Paterson, M. (2010). *Climate Capitalism: Global Warming and the Transformation of the Global Economy*. New York: Cambridge University Press.

Ni, H.G., & Zeng, E. (2009). Law enforcement and global collaboration are the keys to containing e-waste tsunami in China. *Environmental Science & Technology, 43*(11), 3991–3994.

Nicola, S. (2011, 16 September). KfW to Provide 100 Billion Euros to Aid German Energy Transition. *Bloomberg*. Retrieved from http://www.bloomberg.com/news/2011-09-19/kfw-to-provide-100-billion-euros-to-aid-german-energy-transition.html.

Noorgard, R. B. (1984). Coevolutionary agricultural development. *Economic Development and Cultural Change, 32*, 525–546.

O'Connor, J. (1991). On the two contradictions of capitalism. *Capitalism Nature Socialism, 2*(3): 107–109.

O'Neill, S. & Nicholson-Cole, S. (2009). "Fear won't do it": Promoting positive engagement with climate change through visual and iconic representations. *Science Communication, 30*(3): 355–379.

Olivier, J. G., & Peters, J. (2010). *No Growth in Total Global CO$_2$ Emissions in 2009*. Netherlands Environmental Assessment Agency.

Ontario. (2010). Fine Particulate Matter. Ministry of the Environment. Retrieved from http://www.airqualityontario.com/science/pollutants/particulates.php.

Oppenheimer, M. et al. (2007). The limits of consensus. *Science 317*: 1505–1506.

Oreskes, N., & Conway, E. M. (2011). *Merchants of Doubt*. New York: Bloomsbury.

Pagden, A. (1993). *European Encounters with the New World: From Renaissance to Romanticism*. New Haven CT: Yale University Press.

Pandey, B. H., & Okazaki, K. (2005). Community-based disaster management: Empowering communities to cope with disaster risks. *Regional Development Dialogue, 26*(2), 52–62.

Paterson, M. (2008). Post-hegemonic climate politics? *British Journal of Politics and International Relations, 11*, 140–158.

Paton, G. J. (2011). *Seeking Sustainability: On the Prospect of an Ecological Liberalism.* New York: Routledge.

Pearce, F. (2010, 7 July). Climategate inquiry: No deceit, too little co-operation. *New Scientist.* Retrieved from http://www.newscientist.com/article/dn19143-climategate-inquiry-no-deceit-too-little-cooperation.html.

Peck, J., & Tickell, A. (2002). Neoliberalizing space. *Antipode, 34*(3), 380–404.

Peet, R., Robbins, P., & Watts, M. J. (2011). Global nature. In R. Peet, P. Robbins, & M. J. Watts (Eds.), *Global Political Ecology* (pp. 1–48). New York: Routledge.

Peluso, N. L. (1992). *Rich Forests, Poor People: Resource Control and Resistance in Java.* Berkeley, CA: University of California Press.

Peluso, N. L., & Vandergeest, P. (2011). Taking the jungle out of the forest: Counter-insurgency and the making of national natures. In R. Peet, P. Robbins, & M. J. Watts (Eds.), *Global Political Ecology* (pp. 252–284). New York: Routledge.

Pepper, D. (1996). *Modern Environmentalism: An Introduction.* New York: Routledge

Percival, V. & Homer-Dixon, T. (1998). Environmental scarcity and violent conflict: The case of South Africa. *Journal of Peace Research, 35*(3), 279–298.

Perrow, C. (1999). *Normal Accidents: Living with High-Risk Technologies* (2nd ed.). Princeton NJ: Princeton University Press.

Perrow, C. (2006). Culture, structure, and risk. In I. Richter, S. Berking, & R. Muller-Schmid (Eds.), *Risk Society and the Culture of Precaution* (pp. 47–58). New York: Palgrave Macmillan.

Petersen, A. (2011). Climate simulation, uncertainty and policy advice—the case of the IPCC. In G. Gramelsberger & J. Feichter (Eds.), *Climate Change and Policy: The Calculability of Climate Change and the Challenge of Uncertainty* (pp. 91–112). New York: Springer.

Pielke Jr., R. A. (2007). *The Honest Broker: Making Sense of Science in Policy and Politics.* New York: Cambridge University Press.

Pittaway, E., Bartolomei, L., & Rees, S. (2007). Gendered dimensions of the 2004 tsunami and a potential social work response in post-disaster situations. *International Social Work, 50*(3), 307–319.

Plaut, M. (2006, 26 September). Ivory Coast waste "was not toxic." *BBC News.* London, UK. Retrieved from http://news.bbc.co.uk/2/hi/africa/5380296.stm.

Polanyi, K. (1944). *The Great Transformation.* Boston: Beacon Press.

Pollock, S. (1999). *Ancient Mesopotamia: The Eden That Never Was.* New York: Cambridge University Press.

Ponting, C. (2007). *A New Green History of the World: The Environment and the Collapse of Great Civilizations* (2nd ed.). London: Vintage.

Preston, F. (2012) A global redesign? Shaping the circular economy. Chatham House. Briefing paper 2012/02.

Proctor, J. (1998). The social construction of nature: Relativist accusations, pragmatist and critical realist responses. *Annals of the Association of American Geographers, 88*(3), 352–376.

Prudham, S. (2004). Poisoning the well: Neoliberalism and the contamination of municipal water in Walkerton, Ontario. *Geoforum, 35*, 343–359.

Punt, A. E., & Smith, A. D. M. (2001). The gospel of maximum sustainable yield in fisheries management: Birth, crucifixion and reincarnation. In J. D. Reynolds, G. M. Mace, K. H. Redford, & J. G. Robinson (Eds.), *Conservation of Exploited Species* (pp. 41–66). New York: Cambridge University Press.

Qin, A. (2013, 28 January). Taste for shark fin fades slightly in China. *New York Times.* Retrieved from http://www.nytimes.com/2013/01/29/world/asia/taste-for-shark-fin-fades-slightly-in-china.html?_r=0.

Querengesser, T. (2007, 10 November). Is DDT Africa's last hope? *Globe and Mail,* p. A9.

Redclift, M. (2011). The response of the hermeneutic social sciences to a "post carbon world." *International Review of Social Research, 1*(3), 155–166.

Redman, C. L. (1999). *Human Impact on Ancient Environments.* Tuscon, AZ: University of Arizona Press.

Reinhart, C., & Rogoff, K. (2009). *This Time is Different: Eight Centuries of Financial Folly.* Princeton: Princeton University Press.

Renn, O. (2008). *Risk Governance.* London, UK: Earthscan.

Rice, J. (2009). The transnational organization of production and uneven environmental degradation and change in the world economy. *International Journal of Comparative Sociology, 50*(3–4), 215–236.

Rittel, H., & Webber, M. (1973). Dilemmas in a general theory of planning. *Policy Sciences, 4,* 155–169.

Robbins, P. (2012). *Political Ecology* (2nd ed.). Malden, MA: Wiley-Blackwell.

Roberts, J. T., & Grimes, P. (2002). World-system theory and the environment: Toward a new synthesis. In R. E. Dunlap, F. H. Buttel, P. Dickens, & A. Gijswijt (Eds.), *Sociological Theory and the Environment* (pp. 167–194). Lanham, MD: Rowman & Littlefield.

Roberts, J. T., & Parks, B. (2009). Ecologically unequal exchange, ecological debt, and climate justice: The history and implications of three related ideas for a new social movement. *International Journal of Comparative Sociology, 50*(3–4), 385–409.

Roberts, P. (2005). *The End of Oil: On the Edge of a Perilous New World.* New York: First Mariner.

Rodriguez, M. (2004). *Global Environmentalism and Local Politics.* Albany, NY: SUNY Press

Rome, A. (2003). Give Earth a chance: The environmental movements of the sixties. *Journal of American History, 90,* 525–554.

Rosa, E. A., & Clarke, L. (2012). A collective hunch? Risk as the real and the elusive. *Journal of Environmental Studies and Sciences, 2,* 39–52.

Rosa, E. A., & Richter, L. (2008). Durkheim on the environment. *Organization & Environment, 21*(2), 182–187.

Rowell, A. (1996). *Green Backlash: Global Subversion of the Environmental Movement.* New York: Routledge.

Rubin, J. (2009). *Why Your World Is About to Get a Whole Lot Smaller.* Toronto: Random House.

Rubin, J. (2012). *The End of Growth.* Toronto: Random House

Rudel, T., Roberts, J.T., & Carmin, J. (2011). Political economy of the environment. *Annual Review of Sociology, 37,* 221–238.

Ryan, P., Moore, C.J., van Franeker, J.A., & Moloney, C. (2009). Monitoring the abundance of plastic debris in the marine environment. *Philosophical Transactions of the Royal Society B, 364*(1526), 1999–2012.

Saarikoski, H. (2007). Objectivity and the environment: Epistemic value of biases. *Environmental Politics, 16*(3), 488–498.

Sandor, J.A., & Nash, N.S. (1989). Significance of ancient agricultural soils for long-term agronomic studies and sustainable agriculture research. *Agronomy Journal, 83*(1), 29–37.

Sassatelli, R. (2007). *Consumer Culture: History, Theory and Politics.* Thousand Oaks, CA: Sage.

Savoie, D. J. (2010). *Power: Where Is It?* Montreal and Kingston: McGill-Queen's University Press.

Schnaiberg, A. (1980). *The Environment: From Surplus to Scarcity.* New York: Oxford University Press.

Schneider, N. (Ed.). (2008). *A Breath of Fresh Air.* Vancouver: Fraser Institute.

Schofer, E., & Hironaka, A. (2005). The effects of world society on environmental protection outcomes. *Social Forces, 84*(1), 25–47.

Scoones, I. (2008). Mobilizing against GM crops in India, South Africa and Brazil. *Journal of Agrarian Change, 8*(2–3), 315–344.

Seiler, C. (2008). *Republic of Drivers: A Cultural History of Automobility in America.* Chicago: University of Chicago Press.

Shandra, J. M., Shircliff, E., & London, B. (2011). The International Monetary Fund, World Bank, and structural adjustment: A cross-national analysis of forest loss. *Social Science Research, 40*(1), 210–225.

Shapin, S. (1996). *The Scientific Revolution.* Chicago: University of Chicago Press.

Shapin, S. (2008a). *The Scientific Life: A Moral History of a Late Modern Vocation.* Chicago: University of Chicago Press.

Shapin, S. (2008b). Science and the modern world. In E. J. Hackett, O. Amsterdamska, M. Lynch, & J. Wajcman (Eds.), *The Handbook of Science and Technology Studies* (pp. 433–448). Cambridge, MA: MIT Press.

Shapin, S. (2010). *Never Pure: Historical Studies of Science as if It Was Produced by People with Bodies, Situated in Time, Space, Culture, and Society, and Struggling for Credibility and Authority.* Baltimore: John's Hopkins University Press.

Sharpe, A., Arsenault, J.-F., Murray, A., & Qiao, S. (2008). The valuation of the Alberta oil sands. Research report no. 2008-7. Ottawa: Centre for the Study of Living Standards.

Shepard, P., & McKinly D. (1969). *The Subversive Science: Essays Toward an Ecology of Man.* Boston: Houghton Mifflin.

Sherwell, P., & Chamberlin, G. (2006, 17 September). DDT in Africa saves babies' lives, says WHO. *The Telegraph.* Retrieved from http://www.telegraph.co.uk/news/worldnews/1529080/DDT-in-Africa-saves-babies-lives-says-WHO.html.

Simmons, A. (1999). *Faunal Extinction in an Island Society.* New York: Kluwer Academic.

Simon, J. (1981). *The Ultimate Resource.* Princeton NJ: Princeton University Press.

Simon, J. (1996). *The Ultimate Resource 2.* Princeton NJ: Princeton University Press.

Slovic, P. (2000). *The Perception of Risk.* London: Earthscan.

Slovic, P. (2010). *The Feeling of Risk.* Washington DC: Earthscan.

Smith, K. (2001). *Environmental Hazards: Assessing Risk and Reducing Disaster* (3rd ed.). New York: Routledge.

Smith, M. (2001). "Silence, Miss Carson!" Science, gender, and the reception of *Silent Spring. Feminist Studies, 27*(3), 733–752.

Sonnenfeld, D. A., & Mol, A. P. J. (2006). Environmental reform in Asia: Comparisons, challenges, next steps. *Journal of Environment & Development, 15*(2), 112–137.

Sontheimer, S. (Ed.). (1991). *Women and the Environment.* London: Earthscan

Sorenson, M. P., & Christiansen, A. (2013). *Ulrich Beck: An Introduction to the Theory of Second Modernity and the Risk Society.* New York: Routledge.

Soto Am, S. C., & Sonnenschein, C. (2010). Environmental causes of cancer: Endocrine disruptors as carcinogens. *Nature Reviews Endrocrinology, 6*(7), 363–370.

Spaargaren, G., & Mol, A. P. J. (2009). Sociology, environment, and modernity: Ecological modernization as a theory of social change. In A. P. J. Mol, D. A. Sonnenfeld, & G. Spaargaren (Eds.), *The Ecological Modernisation Reader: Environmental Reform in Theory and Practice* (pp. 56–79). New York: Routledge.

Spaargaren, G., Cohen, M. J., Spaargaren, G., & Sonnenfeld, D. A. (2009). Greening lifecycles and lifestyles. In A. P. J. Mol (Ed.), *The Ecological Modernisation Reader: Environmental Reform in Theory and Practice* (pp. 257–274). New York: Routledge.

Stallings, R. A., & Quarantelli, E. L. (1985). Emergent citizen groups and emergency management. *Public Administration Review, 45*, 93–100.

Stehr, N., & Grundmann, R. (2011). *Experts: The Knowledge and Power of Expertise.* New York: Routledge.

Storm, S. (2009). Capitalism and climate change: Can the invisible hand adjust the natural thermostat? *Development and Change, 40*(6), 1011–1038.

Strydom, P. (2002). *Risk, Environment and Modernity: Critical Issues for Social Theory.* Buckingham: Open University Press.

Swart, N. C., & Weaver, A. J. (2012). The Alberta oil sands and climate. *Nature Climate Change, 2*, 134–136.

Szaro, J., Hernandez, P., Singh, A., & Fagan, J. (2011). *Warning: BPA Toxicity: Don't Heat Food with "Plastic."* New Brunswick, NJ: Rutgers University. Retrieved from http://hdl.rutgers.edu/1782.1/rucore00000002167. Manuscript.000064801.

Szasz, A. (2007). *Shopping our Way to Safety.* Minneapolis: University of Minnesota Press.

Tainter, J. (2006). Archaeology of over-shoot and collapse. *Annual Review of Anthropology, 35*, 59–74.

Tait, C. (2012a, 13 June). Seeking a new way to tap the oil sands. *Globe & Mail*. B1.

Tait, C. (2012b, 14 June). BP report suggests fears of oil scarcity overblown. *Globe & Mail*. B6.

Taylor, M. S. (2007). Buffalo hunt: International trade and the virtual extinction of the North American bison. National Bureau of Economic Research, Cambridge MA. Working paper 12969.

Tencer, D. (2011, 23 August). Number of cars worldwide surpasses 1 billion: Can the world handle this many wheels? *Huffington Post Canada*. Retrieved from http://www.huffingtonpost.ca/2011/08/23/car-population_n_934291.html.

Tollefson, J. (2012). Ocean-fertilization project off Canada sparks furore. *Nature, 490*(7421), 458–459.

Tovey, H. (2003). Theorising nature and society: The invisibility of animals. *Sociologia Ruralis, 43*(3), 196–215.

Transport Canada. (2011). *Canadian Motor Vehicle Traffic Collision Statistics: 2009* (No. TP 3322). Ottawa: Transport Canada.

Tranter, B. (2011). Political divisions over climate change and environmental issues in Australia. *Environmental Politics, 20*(1), 78–96.

Trossle, R. (2011). Why another food commodity price spike? *Amber Waves, 9*(3), 1–7.

UNEP. (2009). *Recycling—from e-waste to resources*. United Nations Environment Programme. Retrieved from http://www.unep.org/PDF/PressReleases/E-Waste_publication_screen_FINALVERSION-sml.pdf.

Urry, J. (1995). *The Tourist Gaze*. Thousand Oaks: Sage.

Urry, J. (2011). *Climate Change and Society*. Cambridge UK: Polity

Vaillancourt, J. (2010). From environmental sociology to global ecosociology. In M. Redclift & G. Woodgate, *The International Handbook of Environmental Sociology* (pp. 48–62). Northampton, MA: Edward Elgar.

Van Asselt, M. B. A., & Vos, E. (2008). Wrestling with uncertain risks: EU regulation of GMOs and the uncertainty paradox. *Journal of Risk Research, 11*(1–2), 281–300.

Vandenbergh, M. P. (2007). The new Wal-Mart effect: The role of private contracting in global governance. *UCLA Law Review, 54*, 913–970.

Vanderklippe, N. (2012, 5 June), Crude glut and price plunge put oil sands plans at risk. *Globe & Mail*. B1.

Varano, S. P., Schafer, J. A., Cancino, J. M., Decker, S. H., & Greene, J. R. (2010). A tale of three cities: Crime and displacement after Hurricane Katrina. *Journal of Criminal Justice, 38*(1), 42–50.

Veblen, T. (1899). *Theory of the Leisure Class*. New York: Macmillan

Victor, P. A. (2010). Ecological economics and economic growth. *Annals of the New York Academy of Sciences, 1185*, 237–245. © 2010 New York Academy of Sciences

Vogel, D. (1997). *Trading Up: Consumer and Environmental Regulation in a Global Economy*. Cambridge, MA: Harvard University Press.

Wackernagel, M. & Rees, W. (1996). *Our Ecological Footprint: Reducing Human Impact on the Earth*. Gabriola Island BC: New Society Publishers.

Wada, Y., et al. (2010). Global depletion of groundwater resources. *Geophysical Research Letters, 37*, 1–5.

Waguespack, N., & Surovell, T. (2003). Clovis hunting strategies, or how to make out on plentiful resources. *American Antiquity, 68*(2), 333–352.

Walker, P. A. (2005). Political ecology: Where is the ecology? *Progress in Human Geography, 29*(1), 73–82.

Wallerstein, I. (1974). *The Modern World-System: Capitalist Agriculture and the Origins of the European World-Economy in the Sixteenth Century*. New York: Academic Press.

WCED (World Commission on Environment and Development). (1987). *Our Common Future*. New York: Oxford University Press.

Weart, S. 2008. *The Discovery of Global Warming*. Cambridge, MA: Harvard University Press.

Webster, P. (2006). Canadian petrochemical plants blamed for gender imbalance. *The Lancet, 367*(9509), 462–463.

Weinhold, B. (2011). Alberta's oil sands: Hard evidence, missing data, new promises. *Environmental Health Perspectives, 119*(3), 126–131.

Weisman, A. (2007). *The World Without Us.* New York: St. Martin's Press.

Wilcox, M. (2010). Marketing conquest and the vanishing Indian. In P. McAnany & N. Yoffee (Eds.). *Questioning Collapse: Human Resilience, Ecological Vulnerability, and the Aftermath of Empire* (pp. 113–141). New York: Cambridge University Press.

Williams, M. (2003). *Deforesting the Earth: From Prehistory to Global Crisis.* Chicago: University of Chicago Press.

Williams, M. (2000). Dark ages and dark areas: Global deforestation in the deep past. *Journal of Historical Geography, 26*(1), 28–46.

Wilson, G. A. (2012). *Community Resilience and Environmental Transitions.* New York: Routledge.

Wisner, B., Gaillard, J., & Kelman, I. (2012). Framing disaster: Theories and stories seeking to understand hazards, vulnerability and risk. In B. Wisner, J. Gaillard, & I. Kelman (Eds.), *The Routledge Handbook of Hazards and Disaster Risk Reduction* (pp. 18–33). New York: Routledge.

Woodgate, G., & Redclift, M. R. (1998). From a "sociology of nature" to environmental sociology: Beyond social construction. *Environmental Values, 7*(1), 3–24.

World Bank. (2012). *World Bank Statistics, Energy & Mining.* Washington DC: World Bank. Retrieved from http://data.worldbank.org/topic/energy-and-mining.

Worm, B., & et al. (2006). Impacts of biodiversity loss on ocean ecosystem services. *Science, 314*(5800), 787–790.

Worster, D. (1994). *Nature's Economy: A History of Ecological Ideas* (2nd ed.). New York: Cambridge University Press.

Wright, E.O. (2006). Class analysis. In R. Levine (Ed.), *Social Class and Stratification* (2nd ed., pp. 143–161). New York: Rowman and Littlefield.

WSJ. (2009, 26 May). Malaria, politics and DDT. *Wall Street Journal.* Retrieved from http://online.wsj.com/article/SB124303288779048569.html.

WTO. (2012). *World trade 2011, prospects for 2012* (No. 658). New York: World Trade Organization. Retrieved from http://www.wto.org/english/news_e/pres12_e/pr658_e.htm#chart1.

Wynne, B. (2002). Risk and environment as legitimatory discourses of technology: Reflexivity inside out? *Current Sociology, 50*, 459–477.

Wynne, B. (2003). Seasick on the third wave? Subverting the hegemony of propositionalism. *Social Studies of Science, 33*(3), 401–417.

Wynne, B. (2011). *Rationality and Ritual: Participation and Exclusion in Nuclear Decision-Making* (2nd ed.). London: Earthscan.

Xenos, N. (2010). Everybody's got the fever: Scarcity and US national energy policy. In L. Mehta (Ed.) *The Limits to Scarcity: Contesting the Politics of Allocation* (pp. 31–48). Earthscan: London.

Yamamura, E. (2010). Effects of interactions among social capital, income and learning from experiences of natural disasters: A case study from Japan. *Regional Studies, 44*(8), 1019–1032.

Yates, D. (1996). *The Rentier State in Africa.* Trenton NJ: Africa World Press.

Yearley, S. (2009). Sociology and climate change after Kyoto: What roles for social science in understanding climate change? *Current Sociology, 57*, 389–405.

Yearley, S. (2010). Science and the environment in the twenty-first century. In M. R. Redclift & G. Woodgate (Eds.), *The International Handbook of Environmental Sociology* (2nd ed., pp. 212–225). Northampton, MA: Edward Elgar.

Yoffee, N. (2010). Collapse in Ancient Mesopotamia: What happened, what didn't. In P. McAnany & N. Yoffee (Eds.), *Questioning Collapse: Human Resilience, Ecological Vulnerability, and the Aftermath of Empire* (pp. 176–203). New York: Cambridge University Press.

York, R. & Clark, B. (2010). Critical materialism: Science, technology and environmental sustainability. *Sociological Inquiry, 80*(3), 475–499.

York, R., Rosa, E., & Dietz, T. (2003). Footprints on the Earth: The environmental consequences of modernity. *American Sociological Review, 68*(2), 279–300.

York, R., Rosa, E., & Dietz, T. (2010). Ecological modernization theory: Theoretical and empirical challenges.

In M. Redclift & G. Woodgate, *The International Handbook of Environmental Sociology* (pp. 77–90). Northampton, MA: Edward Elgar.

Young, N. (2012). Visions of rootedness and flow: Remaking economic identity in post-resource communities. In J. R. Parkins & M. G. Reed (Eds.), *Social Transformation in Rural Canada* (pp. 232–248). Vancouver: UBC Press.

Young, N., & Coutinho, A. (2013). Government, anti-reflexivity, and the construction of public ignorance of climate change: Australia and Canada compared. *Global Environmental Politics, 13*(2), 91–110.

Young, N., & Dugas, E. (2011). Representations of climate change in Canadian national print media: The banalization of global warming. *Canadian Review of Sociology, 48*(1), 1–22.

Young, N., & Dugas, E. (2012). Comparing climate change coverage in Canadian English and French-language print media: Environmental values, media cultures, and the narration of global warming. *Canadian Journal of Sociology, 37*(1), 25–54.

Young, N., & Matthews, R. (2010). *The Aquaculture Controversy in Canada: Activism, Policy, and Contested Science.* Vancouver: UBC Press.

Youngman, N. (2009). Understanding disaster vulnerability. In K. A. Gould & T. L. Lewis (Eds.), *Twenty Lessons in Environmental Sociology* (pp. 176–190). New York: Oxford University Press.

Zalasiewicz, J., et al. (2008). Are we now living in the Anthropocene? *GSA Today, 18*(2), 4–8.

Zhang, X., Chang, S., & Martinot, E. (2012). Renewable energy in China: An integrated technology and policy perspective. *Energy Policy, 51*, 1–6.

Zimmerer, K. S., & Bassett, T. J. (2003). Approaching political ecology: Society, nature, and scale in human-environment studies. In K. S. Zimmerer & T. J. Bassett (Eds.), *Political Ecology: An Integrative Approach to Geography and Environment-Development Studies* (pp. 1–28). New York: Guilford.

Zimmerman, E.W. (1951). *World Resources and Industries.* New York: Harper.

Index